[the] vegetable eater (n)   \\'vej-tə-bəl 'ē-tər\\

1. anyone who eats (or wants to eat) vegetables.

2. a person focused on the abundant, delicious produce in the center of their plate—*not* on what is absent from it.

3. this book; an essential collection of produce-inspired main dish recipes made to welcome, nourish, and delight everyone at the table.

THE VEGETABLE EATER

The New Playbook for Cooking Vegetarian

CARA MANGINI

Workman Publishing
New York

Workman
Workman Publishing
Hachette Book Group, Inc.
1290 Avenue of the Americas
New York, NY 10104
workman.com

Workman is an imprint of Workman Publishing, a division of Hachette Book Group, Inc. The Workman name and logo are registered trademarks of Hachette Book Group, Inc.

Design by Becky Terhune
Cover photo by Erin Scott
Photos on pages 35, 187, and 257 by Rachel Joy Barehl
Photo on page 179 © copyright Shutterstock/The Picture Pantry

The publisher is not responsible for websites (or their content) that are not owned by the publisher.

Workman books may be purchased in bulk for business, educational, or promotional use. For information, please contact your local bookseller or the Hachette Book Group Special Markets Department at special.markets@hbgusa.com.

Library of Congress Cataloging-in-Publication Data is available.

ISBN 978-1-5235-1494-6

First Edition March 2024

Printed in China on responsibly sourced paper.

10 9 8 7 6 5 4 3 2 1

For Stella and Nico
and a lifetime of meals
around a table with you.

CONTENTS

WELCOME!

I am so glad you're here. You are already a vegetable eater. Whether you regularly cook vegetarian, or you squeeze in some veggies some of the time, this book is destined to become a trusted guide to creating vegetable-centered meals that are exciting, satisfying, and achievable, like second nature. In these pages, you will learn foundational techniques to reimagine and reinvigorate your repertoire. Ultimately, I hope you will come to treasure this collection of adaptable recipes as one that you can rely on and enjoy all throughout the year. As you use this book to cook dinner on Tuesday nights, map out the week's sustaining lunches, convene friends for weekend brunch, and gather with loved ones for seasonal celebrations, I am confident that you will discover the joy, beauty, and feel-good effects of putting vegetables at the center of your plate.

Let's get started. Together, we are going to turn vegetables into complete meals—the kind of super-satisfying, wildly delicious main dishes that you and everyone at your table will love.

Together, we are going to turn vegetables into complete meals— the kind of super- satisfying, wildly delicious main dishes that you and everyone at your table will love.

HOW DOES IT WORK?

With *The Vegetable Eater*, you decide your own path. You'll find dozens of essential dishes, mostly familiar-sounding ones—the kind of everyday meals that appeal to your ever-evolving appetite. Come here when you are feeling like a truly yummy plant-based burger, a comforting bowl of pasta, or a hearty stew. Return when it's lasagna time, taco Tuesday, or pizza night. Short on time? Turn to sheet pan meals, grain bowls, and stir-fries. When it's your turn to host Sunday night dinner, a special brunch, or a holiday meal, you will find just the right thing here. Will you serve a rustic shepherd's pie, a make-ahead strata, or an elegant beet Wellington? From healthful big salads to showstopper vegetable galettes, there are plenty of recipes to satisfy any craving—in fact, three different recipes for each type of dish, so that as the season changes, you can apply what you've learned to create meals with new main characters.

Throughout this book, you'll find resources on how to handle and prepare a variety of vegetables (and fruits), plus notes about ingredients, shortcuts, swaps, and yields. You'll also find helpful vegetable butcher tips and illustrations showing you the best method for washing greens, the easiest way to break down a butternut squash, and more. Vegetables will become familiar friends, your constant kitchen companions. The most meaningful lessons, however, are uncovered through hands-on cooking. Follow the recipes, get to know them, then consider the many ideas I share for variations. Your vegetable education will come through repetition, practice, and discovery. As you dip in and out of the book, cooking your way through it, you will sharpen your skills and gain confidence. Soon you'll mix and match the best produce of the moment to turn it into a meal of your own design. These dishes will become your go-tos, the ones you regularly riff on—allowing you to make this way with vegetables your very own.

The Seasons

One of the greatest joys of being a vegetable eater is cooking in tune with the seasons and connecting with nature and produce in its prime. Here you will learn the techniques at the core of the recipes in the spring, swap out ingredients for summer, and then again in the fall. There is nothing like the anticipation of

an ingredient—asparagus, young onions, and garlic in the spring, sweet corn, green beans, and tomatoes in the summer, and winter squashes, hearty greens, and all kinds of roots in the fall. Fully and completely enjoy each one when it is at its best (and until the last one is gone). Then get excited about and creative with what is to come.

The Order of Things

This book is broken into a series of simple lessons for satisfying produce-inspired mains. (These are must-know dishes like The Kale Salad, The Saucy Noodle Bowl, and The Pot of Beans.) Generally, within each you will find late-winter or spring recipes offered first, spring into summer next, and late-summer into fall or fall into winter last. Of course, the seasons are fluid and different depending on where you live, so look around (and check out Recipes by Season, starting on page 318, for inspiration). Many recipes can be enjoyed year-round or in multiple seasons. Also, I offer lots of ideas for seasonal swaps and tweaks (plus frozen and canned options when appropriate). Select recipes based on whatever produce is looking good to you now.

All Plants

Most recipes are plant-based or can easily be adjusted to suit our fully plant-based vegetable eaters. When an adjustment isn't obvious, look for my "All Plants" notes in the sidebars.

There are no prerequisites to getting started, but I recommend these basic steps to help you prepare for cooking the dishes in this book (and for a lifetime of vegetable-centered cooking).

STEP 1
PREP YOUR PANTRY

A well-stocked pantry will support you with the ingredients to cook most of the recipes in this book. With a diverse mix of items from several categories, you will also be able to build your own dishes and freestyle.

BEANS (CANNED): chickpeas (my #1), black beans, cannellini beans

BEANS AND LENTILS (DRY): black beans, cannellini beans, cranberry beans, pinto beans, French lentils, brown and black lentils, plus an array of unique heirloom bean varieties

BREAD: Keep a good-quality loaf of bread and crusty, sliced sandwich bread in the freezer.

CHEESE (as needed): Many dishes either don't call for cheese or list it as optional. For recipes with an essential cheese component, you are welcome to use a favorite plant-based cheese or to substitute other cheeses to suit you. I keep Parmigiano-Reggiano on hand at all times and some combination of a sharp Cheddar, jack, and feta.

CITRUS: Lemons, limes, and oranges, too. (Keep them in the fridge unless you are certain that you will use them within a couple of days.)

DRIED FRUIT: Raisins, currants, cranberries, apricots, cherries, dates; on its own or quick-pickled dried fruit can add just the right amount of sweet to lift a dish.

EXTRACTS: almond and pure vanilla

FLOURS: all-purpose (unbleached), almond, bread flour, rye, spelt, whole wheat

TOASTING NUTS AND SEEDS

Toast nuts and seeds in a toaster oven (my preference for small quantities), a dry skillet over medium heat (my preference for pine nuts and seeds), or in the oven (for larger quantities of nuts and large seeds). Toast until fragrant and evenly darker in color (just a shade or two). Do not let them get too dark or unevenly toasted.

TO USE AN OVEN OR TOASTER OVEN: Heat the oven to 350°F. Spread the nuts or larger seeds (like pepitas) out in a single layer on a sheet pan. Bake, checking them often and turning them once or twice, until fragrant and deeper in color, 6 to 10 minutes for most whole nuts. (Pine nuts, seeds, and sliced almonds will cook faster, so check them early.) Let them cool completely and taste for doneness—crunchy, evenly toasted, and flavorful. Toast again briefly if needed. (The toaster oven works well for small quantities, up to 1 cup. You can even just use the "toast" setting if you watch them closely.)

TO USE A SKILLET: Place the seeds in a dry heavy skillet over medium heat. Cook, tilting and swirling the pan frequently (stirring almost constantly for small seeds), until they become golden and fragrant, 3 to 5 minutes.

TAKE NOTE: Nuts and seeds can become rancid quickly. Store large raw quantities in airtight containers in the freezer for up to 6 months (no need to defrost them before you toast them). It's best to toast nuts just before you use them for optimal flavor, but you can store them in an airtight container in a cool cabinet for up to a week.

GRAINS AND PSEUDOGRAINS: medium-grain #2 bulgur, couscous, farro, freekeh, millet, quinoa, and spelt berries

MILKS: We will use unsweetened almond milk and canned coconut milk most often here. A handful of recipes call for buttermilk, heavy cream, milk, or half-and-half; buy them as needed. Feel free to substitute your favorite plant-based versions.

MISO: white or red miso for sauces (generally, the darker the miso the stronger the taste)

MUSHROOMS (DRIED): dried porcini and/or shiitake, offering powerful umami flavor to meatballs, soups, stews, and sauces

NOODLES: a variety of pasta, soba, ramen noodles, udon

NUT AND SEED BUTTERS: smooth natural (no sugar added) peanut butter, almond butter, and tahini to add creaminess to sauces, dips, and dressings

NUTS AND SEEDS: almonds (whole and sliced), cashews, peanuts, pine nuts, pecans, pistachios, walnuts, chia, ground flaxseed, pepitas, poppy, sesame (black and white), sunflower

OATS: Old-fashioned oats. These are naturally gluten free but often are processed around wheat; so if it is important to you, make sure to buy certified gluten free.

OILS: You'll want a good everyday olive oil that has great flavor and an appealing scent (no off, rancid smell!). For finishing dishes, choose a more flavorful, best-quality olive oil with a deeply fragrant, can't-stop-dipping-into-it kind of flavor. (It will likely be more expensive than the everyday oil.) Use canola oil—always choose organic—for a neutral taste and high-heat cooking. Stock also extra-virgin coconut oil and toasted sesame oil.

OLIVES (AND CAPERS): Pitted green olives such as Castelvetrano (my favorite) or Cerignola, and/or black olives like kalamata, add salty goodness and even balance to many dishes. Capers, extra briny, will do the same.

PEPPER: whole black peppercorns in a mill; grind it fresh each time

PICKLES: pickled onions (see pages 66 and 100) for a pop of sourness and acidity, store-bought or homemade cucumber or zucchini pickles, jarred sweet relish

CHILI OIL

1 Warm ½ cup canola oil (for a neutral taste) or olive oil (for a fragrant, fruity flavor) over low heat until it just begins to shimmer. Add 1 tablespoon Aleppo pepper or 1½ teaspoons crushed red pepper flakes and barely simmer, swirling the pan often, for 30 to 45 seconds until fragrant. (Very small bubbles will gently form and faintly sizzle around the chile flakes.) Transfer the oil to a heat-safe bowl and let it cool completely.

2 When you are ready to serve, you can keep the chile flakes in the oil or strain them out for milder heat.

3 Store in the refrigerator for up to 2 weeks.

VARIATION: Add grated garlic to the hot oil. Adjust the heat level with the amount of pepper flakes.

PIZZA DOUGH: Keep a couple of balls of dough in the fridge or freezer (the recipes in this book make extra!). Thaw frozen dough in the refrigerator overnight or in the morning before pizza night and then bring it to room temperature before using.

RICE: short-grain brown rice and brown and white basmati rice for everyday cooking; black rice, wild rice, sushi rice, bomba (paella) rice, and Arborio rice (for risotto) as needed. (And here's a shortcut—shhhh—frozen brown rice and jasmine or basmati rice is a lifesaver when you're short on time. It cooks through in minutes in the microwave. You can buy frozen rice and grains or make your own and freeze it after it has completely cooled.)

SALT: Fine sea salt for seasoning dishes (it is less processed and more pure than table salt and it contains health-supportive trace minerals); flaky salt (such as Maldon) for finishing

SAUCES (JARRED): Keep a favorite store-bought tomato sauce (such as Rao's Marinara), enchilada sauce (such as Hatch Green Chile Enchilada Sauce or Siete Red or Green Enchilada Sauce), and fresh tomato salsa in stock.

SPICY THINGS: Harissa, red curry paste, chili oil, chili crisp, chili paste or sauce such as sambal oelek, and sriracha, just to name a few, lend some heat and just the right amount of zing to many dishes. Add a little at a time and adjust to taste. To make a simple chili oil, see box; for a more sophisticated one see Garlic-Scallion Chili Oil on page 177.

STOCK: Make your own and freeze it (see page 57). Or keep boxed low-sodium vegetable stock or a favorite vegetable broth base on your shelf.

TAMARI OR SOY SAUCE: Both are made from fermented soybeans, but tamari is typically made without wheat (check the label). I prefer tamari, which I find more balanced (and which I used in testing these recipes). You can also use coconut aminos as a soy-free substitute. All of these products vary greatly by producer, so taste and adjust accordingly.

SPICES: Aleppo pepper, allspice, ancho chile powder, cardamom, chili powder, cinnamon, ground cloves, curry powder, garam masala, garlic powder, ground coriander, ground ginger, ground cumin, fennel seeds, Italian seasoning, nutmeg, dried oregano, paprika and smoked sweet paprika, saffron, star anise, sumac, and ground turmeric.

STIR-FRY SAUCES: hoisin or vegetarian stir-fry sauce or oyster sauce.

SWEETENERS: Pure maple syrup (my #1), raw local honey, natural cane sugar, light brown sugar. (Use agave in place of honey if you wish.) White sparkling sugar or turbinado sugar for finishing baked goods.

TOMATOES (CANNED): paste, puree, diced, and whole

VINEGAR: a variety for versatility in

STANDARDS TO COOK BY

For the greatest success, I suggest following these simple ingredient standards, which are what I relied on when developing and testing the recipes in the book.

- **OLIVE OIL** is extra-virgin.

- **CANOLA OIL** is always organic and can be substituted with other neutral vegetable oils.

- Use toasted (dark) **SESAME OIL** wherever sesame oil is called for (store in the fridge; it perishes quickly).

- **SALT** is always fine sea salt.

- **BLACK PEPPER** is freshly ground.

- **CITRUS JUICES** are freshly squeezed. **CITRUS ZEST** is freshly grated.

- **MAPLE SYRUP** is pure.

- **GRANULATED SUGAR** should be minimally processed cane sugar or conventional granulated sugar.

- I prefer **TAMARI** to **SOY SAUCE,** but you can use them interchangeably. Saltiness and sweetness vary by product and manufacturer, so adjust to taste.

- **GARLIC CLOVES** vary greatly in size so use your best judgment, adjusting to your preference and taste. (I've included an exact measurement of minced garlic when I think it matters—in these instances, the associated number of cloves is an approximation.)

- Trim **SCALLIONS** and use white and all green parts unless otherwise specified.

- When I call for delicate fresh herbs like **CILANTRO**, **DILL**, and **PARSLEY**, you can include thin stems. (No need to fuss!)

- **FLOUR** (for baked goods) is stirred, spooned, and leveled; 1 cup all-purpose flour equals approximately 4.5 ounces.

- **PARMESAN** is always freshly grated. "Finely grated" means with a fine Microplane grater, which produces very fine, pillowy ribbons that melt into a dish (1 ounce = about 1 cup). For topping some pastas and soups, I suggest "coarsely grated" Parmesan for concentrated flavor and texture. This means finely processed in a food processor. Break it into chunks and pulse briefly until it forms fine granules like very coarse sea salt (2 ounces = about ½ cup).

vinaigrettes and sauces: apple cider vinegar (unfiltered), balsamic vinegar, distilled white vinegar (used on occasion), red wine vinegar, unseasoned rice wine vinegar, white wine (or champagne) vinegar

YOGURT AND SOUR CREAM: All types of plain yogurt and sour cream are welcome, including plant-based options, for when you need to add something creamy and a little sour.

> **PANTRY EXTRAS (AS NEEDED):** Active dry yeast, breadcrumbs (Italian-style and panko), canned pumpkin, pickled ginger, puff pastry, nori, walnut oil, wasabi, wine (dry white, mirin, sherry)

STEP 2
GATHER YOUR TOOLS

These are my ten essentials (in alphabetical order) for working with vegetables—that is, other than knives (the #1 tool for vegetables, see page 9).

The Top Ten Tools

1. BLENDER: For super silky soups, sauces, and dressings, I recommend a high-speed blender. A handheld immersion-style blender yields a coarser puree, but it is easy to use, clean, and store.

2. BOWLS: Keep a stack of large metal mixing bowls and seek out an extra-large (at least 8-quart) one, which will come in handy when you are washing or tossing (to dress) large quantities of greens or other vegetables.

3. CITRUS JUICER: I prefer a handheld citrus squeezer to get every last drop out of the fruit. You can use any reamer.

4. FOOD PROCESSOR: If you have the space, leave a food processor (standard size or larger) on the counter and you will be much more inclined to use it. I call for it often to cut down on heavy prep and to make doughs, batters, sauces, and more. Safely store the shredding and slicing blades nearby; we will use them, too. I often use a mini food processor for combining salsas, grinding nuts, grating Parmesan, whipping cheese, blending oil, or making a small-batch pesto, dip, or creamy vinaigrette.

5. GRATERS: A box grater or an extra-coarse or ribbon Microplane, and a fine rasp-style Microplane, are essential. I use the latter for grating hard cheeses like Parmesan, as well as garlic.

6. KITCHEN TOWELS: Gauzy cotton tea towels are the best kind for standard use as well as for drying, wrapping, and storing lettuces and greens. They also work like cheesecloth when you need to squeeze and release liquid from shredded zucchini. Keep a good stock of sturdy lint-free kitchen towels that you can often use in place of paper towels.

7. SCALE: I'd like to highlight and underline it—a digital scale is a must.

8. STRAINERS: Prepping and cooking vegetables require a lot of strainers: 1. A large stainless-steel colander with larger holes to drain just-washed veggies and pasta; 2. A small, 2-cup version of the large colander to drain berries and canned beans; 3. A small handheld double-mesh strainer to wash and drain grains; 4. A freestanding wire colander to strain grains and cooked vegetables; 5. A spider (a mesh strainer attached to a long handle) for carefully removing vegetables and pasta from boiling liquid without having to drain it.

9. TOASTER OVEN: I use mine constantly for toasting nuts (fast and easy) and bread, melting cheese, and reheating and re-crisping single portions of so many dishes.

10. VEGETABLE PEELERS: A swivel peeler for cylindrical/long vegetables and a Y-shaped peeler for round ones. I love a peeler with a julienne blade to produce pretty ribbons.

OTHER HELPFUL TOOLS AND SUPPLIES: electric kettle; potato masher; silicone brush; portion scoops (ice cream scoops); 2½- to 3-inch round pastry cutters; rolling pin; collapsible steamer basket; handheld mixer; waffle iron; surgical gloves or other food-safe gloves; multiple sets of measuring cups and spoons; 1-cup, 2-cup, and 4-cup liquid measures; a ruler; plenty of 13 × 18-inch sheet pans; a 9½ × 13-inch quarter-sheet pan; a 3-inch handheld strainer for citrus juice and draining capers and olives; wire cooling racks

---

TAKE NOTE: Serving Dishes
Vegetable-forward food is beautiful, so acquire some white ceramic serving bowls and dishes or handcrafted colorful ones that will show off your work. For serving dishes family-style, I regularly use large shallow serving bowls, a large round platter, and a large wooden board.

Pots and Pans

- A large 12-inch (or larger) stainless-steel skillet with lid. You can use a large cast-iron one if that is your preference. Cast iron gets very hot and stays hot, so you may need to adjust the heat as necessary.

- A medium 10-inch skillet. This can be stainless steel, cast iron, or a nontoxic nonstick skillet.

- A small saucepan and a medium saucepan or heavy-bottomed pot
- A large pot for boiling pasta and making stock
- A large Dutch oven or large, deep sauté pan with lid for stews and long-cooking sauces

> **TAKE NOTE:** A 14-inch, flat-bottomed carbon steel wok is extremely useful for stir-frying and, in general, comfortably cooking large quantities of vegetables. A cast-iron grill for your stovetop or a grill pan is helpful, too.

STEP 3
PREP YOUR KNIVES AND WORK SURFACE

Build Your Knife Kit

You do not need a big block of knives—it just takes up valuable counter space. I recommend the following for your kit:

- **A GOOD-QUALITY, ALL-PURPOSE 8-INCH CHEF'S KNIFE** that can take on almost all cutting jobs. A stainless-steel or high-carbon stainless-steel knife should last you a lifetime if you look after it. Don't put it in the dishwasher, and store it carefully so as not to damage its tip and blade.

- **A PARING KNIFE** with a 3- to 4-inch blade for precise maneuvering and detailed work

- **A SERRATED KNIFE**, 8 to 12 inches long, with moderately deep, pointed serrations

- **A HANDHELD VEGETABLE SLICER OR JAPANESE MANDOLINE.** Keep focused and use a metal mesh glove until you feel comfortable.

Sharp Knives Are Safe Knives

It's important to maintain your knife's edge and keep it sharp for performance and safety. A sharp knife produces clean, easy cuts. A dull knife requires you to apply more force and can slip and cause injury.

TO HONE YOUR KNIVES: A knife's cutting edge is made up of very fine, almost invisible teeth that can easily get knocked out of alignment with regular use and when cutting hard materials. This will make a knife seem dull even when it's not. You can straighten the edge of your knife by running it along a honing or sharpening steel. Ideally, hone your knife before each use; at the very least, do it before and after big cutting jobs.

TO SHARPEN KNIVES: When your knife is dull and is performing poorly no matter how many times you hone it, it's time to sharpen it—a process that essentially creates a new edge by removing metal from the blade. Look around for a professional knife sharpener or sharpening service.

Secure Your Work Surface

You need a firm and stable surface that will allow you to work safely with ease and control. My recommendations:

A large (ideally) or mid-size wooden cutting board or butcher block. Wooden boards just feel good under your knife and will likely last forever if you take care of them. You can get by with a mid-size board that is 16 to 18 inches by 12 inches, but a larger 15 by 20 inches is recommended. I like eco-conscious teak for its durability and balance. It's soft enough that it is gentle on the knife's edge, but hard enough to produce nice, clean cuts. It's also relatively easy to maintain compared to other woods. I like one from Teakhaus (without a juice canal).

A couple of dishwasher-safe smaller, mid-size plastic or composite cutting boards with rubber "feet" or grips. These are good for small, quick jobs like chopping a handful of herbs or slicing a tomato or avocado—or if you don't want to take care of a wooden board.

NOTE: If your board is slipping, place a damp kitchen towel or paper towel underneath it.

STORE-BOUGHT, PRE-PREPPED VEGETABLES

Many vegetables are available precut and packaged (often, even, prewashed). Most do not compete with fresh whole vegetables (especially in-season, local ones), but they can work just fine when you are short on time or options. Just take note: They can be more expensive, they aren't always prewashed, and many types will perish very quickly. Make sure they look fresh: Watch for dryness or too much moisture in the package. Use them right away.

- **DELICATE SALAD GREENS** such as baby arugula, baby spinach, mixed greens, romaine, and other lettuces. (These are the most consistently reliable and delicious of the packaged options. I use them often.)

- **PRECOOKED AND PEELED BEETS:** Use a paring knife to trim the stem end if it has been left on the beets. (Pay attention to labels—some precooked beets are marinated in vinegar.)

- **CURLY KALE:** Remove thick stems. Although prepackaged curly kale is not ideal for a fresh salad, it can be used successfully in soups and stews.

- **BROCCOLI AND CAULIFLOWER:** Trim dry or browning machine-cut ends and cut the florets down into smaller pieces.

- **SHELLED ENGLISH PEAS, SUGAR SNAP PEAS, SNOW PEAS:** Watch for too much moisture/condensation on the peas or the package interior.

- **BUTTERNUT SQUASH:** The cuts are rarely uniform, so consider it only for purees, mashes, and soups.

STEP 4
BRUSH UP ON THE BASICS: VEGETABLE PREP 101

Remove Stems and Leaves

Remove stems and leaves from root vegetables like beets, carrots, celery root, radishes, and turnips before you refrigerate them. The leaves perish faster than the roots and they also pull moisture from the roots. (Snip the stems and leaves off of kohlrabi, too.) Don't cut into the root, just trim the stems an inch from the root. Store the roots on their own. Store the leaves and stems separately if you would like to use them; or discard them.

> **TAKE NOTE: How to Revive Vegetables That Need a Lift**
> Before you compost wilted greens, endives and chicories, romaine lettuce, slightly soft beets, cabbage, radishes, and turnips, and close-to-flabby carrots, give them a soak in cold water or, even better, ice water. If they aren't too far gone, this offers a last chance to bring them back to life.

Best Practices: Washing and Drying

Always wash vegetables. (Washing is assumed in every recipe.) Make sure to give extra care to leafy greens and lettuces; multilayered vegetables like fennel, leeks, and scallions; and the base of stalks like celery and bok choy where dirt tends to settle. Give root vegetables a gentle, quick scrub with your fingers or a brush. Asparagus, broccoli, and cauliflower just need a rinse. When baking produce or using it raw in a dish, dry it well. In some cases, mushrooms just need cleaning with a damp towel to avoid adding moisture to a dish.

The Dunk-and-Shake Method

Good for: all types of hearty greens and delicate lettuces, herbs, and small loose vegetables like green beans, snow peas, sugar snap peas, baby artichokes, and Brussels sprouts. Also good for quartered cabbage heads and halved or quartered fennel.

Fill a bowl with cold water. For vegetables with long stems and leaves, first separate the stems from the leaves (and treat each like a separate vegetable). Immerse the leaves, stems, or veggies in the water. Agitate them, swishing them back and forth, more gently for delicate items and more vigorously for others. Lift the leaves so as not to disturb any sand or dirt that has settled at the bottom of the bowl. Drain the water and repeat as necessary until there is no visible dirt remaining. (Don't use more water than you need!) Rub stems under water to help remove any stubborn dirt.

To dry, place vegetables in a colander to drain. For vegetables that will be enjoyed raw and those that will be fried, grilled, roasted, or sautéed, wrap them in a lint-free kitchen towel and pat them mostly dry. For cabbage, lettuces, or hearty greens headed for a salad or slaw, use a salad spinner to remove as much excess water as possible. For vegetables on their way to a soup, stew, or steamer, just let excess water drain thoroughly; a little excess water is fine.

The Dunk-and-Scrub Method

Good for: root vegetables and potatoes

Place the vegetables in a bowl and fill it with enough cold water to cover. Agitate them, then use your fingers to rub and scrub off dirt. You can also use a vegetable brush to scrub gently. Lift the vegetables out of the bowl and give them a quick rinse to remove any remaining dirt. Drain in a colander and pat mostly dry with a lint-free kitchen towel.

Supreme
(segment citrus)

Extra-small dice
(brunoise), ⅛ inch

Small dice (finely diced),
¼ inch

Garlic: smashed,
sliced, minced

Matchsticks,
minced

Wide ribbons with a
vegetable peeler

Minced
(very finely chopped)

Quarter moons

Half moons

Chopped
(not uniform in size)

Chiffonade
(thin or thick ribbons)

Medium dice, ½ inch

Large dice, ¾ inch

Slabs

Sticks

Thinly sliced

Rounds

⅛ inch coins

¼ inch coins

1/16 inch coins

Thinly sliced on a diagonal

Steak

1-inch slices on a diagonal

Shredded

ENTRÉE-WORTHY SALADS.

THE GREEN SALAD   16

Every Season Green Salad with House Lemon Vinaigrette 18 • Baby Beet and Blueberry Salad with Avocado and Basil Vinaigrette 21 • Delicata Squash and Apple Salad with Arugula and Maple Vinaigrette 23

THE KALE SALAD   25

Kale and Watermelon Panzanella 26 • Lacinato Kale and Jalapeño-Pickled Golden Raisins with Avocado Dressing and Corn Nuts 28 • Kale-Radicchio Caesar with Crispy Chickpea "Croutons" 29

THE GRAIN SALAD   31

Asparagus-Spinach Farro Salad with Almonds and Orange-Sesame Vinaigrette 33 • Tomato–Green Bean Freekeh Salad with Pistachios and Lemon-Feta Vinaigrette 34 • Lemony Rainbow Carrot Couscous Salad 36

THE BEAN SALAD   37

Parisian-Style Lentil and Crudités Salad 39 • Tomato-Bean Salad with Shaved Fennel, Spinach, and Tomato Vinaigrette 40 • Marinated "Agrodolce" Sweet Peppers and Cannellini Bean Salad 41

The Green Salad

This is a hearty, big salad of greens with plenty of thoughtful mix-ins that make it a crave-worthy, deeply satisfying, and nutrient-rich meal to enjoy every day. Make the composed versions on the following pages, and learn to throw one together with the hodgepodge of ingredients that you have on hand.

Greens + Veg + Legumes + Fruit + Nuts or Seeds + Grains + Extra Richness

THE BASIC STEPS

1 SELECT YOUR GREENS

- **Crunchy/Mild:** cabbage, iceberg, little gems, romaine
- **Delicate/Mild:** baby greens like a "spring mix," butter lettuce, red-leaf lettuce
- **Delicate/Spicy:** arugula, baby mustard greens
- **Hearty/Strong:** kale, spinach, Swiss chard (chop these into small bite-size pieces)
- **Crunchy/Bitter:** chicories and endives like Belgian endive, escarole, frisée, radicchio

2 ADD MORE VEGETABLES

- **Raw and Fresh:** carrot, cucumber, fennel, jicama, radish, tomatoes
- **Raw or Roasted:** asparagus, Brussels sprouts, celery root, corn, kohlrabi, onion, peppers, turnips
- **Roasted:** artichokes, beets, broccoli, cauliflower, mushrooms, potato, rutabaga, sweet potato, winter squash
- **Blanched:** shelled edamame, freshly shelled peas, sugar snap peas, snow peas
- **Leafy Herbs:** basil, chives, cilantro, dill, mint, or tarragon
- **Pickled anything**, always

3 ADD LEGUMES

- **Canned Beans:** chickpeas (top choice for consistent texture), black beans, kidney beans, white beans like cannellini or Great Northern
- **Made-at-Home Beans:** any common varieties or heirloom varieties like giant corona beans, cranberry beans, flageolets, or gigante beans
- **Cooked Black or French Lentils**

4 ADD FRUIT (FOR SWEETNESS): apple, berries, grapes, oranges and other citrus; pear, persimmon, stone fruit (such as peach or plum), dried fruit (such as cherries, cranberries, dates, or raisins)

5 TOSS IN TOASTED NUTS AND SEEDS (FOR CRUNCH): almonds, cashews, hazelnuts, pecans, pepitas, pine nuts, pistachios, poppy seeds, sesame seeds, sunflower seeds, walnuts

6 GIVE IT A GRAIN (FOR SOMETHING HEARTY/STARCHY): bulgur, farro, fonio, freekeh, millet, quinoa, spelt berries, wheat berries, wild rice

7 ADD EXTRA RICHNESS: diced avocado, any cheese, pan-seared tofu (see page 151). Note: A creamy dressing, like Green Goddess Dip on page 224, will also work here.

8 DRESS IT: Follow a simple ratio of 1 part vinegar or citrus juice to 3 parts good olive oil. Stop there or dress it up with minced shallot, a smashed garlic clove (allow to marinate in the mixture), Dijon mustard, herbs, miso, soy sauce, tahini, or something sweet like agave, honey, maple syrup, or sugar.

A quick sesame dressing is excellent on a simple side salad (especially with the stir-fries in this book): Grind 3 tablespoons toasted white sesame seeds in a small food processor to a fine powder. Add 1 tablespoon wine vinegar, 1 tablespoon soy sauce, ¼ teaspoon grated peeled ginger, 2 teaspoons maple syrup, and 1 teaspoon toasted sesame oil. Blend until evenly combined.

Or try any of the other flavorful dressings and vinaigrettes used throughout the book (see page 317 for a complete list). Whichever you choose, season the salad and add enough dressing to make it taste good!

TIPS AND TAKEAWAYS

- Keep prewashed lettuce on hand. Consider mixing a variety of greens for interesting textures and flavors: delicate, hearty, crisp; mild, bitter, spicy.

- Use the Dunk-and-Shake Method (page 11) to wash lettuces and other leafy greens.

- Spin it in a salad spinner to dry it or, when short on time, gently shake off excess water and pat dry. For extra crisp lettuce, wash and mostly dry the lettuce leaves then wrap them in a large tea towel. Place the wrapped lettuce leaves in a bowl in the refrigerator until you are ready to prepare the salad.

- Stock up on your favorite dressing, wine vinegars like apple cider, balsamic, champagne, sherry, red and white wine, and rice wine vinegar; find a good-quality olive oil that tastes amazing.

- Chop it. Before adding to your salad bowl and dressing, break down large-leaf lettuces, cabbage, and even baby spinach into bite-size pieces or ribbons to evenly distribute vinaigrette and make each forkful balanced.

- Use a large bowl to toss the salad. All the ingredients need room to move and dress evenly.

- Add something sweet and something crunchy: raw or dried fruit and toasted nuts or seeds are my recommendation. Together, they also bulk up a salad and give it entrée status. Also consider candied nuts, toasted Parmesan crisps (aka Frico, below), croutons, crispy chickpeas (see page 29); or simply sweeten your dressing.

Frico (Toasted Parmesan Crisps)

MAKES 4 FOUR-INCH ROUNDS

Heaping 1 cup finely grated Parmesan cheese

Heat the oven to 400°F with a rack in the middle position. Line a sheet pan with parchment paper or a silicone baking mat. Evenly divide the shredded cheese into 4 separate mounds on the baking sheet. Use a fork to gently spread out each pile into a flat, even round, making sure the cheese strands are mostly overlapping. Bake for 6 to 8 minutes until bubbling and a light golden brown in color (do not overbake!). Use a metal spatula to slide under the frico and transfer them to a cooling rack. Let cool.

NOTE: This recipe doubles easily—just use two sheet pans spaced evenly apart in the oven.

Every Season Green Salad
with House Lemon Vinaigrette

SERVES 2 AS A MAIN,
6 TO 8 AS A SIDE

INGREDIENT INFO: Bulgur comes in a range of sizes, from fine grain to extra coarse. If you are unsure of what size you are working with, cook the bulgur according to the package instructions. For a gluten-free option, try quinoa or fonio.

MAKE AHEAD: The prepped veg and mix-ins keep for days. Double the prep to enjoy individual salads throughout the week.

HOW TO USE A MANDOLINE: Set the slicer to cut at about ⅟₁₆-inch. Carefully press each root against the blade. Using even pressure, glide back and forth to make even slices. Don't try to slice too quickly, but do build some momentum in order to easily push food through the blade. Wear a protective glove until you build comfort.

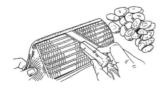

Greens plus a generous serving of goodies—shaved carrot and radish, bulgur, chickpeas, dried cranberries, and feta—come together with a standout citrusy dressing to make an entrée-worthy salad that is perfect all throughout the year. Use a mandoline slicer (or a chef's knife) to produce extra-thin cuts of raw veggies for this salad. The recipe for House Lemon Vinaigrette makes more than double what you'll need. Keep it in the fridge at all times—ready to dress a simple side of greens.

¼ cup fine- or medium-grain bulgur (or ⅔ cup cooked and cooled bulgur, see Ingredient Info)

¾ cup water

5 ounces mixed baby greens or other in-season lettuces (up to 8 ounces)

1 large or 4 to 5 small carrots, sliced into ⅟₁₆-inch coins

4 small radishes or 1 medium watermelon radish, sliced into ⅟₁₆-inch coins

⅔ cup canned chickpeas, drained, rinsed, and patted dry

½ cup sweetened dried cranberries

½ cup freshly crumbled feta cheese, plus more for topping (optional)

House Lemon Vinaigrette (page 21)

Fine sea salt and freshly ground black pepper

---

1 Combine the bulgur and water in a small pot and bring to a boil over medium-high heat. Reduce the heat to low, cover, and simmer for 10 minutes; remove from the heat and let it sit, covered, for 5 minutes. Fluff with a fork and cool.

2 In a large bowl, combine the greens, carrot, and radishes. Gently toss them together with clean hands, separating and evenly distributing the raw vegetables. Add the bulgur, chickpeas, cranberries, and feta (if using). Drizzle with ¼ cup of the vinaigrette and gently toss the salad, evenly distributing the dressing and ingredients. Add more dressing if needed and adjust salt and add pepper to taste. Transfer to a large serving bowl or individual salad bowls. If desired, top with more feta and black pepper.

House Lemon Vinaigrette

MAKES ABOUT 1 CUP

2 tablespoons freshly squeezed
lemon juice

¼ cup rice wine vinegar

2½ tablespoons pure maple syrup

1¼ teaspoons Dijon mustard

¾ teaspoon fine sea salt

½ cup plus 2 tablespoons extra-virgin
olive oil

Whisk together the lemon juice, vinegar, maple syrup, mustard, and salt in a
medium bowl. Slowly stream in the oil while you whisk quickly and constantly,
continuing until the mixture emulsifies. Refrigerate for up to 3 weeks.

Baby Beet and Blueberry Salad
with Avocado and Basil Vinaigrette

SERVES 2 AS A MAIN,
4 TO 6 AS A SIDE

SHORTCUT: Use 1 pound of
precooked and packaged
beets. To concentrate
their flavor, spread them
on a sheet pan, toss them
in a light drizzle of olive
oil, salt, and pepper, and
then broil them until they
sizzle and blacken slightly
around the edges, 5 to 8
minutes, carefully shaking
the pan halfway through.

PREP TIP: If you want to
protect your hands from
beet juice stains, use
food-safe kitchen gloves
when you peel and cut
the beets.

When blueberries are spilling over the tables at farmers markets and baby beets
are stacked high, it's time to make this gorgeous salad. The pickled onions are an
extra step if you don't already have a larger batch (see page 100) in the fridge, but
they add brightness to the salad, even if you just give them a rest in the vinegar
mixture while you pull together the salad.

1¼ pounds Chioggia, red, and/or
golden baby beets (see Shortcut)

¾ cup plus 3 tablespoons water

4 tablespoons apple cider vinegar

2 tablespoons extra-virgin olive oil

¾ teaspoon fine sea salt, plus more
as needed

1 small red onion, thinly sliced

½ teaspoon sugar

Basil Vinaigrette (recipe follows)

5 ounces baby butter lettuce leaves
(or little gems, romaine, or mixed greens)

Freshly ground black pepper

⅔ cup fresh blueberries

1 large avocado, diced

2 tablespoons toasted sunflower seeds

Flaky sea salt, such as Maldon, for finishing

2 ounces freshly crumbled or thinly sliced
blue cheese (optional)

(recipe continues)

MAKE AHEAD: The beets and dressing can be made a day in advance, and the pickled onions, up to 5 days ahead.

SWAPS:

- Try other summer herbs like cilantro, mint, and/or dill in place of the basil in the vinaigrette.

- Try the Basil Vinaigrette with tri-color quinoa, halved cherry tomatoes, corn shaved off the cob, and a handful of chopped basil. Use arugula for the greens—but dress it separately and scatter it over the beets and mix-ins.

1 Roast the beets. Heat the oven to 375°F with a rack in the middle position. Combine the beets with the ¾ cup water, 1 tablespoon of apple cider vinegar, the oil, and ½ teaspoon of fine sea salt in a roasting pan. Turn the beets to coat them in the mixture and cover with aluminum foil. Roast until tender—a paring knife should pierce the skin and reach the center without resistance—about 40 minutes. (For larger beets, this could take 60 minutes or longer depending on size.) Remove the beets from the cooking liquid and cool. Peel and cut the beets into bite-size wedges.

2 Make the pickled onions. In a small to medium bowl, combine the onion with the remaining 3 tablespoons of apple cider vinegar, the remaining 3 tablespoons of water, the sugar, and the remaining ¼ teaspoon of fine sea salt. Stir to combine and let stand, stirring occasionally, while the beets cook.

3 Assemble the salad. In a large shallow serving bowl, toss the greens with 3 tablespoons of the dressing or enough to coat the leaves, and season with fine sea salt and pepper to taste. In a small mixing bowl, dress the beets in 1 tablespoon of the dressing and season with fine sea salt and pepper to taste. Gently layer or toss the lettuce leaves with the beets, blueberries, avocado, sunflower seeds, and ⅓ cup to ½ cup of pickled onions. Season with flaky sea salt and pepper to taste. Top with blue cheese if you are adding it and an extra drizzle of basil vinaigrette if you wish.

Basil Vinaigrette

MAKES ABOUT ⅔ CUP

½ cup packed fresh basil leaves (about ¼ ounce)

2 tablespoons white balsamic vinegar (or white wine vinegar)

Fine sea salt

1 tablespoon honey (or agave or maple syrup)

½ cup extra-virgin olive oil

Combine the basil, vinegar, ½ teaspoon fine sea salt, and the honey in a blender and blend to chop the basil. With the blender running on low speed, stream in the oil, then cover and turn up the speed to high. Blend until the dressing is smooth and emulsified. Adjust the salt to taste. Refrigerate in an airtight container for up to 3 days. Whisk well before using.

Delicata Squash and Apple Salad
with Arugula and Maple Vinaigrette

SERVES 2 TO 4 AS A MAIN.
6 TO 8 AS A SIDE

SWAPS:

- Try butternut squash or sweet potato as a stand-in for delicata. Swap pecans, hazelnuts, or pepitas for the walnuts.

- Try other fall fruits like pear or Fuyu persimmon in place of the apple.

BUTCHER TIP: For how to break down delicata squash, see page 24. Shred the radicchio into thin ribbons and let it stand in a bowl of ice water for 15 to 20 minutes until it crisps up. Drain and dry well.

This fall entrée salad is gorgeous and extremely versatile. Delicata squash's thin skin means there's no need to peel it—it's quick work to break down the squash. This translates to easy prep and fast cooking: it'll roast while you pull together the rest of the salad. For a special gathering, add ribbons of radicchio (which add color and some balancing bitterness) and bedazzle it with a handful of pomegranate seeds.

1¼ to 1½ pounds delicata squash (2 small or 1 large squash), cut into ⅓-inch half or quarter moons (see Butcher Tip)

4 tablespoons extra-virgin olive oil

Fine sea salt

1 tablespoon plus 2 teaspoons pure maple syrup

1 tablespoon balsamic vinegar

5 ounces baby arugula

Heaping 1 cup shredded radicchio (4 to 5 leaves), optional

1 large Honeycrisp or Fuji apple, cored and ½-inch diced

Heaping ½ cup walnuts, toasted and chopped

¾ cup coarsely grated ricotta salata cheese (about 2 ounces), optional

Freshly ground black pepper, for topping

---

1 Roast the squash. Heat the oven to 425°F with a rack in the middle position. Place the squash on a sheet pan and toss with 1 tablespoon of oil and ½ teaspoon salt. Spread the squash pieces in a single layer with as much room as possible between them. Roast the squash until golden brown, 18 to 20 minutes, then flip and continue to roast until well browned on both sides and tender, another 7 to 10 minutes. Let cool.

2 Meanwhile, make the dressing. Whisk together the maple syrup, vinegar, and ¼ teaspoon salt in a small bowl. Whisk in the remaining 3 tablespoons of oil until well blended.

3 Assemble the salad. In a large bowl, mix together the arugula and radicchio if you are adding it, and about three quarters of the dressing to lightly and evenly coat the leaves. Toss in the apple, nuts, and squash. Add more vinaigrette to taste. If using the ricotta salata, add most of it and toss, then finish with the rest on top. Top with freshly ground black pepper and serve.

HOW TO BREAK DOWN DELICATA SQUASH:

Trim the ends and cut in half lengthwise. Scoop out the seeds and discard them.

For a small or narrow squash, slice half moons. If extra-wide, cut each half again lengthwise then crosswise to produce quarter moons.

The Kale Salad

Kale, nutrient-dense and super-powered, has many culinary virtues beyond its health benefits that stand out in an entrée-status salad: its own flavor, loads of texture, and sturdy, creviced leaves that hold hearty add-ins and deliver creamy, silky dressings. Kale has real potential to satisfy on a whole other level, and as a salad it deserves special attention as a meal of its own.

HOW TO PREP KALE

Properly washing kale can feel a bit unwieldy so strip the leaves (and discard the stems) before you wash them.

STEP 1: De-stem Kale

Hold the stem firmly with one hand just at the base of the leaf. Apply a pinch grip just above that hand and slide your hand upward along the center rib, stripping off the leaves at the same time. With lacinato kale, the leaves should come right off in one swoop.

Curly kale may require that you snap off the leaves as you slide then return to the stem to pull of any leaves still hanging on.

STEP 2: Wash Kale

Fill the largest bowl you have with enough water to dunk and shake the leaves under the water to release dirt. Lift the leaves, rinse the bowl and repeat until the kale is clean (see The Dunk and Shake Method, page 11). Drain it and dry it well in a salad spinner or blot it dry with a kitchen towel, then wrap it in a clean towel and place it in the refrigerator until you are ready to use it.

STEP 3: Chiffonade or Chop Kale

For lacinato kale, stack the leaves, fold them in half crosswise, then roll into cigar-shaped bundle. Cut through crosswise to produce thin ribbons (see page 164).

To chop curly kale or a lot of any type of kale at once, gather the leaves in a rough pile and roll them in on one another tightly. Use your non-knife hand to hold the mound of kale down. Cut through the bundled stack, making deliberate, even pieces to your desired consistency.

TIPS AND TAKEAWAYS

- Avoid prewashed, precut kale in raw kale salads—its flavor and quality are inferior and it won't last as long (it can become dry or slimy). If you use it, make sure to remove any thick stems and wash the leaves.

- Entrée-size kale salads call for a lot of kale. A large restaurant-size (at least 8-quart) mixing bowl will allow for comfortable, mess-free tossing.

- To temper kale's strong-ish flavor and chewy texture, chop it into bite-size pieces and massage the dressing into the leaves.

- Raw chopped kale lasts for 3 to 5 days if you remove most of the moisture from the leaves before refrigerating. Wrap the leaves (chopped or unchopped) in a large tea towel or store in a paper towel–lined container. A dressed kale salad will last for hours, which makes it a prime candidate for a meal that requires early prep or transport.

- Creamy dressings love kale and kale loves creamy dressings.

Kale and Watermelon Panzanella

SERVES 2 TO 3 AS A MAIN.
4 TO 6 AS A SIDE

PREP TIP: Toast the pepitas in a small dry skillet over medium heat, shaking the pan frequently, until golden and just beginning to pop, 3 to 5 minutes. (Alternatively, toast them on a pan in a toaster oven for a couple of minutes, watching closely.)

BUTCHER TIP: Shave the onion with a handheld mandoline slicer (see page 18) or slice it as thin as possible with a knife.

There is a beautiful moment in the summer when watermelon and just-cut, perky greens arrive at the market, and this salad is here for it! The dish is a take on both a classic Italian tomato bread salad and a Mediterranean-style watermelon–feta salad with all the sweet, sour, crispy, salty, and creamy notes to elevate it.

---

4 cups torn bite-size crusty bread, such as ciabatta (extra-hard crusts removed)

2 tablespoons plus ¼ cup extra-virgin olive oil

Fine sea salt

½ red onion, shaved (see Butcher Tip)

3 tablespoons freshly squeezed lime juice (from 1 to 2 limes)

1 tablespoon balsamic vinegar

¾ teaspoon sugar or maple syrup

3 packed cups stemmed and chopped curly kale (about half a bunch)

4 heaping cups cubed watermelon

3 tablespoons toasted pepitas (see Prep Tip)

1 cup freshly crumbled feta cheese

Freshly ground black pepper

Flaky sea salt, such as Maldon, for finishing (optional)

---

1 Make the croutons. Heat the oven to 375°F with a rack in the middle position. Place the bread on a sheet pan, and toss with 2 tablespoons (or more) of the oil and a generous pinch of salt until well coated and flavorful. Spread out the bread and bake until golden and crisp, 9 to 12 minutes. Do not over toast or burn; the croutons will continue to crisp as they cool.

2 Make the pickled onions. Combine the onion, a pinch of fine sea salt, and 2 tablespoons of the lime juice and let stand, turning occasionally, while you prepare the rest of the salad.

3 Make the dressing. In a small bowl, whisk together the remaining 1 tablespoon of lime juice, the balsamic vinegar, the sugar, and ¼ teaspoon fine sea salt. Stream in the ¼ cup oil, whisking until emulsified.

4 Assemble the salad. Combine the kale in a large serving bowl with 2 tablespoons of the dressing. Toss together or massage the dressing into the kale with clean hands until the leaves are well coated. Pile the watermelon on top, and add three quarters each of the pickled onions, pepitas, and feta. Drizzle with 1 tablespoon of the dressing and toss the watermelon, onions, pepitas, and feta and combine evenly—don't actively combine with the kale at first. Add about three quarters of the croutons and another 1 tablespoon of the dressing. Now toss everything in with the kale to combine. Sprinkle with the remaining pepitas and feta. Add the remaining onion if you wish. Generously season with black pepper and, if using, a light sprinkling of flaky sea salt. Adjust seasoning and dressing to taste. Top with the remaining croutons.

Lacinato Kale and Jalapeño-Pickled Golden Raisins

with Avocado Dressing and Corn Nuts

SERVES 2 TO 4 AS A MAIN,
4 TO 8 AS A SIDE

BUTCHER TIP:

• See page 164 for how to cut the kale into ribbons. Massage the dressing evenly into the kale to help break it down and infuse it with flavor.

• Tossing this salad with a spoon won't allow you to evenly coat the kale leaves.

SWAP: Feel free to replace the corn nuts with crispy breadcrumbs, with or without garlic (see page 79).

This kale salad hits all the right notes with salt, acid, heat, crunch, and richness. All of the components can be prepped ahead (and in fact the raisins should be pickled for at least 30 minutes, ideally overnight). You may think I'm calling for too much dressing and toppings here, but trust me, each element comes together in a spectacular fashion that will make this salad a complete meal on its own.

FOR THE RAISINS

½ cup water

⅓ cup rice wine vinegar

3 tablespoons apple cider vinegar

2 tablespoons sugar

¾ teaspoon fine sea salt

1 cup golden raisins

1 large jalapeño, quartered lengthwise (seeds removed to reduce heat)

FOR THE DRESSING

⅓ cup freshly squeezed lime juice (about 4 small limes)

1 garlic clove, smashed

¾ cup smashed avocado (1 medium-large avocado)

⅓ cup chopped scallions

½ cup water

1 teaspoon fine sea salt

¼ teaspoon freshly ground black pepper

5 tablespoons canola oil

FOR THE SALAD

Heaping ½ cup corn nuts

1 pound lacinato kale (2 bunches), stemmed, washed and dried well, leaves cut into thin ribbons

Fine sea salt and freshly ground black pepper

Scant 1 cup finely grated Pecorino Romano cheese (about 1 ounce)

1 Pickle the golden raisins. Whisk together the water, rice wine vinegar, apple cider vinegar, sugar, and salt in a wide-mouth jar until the sugar and salt dissolve. Add the raisins and jalapeño, stir to combine, and let stand for at least 30 minutes or ideally overnight (or up to 7 days).

2 Make the dressing. In a high-speed blender for the smoothest result (or a food processor for a more textured one), combine the lime juice and garlic and let it stand for 5 minutes. Add the avocado, scallions, water, salt, pepper, and oil and blend until evenly combined and creamy. Scrape down the sides of the vessel and blend again if needed. (If you are using your food processor here, process the corn nuts first (see step 3) and simply rinse the bowl—no need to dry it.)

3 Assemble the salad. Process the corn nuts in the bowl of a food processor until broken down into a fine, gravel-like consistency. In the largest mixing bowl you have, combine the kale and 1 cup of the avocado–scallion dressing and massage the dressing evenly into the leaves. Season lightly with salt and pepper to taste. Drain the raisins and add about ¾ cup of them, half of the corn nuts, and half of the cheese, and gently toss to evenly combine. Add more dressing to taste if needed. Transfer half of the salad to a shallow serving bowl, layer half of the remaining corn nuts and cheese over the top, then transfer the remaining kale to the serving bowl. Evenly sprinkle the salad with the remaining raisins, cheese, and corn nuts, and more black pepper to taste.

Kale-Radicchio Caesar
with Crispy Chickpea "Croutons"

SERVES 4 AS A MAIN,
8 AS A SIDE

TAKE NOTE: The chickpeas are an irresistible snack. (There may not be enough left by the time you need to serve the salad.) If you can't exercise restraint, double the batch using two sheet pans to prevent overcrowding. Also, play with seasoning if you are making a batch for a snack. They will store for days in an airtight container in or out of the fridge.

SWAPS: Replace the kale with romaine or iceberg lettuce or add either to the kale mix. The radicchio is optional but recommended—it adds color, crunch, and a hint of bitterness.

With all its nooks and crannies, curly kale is made to take on a creamy, Caesar-Style dressing. The dressing evokes classic richness and creaminess, but it's lighter (and I think more flavorful) made with miso, yogurt, lemon, and tamari. Crispy chickpeas are a stand-in for traditional croutons. If you want to move away from a Caesar altogether, add some chopped apple and a handful of nuts.

FOR THE CRISPY CHICKPEAS

1 can (15½ ounces) chickpeas, rinsed and drained

1 tablespoon extra-virgin olive oil

Fine sea salt

1 garlic clove, grated on a Microplane

FOR THE CAESAR-STYLE DRESSING

About 2 tablespoons freshly squeezed lemon juice

1 garlic clove, finely grated with a Microplane

2 teaspoons white miso paste

2 teaspoons tamari or soy sauce

1 teaspoon Dijon mustard

¼ teaspoon freshly ground black pepper

⅓ cup low-fat or full-fat plain Greek yogurt

¼ cup extra-virgin olive oil

Fine sea salt

FOR THE SALAD

1 bunch (8 to 10 ounces) kale, stems removed, leaves chopped

3 to 4 cups shredded radicchio (1 small head)

Finely grated Parmesan cheese

Fine sea salt and freshly ground black pepper

(recipe continues)

1 Make the chickpeas. Heat the oven to 350°F with a rack in the middle position. Place a clean kitchen towel or a couple of paper towels on a sheet pan, and spread the chickpeas on top, patting the chickpeas mostly dry. Use your fingertips to gently rub the chickpeas to remove the skins. (Note: You do not have to precisely remove the skin from every chickpea, just remove the ones that are naturally coming off after a gentle rub.) Remove the towel and discard the chickpea skins.

2 Drizzle the chickpeas with the oil, sprinkle with ¼ teaspoon salt, and add the grated garlic. Toss the chickpeas continuously with two spoons or your hands until evenly coated in oil and garlic. (The garlic should not clump in one place.) Spread them out and roast, shaking the pan halfway through, until they are golden and evenly crispy, 40 to 45 minutes. Let the chickpeas cool completely. If needed, season with more salt to taste.

3 Make the dressing. In a medium bowl, combine 1 tablespoon plus 1 teaspoon of lemon juice and the grated garlic, and let stand briefly. Whisk in the miso and tamari vigorously until the miso is mostly broken up and evenly combined. Whisk in the mustard, pepper, and yogurt, then slowly stream in the oil while whisking constantly until the mixture emulsifies and is smooth. Add more lemon juice and salt to taste.

4 Assemble the salad. Combine the kale and radicchio in the largest mixing bowl you have. Use clean hands or two spoons to toss and evenly combine them. Add a little dressing at a time, tossing until evenly coated and to taste. Toss in 1 cup of the Parmesan and then the chickpeas. For serving, top with more Parmesan and salt and pepper.

The Grain Salad

A good grain salad is obviously and inextricably packed with hearty whole grains, but still—it's all about the vegetables. Its sturdy base will hold an array of produce in so many forms—raw, roasted, pickled, steamed, or grilled—and add-ins, lots of add-ins like nuts, seeds, beans, dried fruit, olives, herbs, and cheese. Plus, you can dress the grain salad ahead and it will last for days. Use the following as a guide to freestyle your own grain salads:

Vegetables + Grain + Nut/Seed + Legume + Fresh fruit/Dried fruit + Dressing

You can omit parts of the equation, but the overall ratio is important: the produce must remain the star.

GOOD GRAINS: black rice, bulgur, farro, freekeh, kamut, spelt berries, wheat berries, wild rice

GOOD PSEUDOGRAINS (COOKED AND USED LIKE GRAINS): amaranth, fonio, millet, quinoa (technically gluten-free and protein-rich seeds), couscous (a fine grain-like pasta made with semolina flour)

TIPS AND TAKEAWAYS

- No grain is off limits. Mix, match, and combine! Make a big batch at the beginning of the week. Have a dressing ready, too, like House Lemon Vinaigrette (page 21), Basil Vinaigrette (page 22), or Maple Vinaigrette (see page 23).

- Cook traditional, larger grains like you would pasta in lightly salted boiling water. (Adding grains to already-boiling water produces individual, less sticky and soft grains, which are ideal for use in a salad.) Alternatively, for robust flavor, toast the grains slowly in oil, stirring frequently, until fragrant and golden brown, then add water and a pinch of salt and bring to a boil.

- Cook pseudograins according to package directions (typically 1 cup grains to 1¾ cups water plus a couple of pinches of salt).

- If you overcook grains, spread them out on a sheet pan to dry them out. Stir occasionally as they cool.

- To enhance flavor, toss warm grains with some of the dressing and they will absorb more of it. Reserve dressing to refresh the salad and adjust seasoning to taste.

- Store grain salads in an airtight container and refrigerate them—most will last for 3 to 5 days. If you want it to go the distance, leave out delicate greens and herbs like arugula, spinach, and basil as well as watery raw vegetables like tomatoes and zucchini. (Add these vegetables as you enjoy leftovers.) Let leftovers stand at room temperature briefly, then refresh the salad with dressing (it will likely need it). Adjust seasoning to taste. Nuts will lose their crunch over time; if you mind, you can leave them out and add to serve, too.

Asparagus-Spinach Farro Salad
with Almonds and Orange-Sesame Vinaigrette

SERVES 3 TO 4 AS A MAIN,
6 TO 8 AS A SIDE

SWAPS:

- Instead of asparagus, try blanched sugar snap peas or small, bite-size pieces of blanched, roasted, or steamed broccoli.

- Instead of farro, try soba or udon noodles, quinoa, or wild rice.

TO SUPREME OR "SEGMENT" AN ORANGE:

1. Slice off the ends of the orange and stand it upright on a flat side. Run a sharp knife around the fruit working from top to bottom to remove the skin and pith.

2. Working over a liquid measuring cup to catch juice, slide a paring knife at an angle between the membranes and flesh to remove the flesh.

3. Squeeze or press the remaining "shell" of membranes and fruit to release juices; reserve the juice.

This is a perfect spring salad made for the second asparagus comes into season. Farro, the chewy and mild Italian grain, soaks up the fragrant orange dressing and holds it together, but it doesn't take over. The veggie mix-ins are plentiful, absolutely the focus, so they really get to shine. Make this salad for a hearty lunch or light dinner, or make it a more substantial meal by pairing it with good bread smeared with fresh ricotta and drizzled with tarragon oil (see page 221).

Fine sea salt

1 pound asparagus, woody ends snapped off, tips left intact, stalks cut into ½-inch slices

1 cup dry farro, rinsed and drained

2 large navel oranges or cara cara oranges

1 tablespoon plus 1 teaspoon unseasoned rice wine vinegar

1 tablespoon pure maple syrup

2 teaspoons tamari or soy sauce

Freshly ground black pepper

1 tablespoon plus 1 teaspoon toasted sesame oil

1 tablespoon canola oil

2 packed cups baby spinach, chopped

½ cup sliced almonds, lightly toasted (or cashews, toasted and chopped)

1½ teaspoons sesame seeds

---

1 Bring a medium saucepan or pot of water to a boil over high heat and add about 2 teaspoons salt. Use a spider to carefully drop the asparagus into the boiling water and cook until crisp-tender, about 1 minute. (Do not overcook the asparagus!) Lift the asparagus from the water with the spider and transfer to a colander, rinse under cold water briefly until cool. Add the farro to the boiling water and cook it like pasta until tender, according to the package instructions (usually 20 to 25 minutes). Drain the farro and let it cool briefly.

2 Meanwhile, zest one of the oranges with a fine-gauge Microplane and reserve the zest, about 1 packed teaspoon. Peel and supreme the oranges. Discard the membranes and peels. Cut the orange segments in half.

3 Combine the orange zest, 2 tablespoons orange juice, the vinegar, maple syrup, tamari, ¼ teaspoon pepper, toasted sesame oil, and canola oil in a large mixing bowl (the same one you'll use to toss the salad). Whisk vigorously until well blended.

4 While the farro is still warm, transfer it to the large bowl and toss it with the dressing to coat. Add the asparagus, spinach, almonds, halved orange segments, and sesame seeds and toss until evenly distributed and well coated with dressing. Add more reserved orange juice and adjust salt and pepper to taste.

Tomato-Green Bean Freekeh Salad

with Pistachios and Lemon-Feta Vinaigrette

SERVES 3 TO 4 AS A MAIN,
8 TO 10 AS A SIDE

INGREDIENT INFO: Freekeh grains may be cracked or whole, which affects cooking time; check package instructions to ensure timing is right. I usually cook freekeh a few minutes longer than directed because I like it on the softer side. If you can't find freekeh, farro is the perfect substitute. Coarse bulgur, spelt berries, or wheat berries are good, too.

VARIATIONS: Try swapping sliced or diced cucumbers for the green beans. Hold the pistachios or mix in any other favorite nuts.

At their peak, tomatoes and green beans require so little of us to show off their fresh, summertime flavors, so this uncomplicated but totally delicious freekeh-based salad calls for simple prep and a bunch of hearty complements to make it a meal. The freekeh, a nutty-tasting and chewy whole grain, allows for a creamy dressing and the peppery lemon–feta vinaigrette delivers. Try the dressing also over grilled vegetables paired with any favorite grain.

Fine sea salt

½ pound green beans, trimmed and cut into 1-inch pieces on a diagonal

1 cup dry freekeh (or farro), rinsed and drained

1 cup freshly crumbled feta cheese (4 ounces)

2 teaspoons finely grated lemon zest

2 tablespoons freshly squeezed lemon juice, plus more as needed

Freshly ground black pepper

½ cup extra-virgin olive oil

⅓ cup plus 1 tablespoon toasted pistachios

2 cups cherry or grape tomatoes

1 cup canned chickpeas, rinsed and drained

⅓ cup currants

A handful of favorite summer herbs, chopped (optional)

---

1 Bring a medium saucepan or pot of water to a boil over high heat and add about 1½ teaspoons salt. Fill a medium bowl with cold water and ice and set it near the stove along with a spider or slotted spoon.

2 Carefully drop the green beans into the boiling water and boil until the beans are slightly tender, but still crisp, about 1 minute. Remove the beans with the spider or slotted spoon and drop them immediately into the cold water to cool them. (Shocking the beans in ice water will stop them from cooking and help maintain a bright green color.) Drain the beans. Add the freekeh to the boiling water and cook it like pasta until tender, according to the package instructions, usually 20 to 25 minutes. Drain and cool the freekeh.

ALL PLANTS: Replace the dressing with the House Lemon Vinaigrette. page 21.

3 Meanwhile, make the dressing. In a small food processor blend together the feta, lemon zest, lemon juice, ¼ teaspoon salt, ½ teaspoon pepper, and the oil until it emulsifies and just comes together, scraping down the sides of the bowl as needed, to produce a creamy but slightly coarse puree. Coarsely chop the ⅓ cup of toasted pistachios, and very finely chop the 1 tablespoon of pistachios; set both aside.

4 In a large mixing bowl, gently toss together the cooked freekeh, tomatoes, green beans, chickpeas, and about ½ cup of the dressing. Stir in the coarsely chopped pistachios and the currants. Adjust the salt, pepper, and lemon juice to taste. Top with the finely chopped pistachios. Add a handful of summer herbs if you wish.

Lemony Rainbow Carrot Couscous Salad

SERVES 4 TO 6 AS A MAIN,
8 TO 12 AS A SIDE

TAKE NOTE: This is a big-batch recipe; enjoy it for multiple lunches or as a side.

INGREDIENT INFO: Rainbow carrots are gorgeous here, but the color may transfer to the couscous. If you care, briefly rest the shredded carrots on a kitchen towel to absorb pigment.

SWAPS: You can use pistachios or pine nuts in place of the almonds. Or add more mix-ins like chickpeas, pomegranate seeds, and/or chives—perhaps even a spoonful of harissa in the dressing for a touch of heat.

Couscous functions like a grain in this simple, pretty, and oh-so flavorful carrot-centric salad. The dressing is extra-lemony and bold by design to shine right through the couscous (which has a habit of soaking up and neutralizing more timid dressings).

FOR THE COUSCOUS AND DRESSING

10 ounces dry couscous
   (about 1½ cups plus 2 tablespoons)

½ cup freshly squeezed lemon juice

1 tablespoon plus 1 teaspoon
   brown sugar

½ teaspoon fine sea salt

¼ teaspoon ground turmeric

¼ cup full-fat or low-fat plain yogurt

3 tablespoons extra-virgin olive oil

FOR THE SALAD

1½ pounds carrots, peeled and trimmed
   (see Ingredient Info)

¾ cup raisins

½ cup sliced almonds, toasted

½ cup thinly sliced scallions

Freshly ground black pepper

½ cup loosely packed fresh mint and/or
   parsley, finely chopped

Fine sea salt

1 Make the couscous according to the package instructions. Uncover, fluff with a fork, and let cool.

2 Make the dressing. Whisk together the lemon juice, brown sugar, salt, turmeric, and yogurt in a 2-cup liquid measure. Stream in the oil, whisking constantly and vigorously to combine; set aside.

3 Make the salad. Attach the shredding disc (with small holes) to a food processor and cut the carrots into 2- to 2½-inch lengths to fit the feed tube. Stack the carrots horizontally in the feed tube and process, pushing them down with the pusher against the shredding disc. Alternatively, shred the carrots against the large holes of a box grater. Transfer the carrots to a large bowl.

4 Give the dressing a stir and drizzle about half of the dressing over the carrots, tossing to combine well. Dump the couscous on top of the carrots and drizzle the remaining dressing over it. Use 2 large spoons or a slotted spoon to combine the dressing and couscous, trying not to combine with the carrots to start. Now, toss to combine the couscous and carrots. Stir in the raisins, almonds, scallions, ¼ teaspoon pepper, and the mint. Adjust salt and pepper to taste.

The Bean Salad

In a proper bean-focused salad, beans are not just a nutrient-dense support: they are noticeably and unapologetically the main component. Forget the overdressed, prepacked deli-style salads you've encountered—in partnership with bright seasonal veggies, the Bean Salad has the potential to show off beans' distinctive, delicious character.

GOOD LEGUMES FOR THE BEAN SALAD:
black beans, cannellini beans or any medium white beans like Great Northern or Tarbais or large ones like giant corona beans or gigante beans, chickpeas, cranberry beans, flageolet beans, kidney beans, pinto beans, black or French lentils

GOOD VEGETABLES FOR THE BEAN SALAD:
baby artichokes (roasted or marinated), asparagus (blanched, roasted, sauteed, grilled), broccoli (roasted), Brussels sprouts (roasted or shredded raw), cabbage (raw), carrot (raw or roasted), cauliflower (pickled or roasted), celery (raw), cucumber (raw), eggplant (roasted or grilled), fennel (raw), greens (arugula, kale, spinach), herbs, radish (raw or roasted), peppers (marinated, raw, roasted, or sauteed), tomatoes (raw or roasted), zucchini (roasted or sauteed)

TIPS AND TAKEAWAYS

- When you use canned beans in a bean-based salad, remember to rinse, drain, and dry them well. (Spread them out on a towel-lined sheet pan and pat dry.)

- When you cook dried beans from scratch, you get to explore heirloom varieties, which bring diversity in taste, texture, size, and color to bean salads (and other cooking). You control the texture with cooking time. (Note: They should not be crunchy or overly firm, and should never be mushy.) You also have the ability to enhance beans' natural flavors with whatever you decide to add to the cooking water, such as aromatics, herbs, olive oil, and/or acid like a squeeze of citrus or vinegar. (Just wait to add acid until the beans have become tender as it will toughen the skins and slow down the cooking process.)

- Bean salads, especially those made with canned beans, need a crisp, raw vegetable element like carrot, celery, fennel, or radish, or something crunchy like nuts and seeds to balance their softness. Dress them in a bold, flavorful vinaigrette to elevate them.

- Consider making a bean salad when you are craving a big salad but are low on or out of fresh greens. You can still follow the basic green salad formula, just hold the greens and add more beans, plus a mix of raw, roasted, or pickled vegetables; maybe a grain or small pasta; something sweet like fresh or dried fruit; and something crunchy like nuts or seeds. Cheese and fresh herbs are optional; a bright vinaigrette or a simple 3-to-1 combination of oil and vinegar is not.

- When using from-scratch beans, they don't require too much gussying up. Season them well. Dress the beans in olive oil and lemon or vinegar or a good vinaigrette (while they are warm). Toss with handfuls of arugula or chopped spinach, maybe some roasted vegetables or crunchy raw ones. If you wish, scatter some nuts or cheese over the top.

- Bean salads get even better with extra time to marinate. (The perfect potluck salad!) Overnight is ideal, but even thirty minutes to an hour will give a boost. Just leave out components that wilt (delicate greens) or lose crunch (nuts) when dressing more than four hours ahead.

Parisian-Style Lentil and Crudités Salad

SERVES 4 AS A MAIN,
8 TO 10 AS A SIDE

BUTCHER TIP: Take out the mandoline vegetable slicer to quickly produce thin slices of the raw vegetables (see page 18).

INGREDIENT INFO: Small, green French lentils—especially ones from Le Puy—are ideal here as they hold their shape well, won't absorb too much dressing, and add texture to the salad.

SWAP: The Dijon-sherry vinaigrette is elevated with wonderful nutty flavor if you swap out some of the olive oil for walnut oil, but no pressure to buy a bottle just for this. (Although I think you'll find that you will use a drizzle often to add something special to salad dressings and roasted or pureed vegetables.)

This is my vegetable-forward, springtime take on the classic Parisian bistro salad. Toss the lentils when they are still warm in the delicious vinaigrette and they will absorb its wonderful flavors. If you are lucky enough to get a bunch of celery with its leaves still attached, give them a rough chop and toss them into the salad. Serve warm or cold or at room temperature—it's always a hit.

---

2 cups dry French lentils, picked over and well rinsed (see Ingredient Info)

1 bay leaf

1 tablespoon minced garlic (1 large clove)

Fine sea salt

2 tablespoons sherry vinegar

1 tablespoon Dijon mustard

¼ teaspoon freshly ground black pepper, plus more as needed

4 tablespoons walnut oil (or extra-virgin olive oil)

2 tablespoons extra-virgin olive oil

2 tablespoons minced shallot

3 medium assorted rainbow carrots, sliced into $\frac{1}{16}$-inch coins

3 large celery ribs (preferably with leaves), ribs $\frac{1}{16}$-inch sliced, leaves chopped

4 red radishes, sliced into $\frac{1}{16}$-inch coins then julienned (or left as coins)

½ cup freshly crumbled feta cheese (2 ounces), optional

---

1 Place the lentils, bay leaf, and garlic in a large saucepan and add water to cover by a depth of 1½ inches. Bring to a boil over high heat, then reduce the heat to maintain a low but steady simmer. Add 1 tablespoon salt and stir the lentils. Cook until the lentils are just tender, 18 to 20 minutes.

2 Meanwhile, make the dressing. Whisk together the sherry vinegar, mustard, ½ teaspoon salt, and the pepper in a large bowl. Gradually stream in the walnut oil and olive oil (or 6 tablespoons olive oil if not using walnut oil), whisking quickly and constantly until the mixture emulsifies. Set aside about 2 tablespoons of the dressing.

3 Drain the lentils and garlic well and let them cool briefly while they continue to drain. Remove the bay leaf and transfer the lentils and garlic while still warm to the large bowl with dressing. Add the shallot and toss to combine. Add the carrots, sliced celery, radishes, and about ¼ cup celery leaves, if using, reserving some of each for topping the salad. Add more of the reserved dressing, and season with salt and pepper to taste. Transfer the lentil salad to a shallow serving bowl or individual bowls and top with the reserved raw vegetables and celery leaves. Sprinkle with feta if you wish.

Tomato–Bean Salad
with Shaved Fennel, Spinach, and Tomato Vinaigrette

HOW TO PREP FENNEL:

1. Cut off the stalks and fronds. Trim the base of the bulb. If the outer layer is tough/dry and browning, peel and discard it. Cut the trimmed bulb in half lengthwise through the core.

2. Cut the halves again lengthwise to quarter.

3. Position your knife at an angle against the core; cut and remove it.

4. Shave the quarters lengthwise or crosswise on a mandoline slicer (see page 18) or slice very thinly with a chef's knife.

This recipe, a riff on one we used to make at my restaurant Little Eater, is a luscious mix of summer tomatoes, shaved fennel, spinach, beans, and a sweet and tangy tomato vinaigrette; it turns a couple of cans of beans into an easy yet sophisticated meal. In the late summer, when tomatoes are everywhere, feel free to add up to 2 cups more. Heirlooms or slicers cut into bite-size pieces are welcome.

FOR THE VINAIGRETTE

2 roma or paste tomatoes
(or 1 medium slicer tomato)

1 tablespoon honey (or sugar)

1 teaspoon sherry vinegar
(or golden balsamic vinegar)

½ teaspoon fine sea salt

¼ teaspoon freshly ground black pepper

3 tablespoons extra-virgin olive oil

FOR THE SALAD

1 can (15½ ounces) chickpeas, rinsed, drained, and patted dry

1 can (15½ ounces) cannellini beans, rinsed, drained, and patted dry

Heaping 2 cups Sungold or mixed cherry tomatoes, cut in half

2 small to medium or 1 large bulb fennel, fronds chopped, bulb shaved

1 tablespoon fresh thyme leaves, finely chopped (optional)

½ teaspoon fine sea salt, plus more as needed

3 cups packed baby spinach leaves (about 3 ounces), chopped

¼ cup toasted pine nuts

Freshly ground black pepper

1 Make the vinaigrette. Set a box grater or handheld grater with large holes over a large bowl and grate the tomatoes, stopping when you get to the skin. Set a small fine-mesh sieve into a liquid measuring cup and pour the grated tomato through the sieve, a little at a time if needed, using the back of a spoon to push the juice through the seeds and thick pulp. The goal is to extract as much juice as possible (discard the solids). Pour ⅓ cup of the juice back into the large bowl and add the honey, sherry vinegar, salt, and pepper. Whisk in the oil until blended. Let the dressing stand.

2 Assemble the salad. Add the chickpeas, cannellini beans, tomatoes, fennel, thyme, a handful of chopped fennel fronds, if using, and the salt to the dressing in the bowl. Gently toss to combine evenly. Gently stir in the spinach and pine nuts. Adjust salt and pepper to taste. You can serve this salad cold or at room temperature. To make more than a few hours ahead, combine the beans, dressing, fennel, and thyme, but wait to add the tomatoes, spinach, and pine nuts. Refrigerate leftovers in an airtight container for up to 2 days. Flavors will remain, but know that the spinach will wilt and the tomatoes will lose juices.

Marinated "Agrodolce" Sweet Peppers and Cannellini Bean Salad

SERVES 4 TO 6 AS A MAIN, 8 TO 10 AS A SIDE

PREP TIPS: Use a mix of red, orange, and yellow bell peppers to make this extra colorful. Refrigerate the marinated peppers for up to 3 days in the jar and their flavors will improve.

INGREDIENT INFO: Canned cannellini beans (rinsed, drained, and mostly dried) work just fine here for speed and ease. DIY-cooked cannellini or other white heirloom varieties are an added treat. Soak beans overnight (to reduce cooking time), then steadily simmer with olive oil, salt, and a bay leaf until just tender. Drain and cool the beans.

BUTCHER TIP: See page 42 for how to prep bell peppers.

This antipasti-style bean and pasta salad is packed with a rainbow of sweet peppers, basil, garlic, cannellini beans, orzo or pearl couscous, and buttery olives. It is a salad to please every crowd, and it promises to become your new favorite for late-summer and fall gatherings. The sweet-sour marinating liquid used for the pan-roasted, Italian-style peppers is magic: it doubles as a bold and tangy dressing for the salad.

FOR THE MARINATED PEPPERS

2 tablespoons plus ½ cup extra-virgin olive oil

3 large red, yellow, and/or orange bell peppers (about 1½ pounds), ⅛-inch sliced (see Butcher Tip)

1 teaspoon fine sea salt

¼ cup balsamic vinegar

¼ cup red wine vinegar

3 large garlic cloves, thinly sliced

2 teaspoons sugar

¼ teaspoon freshly ground black pepper

½ cup loosely packed fresh basil leaves

FOR THE SALAD

1 cup dry orzo or pearl couscous

Fine sea salt

2 cans (15.5 ounces each) cannellini beans, rinsed and drained

Heaping ½ cup pitted Castelvetrano olives, thinly sliced into rounds

½ cup golden raisins or dried currants

1 teaspoon toasted fennel seeds (optional but recommended)

¼ cup loosely packed fresh basil, thinly sliced

Freshly ground black pepper

1 Make the marinated peppers. Heat the 2 tablespoons of oil in a large skillet over high heat. Add the peppers and ½ teaspoon of salt and cook, stirring often, until the peppers are tender and have started to blacken on the edges, 7 to 9 minutes. Add another splash of oil if the pan becomes too dry before the peppers are properly cooked.

2 In a large wide-mouth jar (or medium bowl), combine the vinegars, garlic, sugar, the remaining ½ teaspoon of salt, and the black pepper. Gently swirl the vinegars in the jar (or whisk) to combine them and dissolve the sugar and salt. Transfer the hot peppers to the jar and use tongs to turn them until they are fully coated in the vinegar mixture. Let the mixture stand for at least 15 minutes, preferably 30 minutes, turning the peppers in the dressing once if

(recipe continues)

possible. Chop the basil and add it along with the remaining ½ cup of oil. Stir the peppers well, and let the mixture stand for at least another 30 minutes (or up to 3 days in the refrigerator—the longer, the better; bring to room temperature ahead of serving).

3 Make the orzo or couscous. Bring a medium pot of water to a boil, then generously salt it until it tastes like the sea. Cook the pasta until just tender, about 8 minutes (or until al dente according to the package instructions). Drain and rinse under cold water until cool. Allow excess water to drain very well (you don't want a wet salad). Transfer the pasta to a large mixing bowl and stir to separate.

4 Assemble the salad. Use tongs to evenly stir the peppers, garlic, and basil in the marinade. Working in batches, transfer them to the bowl with the pasta, allowing excess marinade to drip back into the jar (reserve the remaining marinade; it will be the dressing for the salad).

5 Add the cannellini beans, sliced olives, raisins or currants, and fennel seeds (if using), and ¼ teaspoon salt. Gently toss the salad together. Whisk the marinade well in the jar and add 1 tablespoon at a time to the salad—up to about ¼ cup—until the salad is dressed and flavorful. Stir in most of the basil, reserving some for topping. Adjust salt and pepper to taste. Transfer the salad to a serving bowl and top with the remaining basil. The salad will keep well, refrigerated, in an airtight container for up to 4 days.

HOW TO PREP BELL PEPPERS:

1. Cut off the top just where the stem meets the body. Trim a sliver off the bottom to create a flat surface. Place the pepper upright. Make a vertical slit down one side.

2. Place the pepper on its side, skin side down. Cut around the pepper's core, carefully cutting through the ribs to release it, with the blade parallel to the board.

3. Unroll the pepper. Cut the pepper into 2 or 3 sheets. Cut each sheet skin-side down into thin strips. (To dice, cut through the strips crosswise.) Discard the stem and cut thin strips around the stem and out of the bottom piece, too.

2

SOUPS. CHILIES. STEWS.

The Puree of Vegetable Soup

This is a creamy puree of (literally-any-vegetable) soup made simply with vegetables and stock. You can also call it a "cream of vegetable soup" as it classically gets some cream to finish, but it really doesn't need cream at all. The end result feels so fancy, but made with a handful of ingredients, it is actually the kind of meal that you can freestyle on a weeknight. Pureed vegetable soups can be made with a wide variety of veg in the starring role—or can mix-and-match an ensemble cast—following this basic formula:

Oil or Butter + Onions or Leeks + Other Aromatics (optional) + Any Vegetable + Stock + Seasoning

TIPS AND TAKEAWAYS

- A puree of vegetable soup requires blending until smooth. Use an immersion stick blender for convenience, draping a kitchen towel over the pot to contain splatters.

- If you are using a high-speed blender to blend hot soup, blend it in batches and don't fill it more than halfway. Use a kitchen towel to hold the lid on tightly, then start pulsing on the lowest speed. Open the lid to release steam, then continue gradually blending, while increasing the time and length of processing and periodically releasing the steam.

- When heating a finished puree, thin it with more stock and adjust the seasoning as needed. For added richness and silky texture, stir in some cream, coconut milk, or butter to finish.

- Top creamy vegetable soup with something crunchy or serve it with crusty bread, toasts, or a toasted sandwich.

- Once completely cool, store leftover soup in an airtight container. Refrigerate for 3 to 4 days or freeze for up to 3 months. Allow frozen soup to thaw overnight in the refrigerator. Reheat soup in a saucepan over medium heat, stirring frequently until simmering. Thin the soup with stock or water and adjust seasoning to taste.

GOOD VEGETABLES FOR PUREED SOUPS (ONE OR A COMBO): artichokes, asparagus, beans, beets, broccoli, cauliflower, carrots, celery, celery root, corn, fennel, mushrooms, rutabaga, sweet peppers, parsnips, peas, potatoes, spinach, sunchokes, sweet potatoes, tomatoes, winter squash, zucchini.

GOOD TOPPINGS FOR PUREED SOUPS: Torn croutons (see page 26); Crispy Garlic Breadcrumbs (page 79); Frico (page 17); a drizzle of olive oil or herb oil; a spoonful of yogurt, sour cream, or crème fraiche; a sprinkle of chopped nuts, seeds, herbs, or cheese; or a dollop of pesto. Finely chopped raw vegetables or fruit. Try also Orange-Pistachio-Kale Gremolata (see page 68) or make your own combination of nuts and herbs.

Celery Root and Potato–Leek Soup

INGREDIENT INFO: Leeks freeze well. Clean and slice (or vice versa), then, spread out to dry. Freeze for up to 6 months.

BUTCHER TIP: See page 202 for how to peel celery root.

HOW TO CLEAN LEEKS:

1. Trim the root ends and cut off the dark green tops. (Reserve the tops; halve and rinse them well if using in stock.)

2. Cut each trimmed leek in half lengthwise (see illustration).

3. Hold them under running water, spreading the layers apart so water runs through each layer to remove dirt. Alternatively, slice the leeks crosswise. Immerse them in a bowl of cold water and shake them back and forth to release dirt. Lift, rinse, and repeat as necessary. Drain and pat dry before cooking.

I've amplified a simple classic with celery root and a leek-scrap stock that comes together while you prepare the roots for cooking. The celery root adds robust flavor and a velvety, creamy texture that doesn't require actual cream. (Make sure you reserve the leek tops and celery root stems, if attached, for the stock.) I like to finish the soup with just a drizzle of good olive oil and serve it with good sourdough bread or torn croutons (see page 26) for topping.

---

3 tablespoons extra-virgin olive oil

2 large leeks, white and light green parts, halved lengthwise and thinly sliced (reserve the tops)

1 pound celery root, peeled and ¾-inch diced

2 large russet potatoes, peeled and ¾-inch diced

1 teaspoon fine sea salt, plus more as needed

¼ teaspoon freshly ground white or black pepper

6 to 7 cups Leek-Top Scrap Stock (recipe follows) or low-sodium vegetable stock

Best-quality olive oil, for topping

---

1 Heat the extra-virgin olive oil over medium heat in a Dutch oven or large soup pot. Add the leeks and cook, stirring occasionally, until they begin to soften, about 5 minutes. Do not let them brown. Add the celery root, potatoes, salt, and pepper and cook, stirring occasionally, until incorporated and beginning to soften, 3 minutes.

2 Add 6 cups of the stock to the mixture and bring it to a boil. Reduce the heat to maintain a low but steady boil. Cook, partially covered and stirring occasionally, until the vegetables are completely soft, 25 to 30 minutes; cool briefly.

3 To puree the soup with an immersion blender, drape a kitchen towel over the pot (to catch any splattering soup), immerse the blender, and blend until completely smooth. To use a high-speed blender, transfer the soup in batches, making sure not to fill the blender more than halfway if the soup is still warm. Secure the top firmly with a towel in hand and blend until smooth. Open the top carefully and slowly; return the soup to the pot.

4 Reheat the soup in the pot over medium-low heat, adding about 1 cup stock or water to thin the soup to your liking. Adjust salt and pepper to taste. Top with a drizzle of your best olive oil.

To store and reheat, see Tips and Takeaways on page 46.

Leek-Top Scrap Stock

MAKES 7 TO 8 CUPS

9 cups water

1½ teaspoons fine sea salt

2 dark green leek tops, cut in half
lengthwise and rinsed well

1 cup roughly chopped celery root stems
or celery ribs

2 carrots, chopped

4 to 6 unpeeled garlic cloves

8 white (or black) peppercorns

Combine the water, salt, leek tops, celery root or ribs, carrots, garlic, and
peppercorns in a medium pot and bring to a boil over high heat. Turn the
heat down and simmer, partially covered, until the vegetables are soft and the
stock is flavorful, about 30 minutes. Strain the stock through a fine-mesh sieve.
Use immediately or let cool completely and transfer to an airtight container.
Refrigerate for up to 5 days or freeze for up to 6 months.

Charred Zucchini Soup
with Sweet Corn and Tomato Crostini

SERVES 4 AS A MAIN
(MAKES 6 TO 7 CUPS)

INGREDIENT INFO: If you
must use larger zucchini,
note that they will release
more liquid. Start with
1½ cups stock and add
more as needed.

BUTCHER TIP: See page
120 for how to shave corn
off the cob.

This soup is easy to make and wonderful served both hot and cold. I've kept
the basic recipe simple and focused, allowing the zucchini to come forward
with subtle bitter notes thanks to the charring in the broiler and some zing and
brightness from the lime juice. I love to serve it as a light meal with a tomato,
corn, and whipped feta crostini on the side.

3 pounds medium zucchini

3 tablespoons extra-virgin olive oil

1 medium yellow onion,
finely diced (about 2 cups)

2 garlic cloves, minced

Fine sea salt

Freshly ground black pepper

2 cups low-sodium vegetable stock,
plus more as needed

2 teaspoons pure maple syrup

1 tablespoon freshly squeezed lime juice,
plus more as needed

2 large ears of sweet corn, cooked and
shaved off the cob (about 2 cups),
for topping (optional)

Best-quality olive oil, for topping

Fresh summer herbs, such as basil,
cilantro, dill, or mint, for topping
(optional)

Sweet Corn and Tomato Crostini with
Feta Crema (page 50), for serving
(optional)

(recipe continues)

VARIATION: Freestyle with other garnishes and pairings—like chopped tomato and fresh herbs on top and good bread (or grilled flatbread; see page 225) with olive oil–drizzled burrata alongside.

1 Heat the broiler and adjust the rack to 6 inches below it.

2 Trim the zucchini, and quarter them lengthwise. Transfer the pieces to a sheet pan, keeping matching halves together. (For large zucchini, cut them in half crosswise, first, then quarter lengthwise.) Brush all sides lightly with 1 tablespoon of oil. Reassemble the matching halves and place them flesh side down on the sheet pan. Broil until very tender and the skin is charring in places, 10 to 13 minutes. (For larger zucchini, you may need 5 minutes more until the flesh is tender and the skin is charring.)

3 Meanwhile, heat 2 tablespoons of oil in a pot or large Dutch oven over medium-low heat. Add the onion, garlic, and ¼ teaspoon salt. Cook, stirring frequently, until tender and translucent and just turning golden in color, not browning, 5 to 7 minutes. Transfer the broiled zucchini and any juices to the pot along with ½ teaspoon salt, ¼ teaspoon pepper, and the vegetable stock. Simmer, stirring occasionally and breaking apart the zucchini, until the zucchini and onion have completely softened, about 10 minutes. Cool briefly.

4 To puree the soup with an immersion blender, drape a kitchen towel over the pot (to catch any splattering soup), immerse the blender, and blend until completely smooth. To use a high-speed blender, carefully transfer the softened zucchini pieces to the blender, followed by all of the remaining bits and liquid. Blend until completely smooth.

5 Stir or blend in the maple syrup, lime juice, and ¼ teaspoon salt. Thin with more stock, if needed, to reach your preferred consistency. Adjust salt, pepper, and lime juice to taste. Return to the pot and reheat until just bubbling or chill if you wish to serve cold.

6 Ladle into bowls, piling each generously with the shaved corn. Drizzle with your best olive oil, and sprinkle with pepper and fresh summer herbs, if using. Serve with the crostini if you wish.

To store and reheat, see Tips and Takeaways on page 46.

Sweet Corn and Tomato Crostini
with Feta Crema

MAKES 8 SMALL TOASTS

8 small slices (about 1½ inch thick) crusty bread

4 ounces freshly cut feta cheese

⅓ cup heavy cream, plus more as needed

2 cups halved or quartered Sungold or cherry tomatoes (depending on size)

1 large ear of sweet corn, cooked and shaved off the cob (see Ingredient Info)

1 tablespoon chopped fresh basil

½ teaspoon balsamic vinegar

1 tablespoon extra-virgin olive oil

Fine sea salt and freshly ground black pepper

INGREDIENT INFO: When it's in season and extra fresh, use raw corn or boil it until just tender, about 2 minutes. Alternatively, broil or grill the corn until tender and charred in places, about 5 minutes.

VARIATION: Replace the feta crema with whole-milk or cashew-milk ricotta.

1 Toast the bread in a toaster oven (or 350°F oven) until lightly crispy and golden. Let cool.

2 For the feta crema, combine the feta and heavy cream in a small food processor and blend until smooth, adding more cream to thin it as needed.

3 Stir together the tomatoes, corn, basil, and balsamic vinegar in a medium bowl. Drizzle in the oil, stirring to combine. Season with salt and pepper to taste.

4 Spread the toasts with the feta crema. Top with the tomato-corn mixture and serve.

Classic Butternut Squash Soup
with Pepitas and Pomegranate

SERVES 4 TO 6 AS A MAIN
(MAKES 9 TO 10 CUPS)

This butternut squash soup is a classic—gently spiced and sweet—the kind you want right when fall gets under way. I prefer it on the thicker side, but you can thin it with stock or with coconut milk to enhance its sweetness and silky texture.

VARIATIONS:

• To peel and cut the squash, see page 52. If that feels too time-consuming, roast it instead: Cut it in half, brush the cut side with olive oil, and roast it at 400°F, cut side down, until tender, 35 to 40 minutes. Let it cool enough to handle. Scoop out and discard the seeds. Scoop out the flesh, being careful not to pull up the skin, and reserve it. Add the roasted squash when you add the stock.

• For natural sweetness and extra fall flavor, leave out all but 1 teaspoon of the brown sugar and add a peeled, cored, and cubed apple.

2 tablespoons extra-virgin olive oil

2 medium-large leeks, rinsed well, white and pale green parts thinly sliced (about 3 cups sliced leeks)

1½ teaspoons fine sea salt, plus more as needed

1 medium-large (2½- to 3-pound) butternut squash, peeled, seeded, and ¾-inch diced (about 7 cups)

1 large sweet potato (12 to 16 ounces), peeled and ¾-inch diced (2 to 2½ cups)

⅛ teaspoon ground cinnamon

⅛ teaspoon freshly grated nutmeg

Pinch of ground cloves

About 7 cups low-sodium vegetable stock, or Butternut Squash Scrap Stock (see sidebar, page 52)

2 tablespoons brown sugar

⅛ teaspoon freshly ground black pepper, plus more as needed

1 teaspoon apple cider vinegar, plus more as needed

Toasted pepitas, for topping (optional; see Prep Tip, page 26)

Pomegranate seeds, for topping (optional)

Crème fraîche, whole-milk Greek yogurt (or alternative), or sour cream thinned with cream, for topping (optional)

(recipe continues)

BUTCHER TIP: See page 47 for how to clean leeks.

BUTTERNUT SQUASH SCRAP STOCK: Fill a large pot with 3 quarts water, then add the leek tops and the squash seeds and guts. Add 8 peppercorns. Bring to a boil, then reduce the heat to maintain a steady simmer and cook until the scraps are completely tender, 45 minutes. Set a fine-mesh sieve over a large heat-safe bowl and strain the stock through it. Discard the solids and reserve the stock. It will keep for up to 5 days in the refrigerator or up to 6 months in the freezer.

1 Heat the oil in a large Dutch oven or soup pot over medium heat. Add the leeks and ½ teaspoon of salt and cook, stirring occasionally, until the leeks begin to soften, about 5 minutes. Stir in the butternut squash, sweet potato, the remaining 1 teaspoon of salt, and the cinnamon, nutmeg, and cloves. Cook to toast the spices and start softening the squash and sweet potato, about 3 minutes.

2 Add 6 cups of the stock, the brown sugar, and the pepper and bring to a boil over high heat. Reduce the heat to maintain a steady simmer and partially cover. Cook, stirring occasionally, until the vegetables are completely tender, about 30 minutes. Let the soup cool briefly.

3 To puree the soup with an immersion blender, drape a kitchen towel over the pot (to catch any splattering soup), immerse the blender, and blend until completely smooth. To use a high-speed blender, transfer the soup in batches, making sure not to fill the blender more than halfway if the soup is still warm. Secure the top firmly with a towel in hand and blend until smooth; return to the pot.

4 Reheat the soup over medium heat. Depending on its current thickness, stir in ½ cup to 1 cup of stock to thin the soup. Add more stock or water to reach your desired consistency. Stir in the apple cider vinegar. Adjust the salt, pepper, and vinegar to taste. Serve hot with a selection of toppings. Reserve remaining stock for reheating leftover soup.

To store and reheat, see Tips and Takeaways on page 46.

HOW TO BREAK DOWN BUTTERNUT SQUASH:

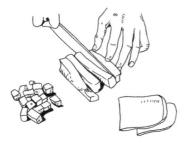

1. Trim the ends. Halve the squash crosswise to separate the bulb from the neck.

2. Stand each half on its widest cut side and, working from top to bottom, slide a chef's knife between the skin and flesh to peel it (see illustration). Go back through with a vegetable peeler or knife to remove any remaining skin or white fibrous flesh. (Alternatively, use a vegetable peeler to peel the squash halves.)

3. Halve the bulb lengthwise and scoop out the seeds.

4. Stand the neck upright on its widest cut surface and make vertical cuts to produce slabs of equal width. Stack a couple of slabs at a time and cut lengthwise into sticks of equal width (see illustration). Cut across the sticks to produce dice of equal width.

5. Cut the bulb into half moon slices. Cut the half moons into dice-like pieces of equal width.

The Farmhouse Soup

The Farmhouse Soup is a hearty, rustic, fill-you-up mixed-vegetable and, sometimes, bean soup. (Think minestrone.) With the right structure in place, it will take on any vegetables that you have around.

THE BUILDING BLOCKS OF A BASIC FARMHOUSE SOUP

1. AROMATIC VEGETABLE BASE: For a hearty, flavorful foundation, start with two or more ingredients: chopped carrots, celery, fennel, garlic, ginger, leeks, onions, peppers. In a large pot, sauté the vegetables in oil or butter (or a combination) until just tender.

2. DRIED BEANS (IF USING): Add soaked beans or unsoaked beans, such as cranberry/borlotti beans, cannellini beans, chickpeas, lentils, lima beans, or any interesting heirloom varieties.

3. STOCK OR WATER: You can use stock, water, or a combination. If you are cooking beans from dry along with aromatics to start the soup (or if you are cooking the beans separately), it's fine to use water at this point. Once the beans are tender, you can use more water to keep them covered while they simmer (or to thin the soup). For a more deeply flavored soup, switch to stock to cook these later additions. I also recommend stock for farmhouse soups that utilize already-cooked beans, canned beans, or no beans.

If you're using soaked beans, add enough water to cover by a depth of a little over 1 inch; for unsoaked beans, add enough to cover by a depth of 2½ to 3 inches. Bring to a boil over high heat and boil for 5 minutes.

Reduce the heat to a low simmer and cook, stirring occasionally, until the beans are tender; generally 30 to 60 minutes for soaked beans and 70 to 90 minutes (or longer) for unsoaked beans. Add more water as needed to keep the beans covered. Alternatively, cook the beans separately and add the beans and their cooking liquid toward the end of cooking (see step 6).

4. FLAVOR BUILDERS: A sprinkle of dried herbs, a couple of sprigs of hearty fresh herbs like rosemary or thyme, a bay leaf, a Parmesan rind, a spoonful of miso or nutritional yeast, tamari. Season with salt and pepper throughout, tasting and adjusting as needed. Try a glug of wine, a splash of good-quality wine vinegar, fresh tomatoes or canned diced tomatoes or tomato puree, but if you are cooking beans in the soup, wait until the beans have become tender. (Acidic ingredients will slow down and toughen the beans.)

5. STARCHY ADD-INS: Add starchy long-cooking vegetables like butternut squash, potatoes, sweet potatoes, or turnips; pasta such as ditalini, orzo, gemelli, or macaroni; or grains like barley, farro, spelt berries, or wild rice. Starchy, long-cooking vegetables generally need to simmer for 15 to 20 minutes. (Time pasta and grain additions according to package instructions and add more water or stock as needed, or cook separately and add to the soup to finish.)

6. QUICK-COOKING (OR COOKED) VEGETABLES: Once the beans and grains are close to tender, add quick-cooking vegetables (cut to roughly the same size) including asparagus, cabbage, corn, fava beans, green beans, kale, peas, radishes, spinach, Swiss chard, escarole, or zucchini. Cook until tender. You can also add already-cooked vegetables, roasted and cut into small pieces, like broccoli, butternut squash, cauliflower, rutabaga, sweet potato, or turnip. (A good use for leftovers.) Add freshly cooked beans with their cooking liquid or rinsed and drained canned beans, and cook until the beans are warmed through and the flavors meld together.

7. FINISH IT RIGHT: Top with fresh herbs, pesto, lemon zest and/or juice, freshly cracked black pepper, a drizzle of your best olive oil, or a sprinkle of good-quality cheese for grating such as Parmigiano-Reggiano or Pecorino Romano.

TIPS AND TAKEAWAYS

- Cooking beans from dry, whether soaked or unsoaked, will add body with starch to a farmhouse soup. Try to soak beans for 2 to 8 hours ahead to cut down on cooking time, as this will preserve some texture in the aromatic vegetable base. Remember, the type of beans will determine how much cooking liquid to use and when to add the beans. Add both unsoaked and soaked beans as soon as you add the liquid. Canned or cooked beans should be added toward the end; they just need to warm up. Try smashing a cup or so and stirring it into the soup to add thickness.

- Consider cooking any pasta separately to ensure it doesn't get mushy or soak up the soup. If you expect leftovers, reserve pasta to add when reheating.

- These soups are undoubtedly tastier after they've spent a night in the fridge, which makes leftovers a boon.

- Once completely cool, store leftover soup in an airtight container. Refrigerate for 3 to 4 days or freeze for up to 3 months. Allow frozen soup to thaw overnight in the refrigerator. Reheat soup in a saucepan over medium heat, stirring frequently until simmering. Thin the soup with stock or water and adjust seasoning to taste.

Spring Vegetable and Orzo Soup
with Parmesan-Miso Broth

SERVES 4 AS A MAIN

TAKE NOTE: If you use store-bought stock, hold back on the salt and instead season to taste.

SWAP: For a heartier soup, replace the orzo with store-bought cheese tortellini. Cook it separately, then add it to the soup just before serving. Let it simmer for 1 minute until the flavors come together.

INGREDIENT INFO: If you can get flowering chives, this is a great place to showcase their beauty and add a pop of onion flavor. Rinse the flowers well and carefully pull apart the petals. Top each soup with a sprinkling of petals.

This is a light but comforting vegetable soup for those chilly spring days that seem to drag on (or pop up out of nowhere). To fully capture the depth and deliciousness of the broth I hope you will make your own stock here. (It's a mindless, hands-off task.) But no matter how the stock comes together for you, once you have it ready to go and the veggies are prepped, you can make this soup in about the time it takes to boil the pasta.

---

6 cups (1½ quarts) Vegetable Stock (page 57) or low-sodium vegetable stock

2 tablespoons red or white miso paste

3-inch Parmesan rind (about 1 ounce) or a small chunk of Parmesan (about ¾ ounce) plus ¾ cup finely grated Parmesan (¾ ounce)

Fine sea salt and freshly ground black pepper

½ cup dry orzo

14 asparagus spears, woody ends discarded, spears sliced into ¼-inch coins, tips left intact

1 cup shelled fresh peas (1 pound in the pod)

4 red radishes, sliced into ¹⁄₁₆-inch coins

2 tablespoons best-quality olive oil, plus more for topping

2 tablespoons ¼-inch chopped fresh chives (or a finely chopped scallion)

---

1 Bring the vegetable stock to a low simmer over high heat in a medium saucepan. Immediately reduce the heat to maintain a steady, low simmer and whisk in the miso until dissolved. Add the Parmesan rind or piece of Parmesan. Season with ½ teaspoon salt and ¼ teaspoon pepper. Stir in the orzo, reduce the heat to medium-low to maintain a low boil, and cook for 5 minutes.

2 Carefully add the asparagus and peas and stir to combine. If needed, adjust the heat to return to and maintain a simmer. Continue to cook the pasta and vegetables until the pasta is tender and the peas and asparagus are crisp-tender, another 4 to 5 minutes (9 to 10 minutes total cooking time).

3 Remove the pot from the heat. Stir in about three quarters of the radishes, the oil, ¼ cup of finely grated Parmesan, and 1 tablespoon of chives. Adjust salt to taste. Ladle the soup into individual bowls for serving. Top each with a generous drizzle of the remaining oil and a generous sprinkle of the remaining Parmesan, and add the remaining radishes and chives. Serve with freshly grated black pepper for topping.

To store and reheat, see Tips and Takeaways on page 54.

Vegetable Stock

MAKES 6 TO 6½ CUPS

TAKE NOTE: When preparing other dishes, reserve and freeze shiitake mushroom stems to use for stock. If you have fresh mushrooms, feel free to use the mushroom caps in addition to the stems or reserve the caps and add to a soup, stew, stir-fry, or pizza.

10 cups (2½ quarts) water

½ large onion, peeled and cut into 6 chunks

1 cup scrubbed and roughly chopped carrots (½-inch pieces)

1 cup roughly chopped celery ribs (½-inch pieces)

1 leek top (6 inches long), halved lengthwise and all layers rinsed well

1 small fennel bulb, halved lengthwise (optional, but recommended)

5 garlic cloves, peeled

10 fresh shiitake mushroom stems (see Take Note) or 5 slices dried shiitake mushrooms

1 bay leaf

3 sprigs fresh thyme

8 peppercorns

1 teaspoon fine sea salt

Combine the ingredients in a large saucepan and bring to a boil over high heat. Immediately reduce the heat to maintain a low simmer. Simmer until the vegetables are soft and the stock is flavorful, 1 hour. Let the stock cool briefly and strain it through a fine, double-mesh colander, gently pressing the cooked vegetables to release liquid without pushing the vegetables through the colander. The cooled stock will keep in an airtight container in the refrigerator for up to 5 days or in the freezer for up to 3 months.

Green Summer Vegetable Soup
with Basil Pesto

SERVES 4 TO 6 AS A MAIN

TAKE NOTES:
- Beware of mushy pasta!
- Check the package instructions and adjust the cooking time accordingly.

SWAPS:
- Feel free to use Great Northern beans, chickpeas, or kidney beans in place of the cannellini beans.
- Fresh pesto is always best, but you can use a favorite store-bought pesto to save time.

ALL PLANTS: Omit the Parmesan from the pesto and add a generous spoonful of miso paste or a couple of tablespoons of nutritional yeast to the base of the soup along with the stock, whisking to dissolve.

This quick-cooking vegetable soup is a showcase for summer's green veggies. You can play around with the vegetables and the type of pasta, or omit the pasta altogether and add farro or more potatoes.

Extra-virgin olive oil

1 yellow onion, ¼-inch diced

2 large celery ribs, ¼-inch diced

3 large garlic cloves, minced

1 pound (2 medium) zucchini, ¼-inch diced

1 cup ¾-inch sliced green beans

Fine sea salt

2 medium red or Yukon gold potatoes, peeled and ¾-inch diced

4 cups (1 quart) low-sodium vegetable stock

4 cups (1 quart) water, plus more as needed

Freshly ground black pepper

2- to 3-inch Parmesan rind (optional), plus coarsely grated Parmesan cheese (optional)

1 cup ditalini or other small pasta

1 can (15½ ounces) cannellini beans, rinsed and drained

½ cup to ¾ cup Basil Pesto (recipe follows)

Freshly squeezed lemon juice

1 Heat 3 tablespoons of the oil in a large (at least 7-quart) Dutch oven or large saucepan over medium heat. Add the onion, celery, and garlic and sauté, stirring occasionally, until translucent and just tender, 3 to 5 minutes. Stir in the zucchini, green beans, and ½ teaspoon salt. Cook until they just begin to soften, stirring occasionally, about 3 minutes.

2 Add the potatoes, stock, water, ¾ teaspoon salt, ¼ teaspoon pepper, and the Parmesan rind if using. Bring to a boil over high heat for 2 minutes to give the potatoes a head start then add the pasta. Give it a stir. Reduce the heat, adjusting as needed, to maintain a steady simmer. Cook, stirring occasionally, until the pasta and potatoes are nearly tender, about 8 minutes. Stir in the cannellini beans and cook until the pasta and potatoes are tender and the beans are warmed through, 2 to 4 minutes more. Remove the pan from the heat and stir in ½ cup of pesto, and 1 tablespoon of lemon juice. Adjust the salt, pepper, pesto, and lemon juice to taste. If you wish, serve with a drizzle of pesto and a generous shaving of Parmesan cheese, more black pepper, and a drizzle of oil.

To store and reheat, see Tips and Takeaways on page 54.

Basil Pesto

MAKES ¾ TO 1 CUP

Blanching the basil helps maintain this pesto's bright green color. If you will be using all of the pesto right away, you can omit step 1 and process the basil leaves in the pesto without blanching them—just make sure not to overprocess the basil in the food processor or it will turn brown. Add a little of the olive oil when you add the basil to help break it down faster.

3 cups loosely packed fresh basil leaves

1 garlic clove

Fine sea salt

⅓ cup lightly toasted pine nuts
   (or walnuts, almonds, or pistachios)

½ cup extra-virgin olive oil, plus more
   as needed

1½ cups finely grated Parmesan cheese
   (about 1½ ounces)

1 Bring a small pot of water to a boil and place a large bowl of ice water next to the stove. Drop the basil leaves into the boiling water just for a few seconds until they wilt. Immediately remove them with a spider or slotted spoon and immerse them in the ice water. Lift the leaves and transfer them to a small colander to drain. Gently squeeze out excess water.

2 Peel, trim, and roughly chop the garlic on a cutting board. Sprinkle with ¼ teaspoon salt and continue to chop, then pulverize the garlic, sliding your knife back and forth on its side and pushing down against the garlic–salt mixture until a paste forms. Transfer the garlic paste and pine nuts to a food processor. Pulse briefly to just combine. Add the basil and pulse about 5 times to chop it, then process on low until just blended. Scrape down the sides of the processor bowl. With the motor running on high, pour the oil through the top feed tube and stop just as it comes together. Scrape down the sides of the bowl again, add the Parmesan, and blend briefly to incorporate it. Adjust the salt and add more oil to taste and to reach your preferred texture. The pesto will keep, tightly covered, in the refrigerator for up to 3 days. You can freeze it for up to 3 months.

Winter Minestrone
with Kale and Farro

SERVES UP TO 6 AS A MAIN

TAKE NOTE: I like farro in minestrone, but you can cook small, tube-shaped pasta like ditalini or macaroni separately and stir it into the soup just before serving. (My kids love it this way.) Most important, do use good-quality dried beans (I like Rancho Gordo's) to ensure freshness, and use the real-deal Parmigiano-Reggiano and your best-quality olive oil for generously topping the soup. These ingredients make all the difference.

Minestrone is a rustic, a-little-of-this and a-little-of-that kind of soup—the kind my grandmother and great-grandmother used to clean out the vegetable drawer. Get comfortable with the basics of this version and it will become a reliable, invaluable meal in your everyday repertoire (with some bread alongside for dipping).

1 cup dried cranberry, borlotti, or cannellini beans, picked through and rinsed (see Shortcuts)

Fine sea salt

¼ cup extra-virgin olive oil

1 large yellow onion, ¼-inch diced

3 large carrots, ¼-inch diced

4 to 5 large celery ribs, ¼-inch diced

6 to 8 garlic cloves, minced

⅓ cup red wine (or 1 tablespoon aged balsamic vinegar)

8 cups (2 quarts) low-sodium vegetable stock

1 bay leaf

1 tablespoon dried Italian seasoning

Finely chopped leaves from 1 sprig (3 inches) fresh rosemary (optional)

½ cup dry farro, rinsed and drained

3-inch Parmesan rind or ½-ounce chunk of Parmesan cheese (optional, but recommended)

6 to 8 cups chopped curly or lacinato kale leaves or 5 ounces chopped baby spinach

1 can (28 ounces) tomato puree

¼ teaspoon freshly ground black pepper, plus more for serving

Best-quality olive oil

Freshly grated Parmigiano-Reggiano cheese, for serving

1 Cook the beans. If you presoaked the beans, drain and rinse them. Place the beans in a medium saucepan and add water to cover by a depth of 1 inch. If using unsoaked beans, place them in a medium saucepan and add water to cover by just over 2 inches. Bring to a boil over high heat and boil vigorously for 5 minutes. Reduce the heat to maintain a low but steady simmer. Add 1 teaspoon salt and give the beans a stir. Gently simmer the beans, stirring occasionally and adding more water as needed, until tender, not overly soft, checking a few beans to ensure consistency. Generally, this takes about 45 minutes for soaked cranberry, borlotti, and cannellini beans and 75 to 90 minutes for unsoaked beans. Remove the beans from the heat and let them stand. (Once they're cool, you can refrigerate them in their broth for up to 3 days.)

· Soak the beans for 6 to 8 hours or overnight and you can cut their cooking time in half. Canned beans don't offer the fullest flavor in this soup, but in a pinch you can use 1 can (15½ ounces) cannellini beans or kidney beans, rinsed and drained; or look for canned borlotti beans at Italian specialty stores.

· Feel free to use precut kale or baby spinach here. Remove any thick kale stalks and give the leaves a rinse.

· Curly kale freezes really well. I like to keep 6 to 8 cups trimmed and cut kale in a zip-top bag in the freezer so that I can make this soup whenever the mood strikes.

SCRAP SAVINGS: If you don't have a rind or chunk of Parmesan, try a generous spoonful of white or red miso paste or nutritional yeast (or skip it).

MAKE A GREENER SOUP: Add another 2 cups kale or spinach leaves, finely chopped zucchini or green beans, and/or a spoonful of pesto on top.

2 Make the soup. Heat the oil in a large Dutch oven or pot over medium-high heat. Add the onion, carrots, celery, and 1 teaspoon salt and cook, stirring occasionally, until the vegetables begin to soften and turn golden in places, 8 to 10 minutes. Stir in the garlic and cook for 60 to 90 seconds until fragrant and it just begins to soften.

3 Carefully add the red wine (or balsamic vinegar) and continue to cook, stirring frequently, for another minute or so until the wine (or vinegar) has been absorbed and cooked off. The vegetables should appear very glossy.

4 Add the vegetable stock, bay leaf, Italian seasoning, and rosemary, if using. Bring to a boil over medium-high heat. Add the farro and Parmesan rind and give it a stir. Reduce the heat slightly to maintain a steady simmer, stirring occasionally, until the farro is al dente, about 20 minutes.

5 Use a slotted spoon to drain and transfer the cooked beans to the soup. Add 2 cups of the bean cooking liquid (or 2 cups of water if the bean broth isn't available). Stir in the kale (or spinach), tomato puree, and pepper. Return the soup to a boil and then reduce the heat again to maintain a gentle simmer. Simmer, stirring occasionally, for 10 to 12 minutes more until the kale is wilted, the farro is tender, and the soup reduces slightly. Add more water, bean cooking liquid, or stock at any point to thin the soup to your liking.

6 Turn off the heat. Remove the bay leaf and Parmesan rind. Stir in 2 tablespoons of your best olive oil. Adjust salt and pepper to taste (considering the final addition of salty cheese at the table).

7 To serve, ladle the soup into individual bowls and top each generously with freshly grated Parmigiano-Reggiano, freshly ground black pepper, and more of your best oil.

To store and reheat, see Tips and Takeaways on page 54.

The "Pot of Beans"

Beans are the humble seeds of dried legumes. But simmer these unassuming pebbles in water with aromatics and salt, and they magically turn themselves into plump, indulgent beans cloaked in a revelatory, rich elixir. Beans have a reputation for taking a long time to cook, but they're actually one of the easiest and most health-supportive meals that you can make.

BEAN COOKING BASICS

1. Check the beans for rocks and debris and remove any you find. Rinse the beans to remove dirt.

2. Soak the beans for 6 to 8 hours to reduce cooking time. (It may feel easier to just soak overnight or up to 24 hours. A short 2-hour soak is worth it, too.) Soaking beans will reduce cooking time and will result in a more uniform texture. It is also said to help with digestion. Don't worry if you haven't planned ahead; see Tips and Takeaways.

3. Select a large heavy-bottomed pot with room for beans to move and cook evenly.

4. Flavorful aromatics make extra-flavorful beans. Sauté onion, carrots, and celery in olive oil or just combine them raw with the beans in the pot. Add whole, smashed cloves of garlic or minced garlic if you wish. (When you are in a hurry, just the addition of smashed garlic cloves and a bay leaf plus good olive oil will produce a delicious pot of beans.) Play around with other aromatics like peppers, fennel, and ginger.

5. Cover the beans with plenty of water: soaked beans by just over 1 inch, unsoaked by a depth of just over 2 inches. Be prepared to add water as needed; the amount will vary depending on the age and type of bean.

6. Bring the beans to a boil. Boil vigorously for 5 minutes, then reduce the heat to maintain a gentle simmer. Generously salt the beans. Add a glug of good olive oil. You can add fresh or dried herbs now.

7. Cook the beans for 45 minutes to 2 hours (or longer as needed) until evenly tender, giving an occasional stir and adding more water as needed. (An electric kettle of hot water at the ready comes in handy here.) The beans should never be crunchy or firm (or mushy). Make sure to taste a few beans, to ensure the whole batch is evenly cooked through.

8. Once the beans are tender, finish simply with more olive oil, salt if needed, and freshly cracked pepper. Add brightness with a squeeze of citrus or a splash of wine vinegar, or top the beans with something pickled. Bring some heat with chili crisp or chili oil. Add freshness with chopped herbs, crunch with raw radish or nuts/seeds, and/or richness with a sprinkle of cheese or diced avocado. (Serve, store, and reheat beans in their delicious broth.)

TIPS AND TAKEAWAYS

- Old beans translate to longer cooking times or never quite cook through at all. It can be difficult to identify old beans, but a dusty bag or cracked skins are good indicators. Try to buy more well-known commodity beans like black beans, chickpeas, pinto beans, and cannellini beans from a trusted supplier that moves through inventory regularly. Even better, consider trying heirloom varieties from a producer like Rancho Gordo or Zürsun Idaho Heirloom Beans.

- Soaking will reduce cooking time, but you don't have to presoak beans. It's fine to just get cooking! Allot plenty of time for unsoaked beans to cook and turn tender. It can take up to double the time.

- To soak beans, place sorted, rinsed beans in a bowl and add water to cover by a depth of about 3 inches. Cover and store in the refrigerator for up to 24 hours. (Drain and replace the soaking liquid if you need to soak for more than 24 hours as the beans may start to germinate!) You can leave out beans for 2- to 4-hour soaks. Drain, rinse, and drain the beans, then start cooking. (Note: Lentils don't require soaking, but they do need extra care when picking through them for small stones and other debris.)

- Salting beans ahead will not make them tough! In fact, if you don't properly salt beans up front you may end up with flavorless beans. Start with about 1¾ teaspoons fine sea salt for 1 pound of beans, added when they come to a boil, plus more to taste as you check the beans for doneness throughout cooking.

- Gently simmer beans to ensure even cooking. You can more vigorously boil beans to cut down on time, but they may break and cook unevenly.

- Store completely cooled beans in an airtight container and refrigerate for 3 to 4 days.

- To reheat beans, add liquid to loosen them, simmer until warmed through, and adjust seasoning to taste.

Stewed Lentils and Carrots

with Olive Oil and Parmesan

SERVES 6 AS A MAIN

This is one of the first dishes I ever learned to make, courtesy of my dear friend Ryan when we were living abroad during college. It was cheap, unbelievably simple, filling, and delicious. There are zero bells and whistles here, but it's a trusted technique for cooking lentils that every vegetable-friendly cook should know. This is exactly what a simple "pot of beans" should be. Serve the lentils on their own with a good baguette or feel free to dress them up. They are always wonderful tossed with pasta (like orecchiette or penne).

---

1 pound green or brown lentils, picked through, rinsed, and drained

2 heaping cups ½-inch diced carrots

4 to 5 garlic cloves, minced

Fine sea salt

1 bay leaf

7 cups water

Best-quality olive oil

Baguette, cooked short pasta, or grain, for serving (optional)

Coarsely grated Parmesan or Pecorino cheese, for serving

½ cup fresh flat-leaf parsley, finely chopped (optional)

Freshly cracked black pepper, for serving

---

1 Combine the lentils, carrots, garlic, 1 teaspoon salt, and the bay leaf in a large Dutch oven or heavy-bottomed pot. Add the water, give it a stir, and bring to a boil over high heat. Reduce the heat to medium and boil, stirring occasionally and skimming the top with a wooden spoon to remove impurities (you'll see a grayish film on the surface of the water), until much of the water has been absorbed, about 12 minutes.

2 Reduce the heat to a gentle simmer until the lentils and carrots are tender and the mixture is stew-like, but not soupy, 10 to 13 minutes. (Add a touch more water if the mixture is too thick and you'd like to loosen it slightly.)

3 Stir in 2 tablespoons olive oil and adjust salt to taste—keeping in mind the salty cheese for serving. Serve on its own or over pasta (or grain), and top with Parmesan, parsley, a drizzle of olive oil, and freshly cracked pepper.

To store and reheat, see Tips and Takeaways on page 63.

Pinto Beans and Rice
with All the Fixings

SERVES 4 AS A MAIN

You can transform a pound of dry pinto beans (or black beans) into a simple meal that you will regularly crave. Simmer the beans in water with onion, carrot, celery, and garlic. Stir in olive oil, cumin, and orange zest. Let the beans hang out in that soupy, yummy elixir—the real prize in any pot of beans—until you are ready to eat. Serve with rice and have fun with the accompaniments.

FOR THE BEANS

1 pound dry pinto beans (or black beans), picked through and rinsed

1 medium onion, ¼-inch diced

2 large carrots, ¼-inch diced

3 celery ribs, ¼-inch diced

4 large garlic cloves, quartered

1 bay leaf

14 cups (3½ quarts) water, plus more as needed

Fine sea salt

3 to 4 thumb-size pieces freshly peeled orange zest (optional)

1 teaspoon ground cumin

3 tablespoons extra-virgin olive oil

¼ teaspoon freshly ground black pepper

¼ cup chopped fresh cilantro (optional)

Cooked brown rice, for serving

FOR THE FIXINGS

15-Minute Pickle-y Onions (recipe follows)

Queso fresco, goat cheese, or sour cream

Thinly sliced radishes

Sliced or smashed avocado or guacamole

Warm tortillas or tortilla chips

Salsa Verde (page 252) or tomato salsa

1 Combine the pinto beans, onion, carrots, celery, garlic, bay leaf, and water in a Dutch oven or large heavy-bottomed pot. Cover and bring to a boil over high heat, then uncover and boil for 5 minutes. Reduce the heat to maintain a steady simmer, about medium heat. Skim any foam that has formed on top. Add 2 teaspoons of salt and stir. Simmer the beans, uncovered, until mostly tender, stirring occasionally and adding more water if the beans dry out at any point, about 1 hour and 15 minutes. (You may want to reduce the heat to medium-low or low if the water is cooking off too quickly and/or as the water reduces toward the end of cooking.)

2 Stir in the orange zest, if using, the cumin, 2 tablespoons of oil, and the pepper. Cook until the beans are completely tender but not mushy or falling apart, and the cooking liquid has been reduced to a soupy stew-like consistency and tastes delicious, at least 10 to 15 minutes. Adjust salt and pepper to taste. (If the beans are not tender after 90 minutes of cooking, add more water, a cup at a time as needed, and continue to simmer until the beans are completely tender.)

(recipe continues)

3 Remove the pan from the heat. Remove the bay leaf and orange zest. Stir in the remaining 1 tablespoon of oil. If you are adding the cilantro, stir it in now or reserve it to sprinkle over the top of the beans upon serving.

4 Serve the beans with the rice and fixings of your choice.

To store and reheat, see Tips and Takeaways on page 63.

15-Minute Pickle-y Onions

MAKES ABOUT 2 CUPS

1 small red onion, thinly sliced

3 tablespoons apple cider vinegar or freshly squeezed lime juice

3 tablespoons water

2 teaspoons sugar

¼ teaspoon fine sea salt

Stir the onion, vinegar, water, sugar, and salt together in a jar or small bowl. Let stand, stirring occasionally, for at least 15 minutes (the longer they sit, the more pickled the onion slices will become). The onions will keep in the refrigerator for up to 5 days.

The Best Cannellini Beans
with Orange-Pistachio-Kale Gremolata

SERVES 4 AS A MAIN

This brilliantly simple recipe for cannellini beans belongs to a dear friend and mentor, Carol White. I have added an orange-forward pistachio-and-kale gremolata for topping. I serve the dish with a hunk of good bread—fresh or brushed with oil and grilled or skillet-toasted. The key to the beans, as Carol always says, is using fragrant sage and really good olive oil, which she adds right to the cooking water. The finished beans should bathe in the magically thickened and delicious cooking liquid. I sometimes use everyday olive oil for cooking and save my best-quality oil for finishing. Feel free to go either way if your everyday olive oil is tasting and smelling great.

(recipe continues)

INGREDIENT INFO: Fresh, unsoaked cannellini beans should take between 70 and 75 minutes to cook; older beans can take 90 minutes or longer. Reduce the heat as the water cooks off, taste throughout, and add water as needed, adjusting the heat to maintain a simmer, until the beans are evenly tender with no hardness. (They should never be mushy!)

TAKE NOTE: If you choose to soak the beans ahead (for at least 6 hours), reduce the first addition of water to 8 cups. Add more water as needed throughout cooking and cut the total cooking time in half, adding more time as needed until the beans become tender.

BUTCHER TIP: For the gremolata, finely mince the kale like you would herbs: Gather the leaves in a rough pile and roll them in on one another, then use your non-knife hand to hold them down. Slice through the stack, making deliberate, even cuts, then continue to further mince the leaves into very small pieces.

FOR THE BEANS

1 pound unsoaked cannellini beans, picked through and rinsed

At least 12 cups (3 quarts) water

4 to 5 large garlic cloves, halved

8 large fresh sage leaves, torn in half

2 tablespoons extra-virgin olive oil

1¾ teaspoons fine sea salt

2 tablespoons best-quality olive oil (or more extra-virgin olive oil)

Freshly cracked black pepper

FOR THE GREMOLATA

1 teaspoon finely grated orange zest (or lemon zest)

2 tablespoons freshly squeezed orange juice, plus more as needed

½ small garlic clove, finely grated with a Microplane (optional)

1 tablespoon extra-virgin olive oil

⅓ cup toasted pistachios (or sliced almonds), very finely chopped

2 cups minced kale leaves

Fine sea salt and freshly ground black pepper

Slices of good crusty bread, toasted or grilled if desired, for serving

1 Make the beans. Combine the cannellini beans and water in a large Dutch oven or heavy-bottomed pot. Bring to a boil over high heat and boil rapidly for 5 minutes, then reduce the heat to maintain a steady, gentle simmer. Add the garlic, sage, extra-virgin olive oil, and salt and simmer, uncovered, stirring occasionally, and reducing the heat as needed every 20 minutes or so as the water cooks off, until the beans are evenly tender and almost all of the liquid has been absorbed, 70 to 90 minutes (possibly longer). Add up to 2 cups of water as needed at any time if the beans have absorbed the liquid before they are evenly tender (conversely, if the beans become tender and there is too much liquid, simply cook it off). The beans should be surrounded by a thick liquid. To finish, stir in your best olive oil and top with cracked black pepper to taste.

2 Meanwhile, make the gremolata. Combine the orange zest, orange juice, and garlic, if using, in a medium bowl; let it sit briefly. Whisk the mixture and stream in the extra-virgin olive oil, whisking until evenly combined. Stir in the pistachios and kale until evenly combined. Season with salt and pepper to taste.

3 Spoon the warm beans into shallow bowls and serve with the gremolata on the side for topping and bread for scooping.

To store and reheat the beans, see Tips and Takeaways on page 63.

The Chili

Just one good chili recipe can make a huge impact—filling in the gaps in your weekly rotation and delivering a delicious meal just when you were all out of ideas. Here you have three. Take the time to make a classic big batch ahead of time with dried beans (the Ultimate Black Bean Chili on page 71). You will be rewarded with portions that you can freeze and defrost when you need a meal on the table, fast. Or throw together a simple chili with canned beans like Easy White Bean Chili with Tomatoes and Sweet Corn (page 73). Every season brings new ideas and new ways with this spiced bean-and-vegetable stew.

TOPPINGS AND ACCOMPANIMENTS

These mix-and-match toppings and go-withs create a buzz and fun at the table.

- finely chopped red onion, sliced scallions, or 15-Minute Pickle-y Onions (page 66)

- fresh cilantro leaves, whole or chopped

- sour cream or plain Greek yogurt

- shredded Cheddar or Monterey Jack cheese, or crumbled Cotija cheese, queso fresco, or feta cheese

- avocado slices or guacamole

- pico de gallo, tomato salsa, or Salsa Verde (page 252)

- lime wedges

- To fill out a chili meal, serve it with something starchy like a simple cooked grain, warm tortillas, or tortilla chips.

TIPS AND TAKEAWAYS

- You can make a good chili with both dried beans and canned beans. Cooking from dried beans allows you to control the texture of the beans and produces the ultimate chili with a flavorful bean-broth base that also adds body to the chili. Canned beans will produce a quick-cooking chili, a virtue of its own.

- Control the thickness of the chili with the amount of liquid that you add. Thin it with vegetable stock or water and adjust salt to taste. Thicken the chili by cooking it down longer or scoop out some beans and smash them with a potato masher or the back of a fork, or puree them in a food processor, then add them back to the chili. (This works especially well with canned beans.)

- The fun is in the toppings, so serve a selection of them at the table.

- Double the recipe to produce freezable leftovers.

- Once completely cool, store leftover chili in an airtight container. Refrigerate for 3 to 4 days or freeze for up to 3 months. Allow frozen chili to thaw overnight in the refrigerator. Reheat over medium heat, adding stock or water to loosen the chili and stirring occasionally until simmering and hot all the way through. You may want to thin the chili with more stock or water and adjust seasoning to taste.

Ultimate Black Bean Chili

SERVES 5 TO 7 AS A MAIN

SERVES 5 TO 7 AS A MAIN

TAKE NOTE:

- I like to use dark chili powder to bring smoky richness and just the right amount of heat to this chili, but any chili powder will work fine.

- Cooking time varies based on the freshness of the beans. This recipe calls for about 1 hour 40 minutes of total cooking with unsoaked beans, but you can reduce the cooking time and use less water to start if you soak the beans in advance.

There's no way around it, dried beans take time to cook; but they cook in enough water here that it does not require babysitting. I am giving you a recipe that yields about 2 to 2½ quarts, but if you want plenty of leftovers, double the recipe (see Variation on page 72). It feels good to make a big-batch recipe that you can serve tonight and also store in the freezer for later—ready simply to defrost when you need a quick lunch or dinner.

---

1 tablespoon chili powder, preferably dark chili powder (see Take Note)

1 teaspoon ground cumin

1 teaspoon dried oregano

½ teaspoon granulated garlic or garlic powder

½ teaspoon dry mustard powder

¼ cup extra-virgin olive oil or vegetable oil

Heaping 1 cup finely chopped yellow onion

1 cup finely chopped carrot

1 cup finely chopped celery

2 tablespoons minced garlic

1 tablespoon minced chipotle peppers in adobo sauce (seeded if you prefer less heat) or 1 teaspoon ground chipotle pepper

1 pound dried black beans, picked through, rinsed, and drained

About 14 cups (3½ quarts) water

2 bay leaves

1 can (28 ounces) tomato puree

2 tablespoons pure maple syrup, plus more as needed

Fine sea salt

1 tablespoon apple cider vinegar (or freshly squeezed lime juice), plus more as needed

Your favorite toppings and accompaniments (see page 69), for serving

---

1 Carefully whisk together the chili powder, cumin, oregano, granulated or powdered garlic, and dry mustard in a small bowl; set aside.

2 Heat the oil in a large Dutch oven or heavy-bottomed pot over medium heat. Add the onion, carrot, and celery and cook, stirring occasionally, until they just begin to soften, about 5 minutes. Stir in the minced garlic, reserved spices, and chipotle peppers (or chipotle powder) and cook, stirring frequently, until the garlic is fragrant and begins to soften, about 2 minutes. Be careful not to let the garlic burn.

(recipe continues)

3 Add the beans, water, and bay leaves. Bring the water to a boil, then reduce the heat to medium-low to maintain a steady simmer. Let the mixture cook, checking the water and stirring a few times throughout cooking, until the beans are just tender, 70 to 80 minutes.

4 Stir in the tomato puree, maple syrup, 1 tablespoon salt, and 1 cup water if needed to loosen. Continue to simmer, partially covered to catch any splattering and stirring occasionally, until the beans are completely tender but still hold their shape, 20 to 30 minutes. Add more water if needed at any point to loosen the chili or to prevent the beans from burning or sticking to the bottom of the pot.

5 Stir in the vinegar. Add water, a little at a time, if you would like to loosen the consistency. (Or turn up the heat to cook off excess liquid and thicken the chili if needed.) Adjust salt, vinegar, and maple syrup to taste. Remove the chili from the heat and remove the bay leaves.

6 Serve the chili with your favorite toppings and accompaniments.

To store and reheat, see Tips and Takeaways on page 69.

To store and reheat, see Tips and Takeaways on page 69.

VARIATION
To double the chili, yielding 4 to 5 quarts

- Use a large Dutch oven or heavy-bottomed pot and double all ingredients except the water, tomato puree, and chipotle peppers in adobo.

- Use 16 cups (4 quarts) water to start, then add another 1 cup when you add the tomato sauce—plus more if you want to loosen it further. Adjust the seasonings to taste.

- Start with 1 tablespoon chopped chipotle pepper and then add more to reach your desired level of heat.

- Use about 42 ounces tomato puree: that's 1½ (28-ounce) cans or 1 large (28-ounce) can plus one small (14- to 15-ounce) can.

Easy White Bean Chili
with Tomatoes and Sweet Corn

SERVES 4 AS A MAIN

TAKE NOTE: When fresh tomatoes and sweet corn are in full swing, give them a try here (use 2 cups diced tomatoes). In the off season, feel free to use a can of diced tomatoes and frozen corn kernels to save on time; you won't compromise flavor. Fire-roasted, canned tomatoes are recommended for added depth of flavor.

This is a quick-cooking, skillet-style chili made for summer nights. It comes together in no time with a couple of cans of cannellini beans, canned or fresh tomatoes, fresh or frozen sweet corn—energized with chili powder, oregano, and a squeeze of lime juice.

---

2 tablespoons olive or canola oil

1 large yellow onion, ¼-inch diced

1 large red bell pepper, ¼-inch diced

½ large or 1 small poblano, ⅛-inch diced (about ½ cup)

¾ teaspoon fine sea salt, plus more as needed

3 large garlic cloves, minced

1 teaspoon chili powder, plus more as needed

½ teaspoon dried oregano

½ teaspoon ground cumin

¼ teaspoon cayenne pepper (optional)

1 can (15 ounces) diced tomatoes and juice

2 cans (15½ ounces each) cannellini beans, rinsed and drained

2 cups low-sodium vegetable stock

1½ to 2 cups sweet corn kernels (from 2 large ears or frozen)

1 tablespoon freshly squeezed lime juice, plus more as needed

FOR THE TOPPINGS

Sour cream

Chopped fresh cilantro

1 large avocado, diced

Lime wedges

---

1 Heat the oil in a large straight-sided sauté pan (or skillet or Dutch oven) over medium-high heat. When it shimmers, add the onion, bell pepper, poblano, and ¼ teaspoon of salt. Cook, stirring occasionally, until the onion and peppers begin to soften and are lightly browning in places, about 5 minutes. Add the garlic, chili powder, oregano, and cumin and cook, stirring frequently, 1 to 2 minutes more until fragrant. Add the cayenne if you wish.

2 Stir in the tomatoes and juices, cannellini beans, the remaining ½ teaspoon of salt, and 1½ cups of vegetable broth. Reduce the heat to medium to medium-low and simmer, stirring occasionally, until the tomatoes are beginning to break down, about 10 minutes. Add the corn and simmer, continuing to stir occasionally, until the tomatoes have broken down, the chili has thickened, and the flavors have come together, 5 to 7 minutes. (If you would like the chili to thicken a bit further, you can cook it for another 2 to 3 minutes here. Alternatively, add the remaining ½ cup of vegetable broth to loosen the chili if you wish.) Stir in the lime juice and adjust the salt, chili powder, and/or lime juice to taste. Serve hot with a selection of toppings.

To store and reheat, see Tips and Takeaways on page 69.

Sweet Potato and Poblano Chili

SERVES 5 TO 6 AS A MAIN

TAKE NOTE: Use 5 cups of stock for the fullest flavor. If using a 4-cup box of stock, you can supplement it with 1 cup of water and use more water to thin the chili as needed.

EQUIPMENT NOTE:
A potato masher is recommended to mash the cannellini beans, but if you don't have one, use the back of a fork to mash them in a small bowl before adding them.

A mix of spices, charred poblano peppers, and sweet potatoes turns a few cans of beans into a hearty cold-weather chili that comes through with complex, can't-get-enough flavor. I enjoy it with a sprinkling of chopped cilantro, and both avocado and sour cream. Tortilla chips are by no means necessary, but I do love them with this chili as a crunchy topping or for dipping.

2 to 3 poblano peppers (5 to 8 ounces), stem removed, halved lengthwise, and seeded

1 teaspoon canola oil

Fine sea salt

2 teaspoons ground cumin

1 teaspoon ground coriander

1 teaspoon dried oregano

¼ teaspoon cayenne pepper

¼ teaspoon ground cinnamon

2 tablespoons extra-virgin olive oil

1 large onion, ¼-inch diced

2 jalapeños, seeds and ribs removed, minced

4 large garlic cloves, minced

1 can (15½ ounces) cannellini beans, rinsed and drained

5 cups low-sodium vegetable stock

1¼ to 1½ pounds sweet potatoes (2 medium), ¾-inch diced

1 bay leaf

2 cans (15½ ounces each) pinto beans, rinsed and drained

1½ tablespoons freshly squeezed lime juice

Lime wedges, for serving

Your favorite toppings (see page 69), for serving

1 Place an oven rack 6 inches from the broiler element and turn on the broiler. Place the poblanos on a sheet pan, drizzle the canola oil over them, and use your hands to evenly coat them all over. Place them skin sides up and broil until the skins are black and charred all over and the flesh is tender, 6 to 9 minutes. Transfer the poblanos with tongs to a small bowl and cover with plastic wrap, foil, or a kitchen towel to cool. When the poblanos are cool enough to handle, peel off and discard the charred skins and dice the flesh. Set aside.

2 Combine 1 teaspoon of salt with the cumin, coriander, oregano, cayenne pepper, and cinnamon in a small bowl; set near the stove.

3 In a large Dutch oven or heavy-bottomed pot, heat the olive oil over medium heat. Add the onion and jalapeños and cook, stirring occasionally, until the onion is sweating and becoming translucent, about 4 minutes. Stir in the garlic and the spice mixture. Cook, stirring frequently, until deeply fragrant, about 2 minutes. Push the onion mixture to the sides of the pan and add the cannellini beans. Use a potato masher to break down the cannellini beans into coarse paste—not all of the beans have to be completely broken down—and stir to incorporate.

4 Add 4 cups of vegetable stock, turn the heat up to high, and bring to a boil. Add the sweet potatoes and bay leaf. Stir to incorporate the ingredients. When the liquid returns to a boil, reduce the heat to maintain a steady simmer, and cook, stirring occasionally, until the sweet potatoes are just becoming tender, about 10 minutes. Stir in the reserved diced poblanos, the pinto beans, another ¾ teaspoon salt, and 1 cup of stock (or water). Adjust the heat to a gentle simmer and cook, stirring more frequently, until the sweet potatoes are tender, the chili has thickened, and all the flavors have come together, another 12 to 14 minutes. You can add more stock or water to thin it. (I like it on the thicker side.) Turn off the heat. Stir in the lime juice. Adjust salt to taste. Remove the bay leaf.

5 Serve in individual bowls with a wedge of lime and your toppings of choice.

To store and reheat, see Tips and Takeaways on page 69.

The Seasonal Stew

When you think of stew, it may not conjure the most appealing dish. But consider artichokes, fennel, lemon, and fava beans with garlicky, crispy breadcrumbs, then butternut squash and kale simmering in coconut milk with sweet curry spices. Now, bring wintery root vegetables into focus–carrots, parsnips, turnips, potatoes–with turmeric, ginger, dried apricots, olives, and honey. You can imagine that with the best-known vegetables of the season leading the way (and extra goodies, adding texture, for topping), the Seasonal Stew is a dynamic one-pot meal that you will crave.

GOOD VEGETABLES FOR STEWS

SPRING INTO SUMMER: asparagus, artichokes, carrots, English peas, fava beans, fennel, greens (kale, spinach, Swiss chard), leeks, mushrooms, potatoes, ramps

SUMMER INTO FALL: carrots, corn, fresh cranberry beans, eggplant, green beans, peppers, potatoes, okra, tomatoes, zucchini

FALL INTO WINTER: cabbage, carrots, celery root, fennel, hearty greens (collards, kale, mustard greens, Swiss chard), leeks, mushrooms, parsnips, potatoes, rutabaga, sweet potatoes, turnips, winter squash

SEASONAL STEW BASICS

1. Choose a combination of aromatic vegetables to make a base: onion, carrots, celery, fennel, garlic, ginger, leeks, peppers.

2. Sauté in a fat like olive oil and/or butter, coconut oil, or coconut milk.

3. Add spices (if using) to toast and liven and/or deglaze with wine or an aged vinegar (if using).

4. Stir in the starring vegetables of your stew. Sauté to soften briefly. Simmer, covered, in vegetable stock, water, wine, tomatoes, or a combination.

TIPS AND TAKEAWAYS

- Control the thickness of your stew with liquid and length of cooking. Add more liquid to thin it. Adjust seasoning to taste. To thicken it, hold back liquid or turn up the heat to cook off excess.

- Check vegetables often for doneness—they should be soft, but with a slight bite. (No one wants mushy stew.)

- Stir in or top with fresh herbs, citrus juice and/or zest, golden toasted nuts or seeds, and/or a touch of something sweet like dried fruit. Experiment—the goal is to give the stew lift and balance.

- Leftovers only get better.

- Cooled stew will keep in an airtight container in the refrigerator for 3 to 4 days. Reheat it in a microwave or on a stovetop, thinned with stock or water and stirred occasionally until just simmering. Adjust seasoning to taste.

5. Add beans if you wish. Stir in cooked beans like cannellini beans or chickpeas (if using) or fresh beans like fava beans or cranberry beans.

6. Toss in extras. Now you can add ingredients that just need to warm through like quick-wilting greens and sweet corn. Olives and dried fruit, salty and sweet, have the power to make a stew pop.

7. Cook to your desired consistency, thick or thin, adjusting the liquid to taste or cooking longer to thicken.

8. Adjust the seasoning to taste; add citrus juice, something sweet like maple syrup or honey, or a touch of sugar. Stir in and top with fresh herbs. Top with something crunchy like nuts or seeds, crispy breadcrumbs (see page 79), hand-torn croutons (see page 26), store-bought Parmesan crisps or homemade Frico (see page 17); creamy like yogurt; or spicy like harissa.

9. Serve over a favorite grain or pseudograin, or with grilled flatbread (see page 221) or toasted crusty bread.

Spring Artichoke Ragout

SERVES 4 TO 6 AS A MAIN

BUTCHER TIP: See page 40
for how to prep fennel.

HOW TO PREP FAVA BEANS:

1. Trim or snap off the top of the pod and pull it down along the curved side of the pod to remove the string. Slide your finger down the seam to open the pod and release the beans.

2. Cook shelled fava beans in a large pot of salted boiling water for 1 minute. Immediately immerse drained beans in a bowl of ice water or rinse with very cold water to stop the cooking process.

3. Remove the tough membrane around each cooked bean by carefully pinching the outer shell with your thumbnail, then gently pushing the bean through to release it (see illustration).

Artichokes melt into stew beautifully. In this French-style ragout (a dish of slowly stewed vegetables), they simmer with onion, carrots, and fennel in plenty of olive oil, white wine, and vegetable stock. In true spring fashion, they come together with fava beans (or fresh English peas), lemon, and tarragon to capture the exact moment of the year. Be generous with your best olive oil for cooking and to finish the dish.

5 tablespoons best-quality extra-virgin olive oil, plus more for topping

1 medium yellow onion, ¼-inch diced

1 small to medium fennel bulb, halved lengthwise, cored, and ⅛-inch sliced

2 small carrots, ¼-inch diced

4 large garlic cloves, smashed

2 to 2½ pounds fresh baby artichokes, trimmed and halved or 12 ounces frozen artichoke heart

Fine sea salt and freshly ground black pepper

½ cup dry white wine

1½ cups low-sodium vegetable stock, plus more as needed

1 bay leaf

2 lemons, one finely zested and juiced, one cut into wedges

1 cup blanched, peeled fava beans (from about 12 ounces of fava pods) or fresh English peas (or frozen peas)

Heaping 1 cup cooked cannellini beans (optional)

1 tablespoon minced fresh tarragon leaves, plus more for topping

Polenta, couscous, or favorite grain, for serving

Flaky sea salt, such as Maldon (optional)

Crispy Garlic Breadcrumbs (recipe follows), for topping

1 Heat the oil in a Dutch oven or a large heavy-bottomed, deep sauté pan over medium heat. Add the onion, fennel, carrots, and garlic and cook, stirring occasionally, until the vegetables just begin to soften and the onion is translucent but not browning, 5 to 8 minutes. Stir in the artichokes, 1 teaspoon fine sea salt, and ¼ teaspoon pepper. Add the wine, stock, bay leaf, and lemon zest. Bring to a gentle boil, then reduce the heat to a low but steady simmer, just under medium heat. Cover and simmer, stirring occasionally and adjusting the heat as needed, until the artichokes are tender and a small amount of liquid remains, 15 to 20 minutes for fresh artichokes and 13 to 15 minutes for frozen artichokes.

2 Uncover and gently stir in the fava beans or peas and cannellini beans (if using). Reduce the heat to medium-low and simmer, gently stirring frequently, until the additional vegetables are warmed through, about 2 minutes. Remove from the heat.

INGREDIENT INFO:

- You can use mature, medium artichokes in place of the baby or frozen artichokes. See How to Prep Baby Artichokes, below (in step 3, quarter them lengthwise, cut out the choke on a diagonal, then cut the flesh lengthwise into bite-size pieces).

- If using cannellini beans, for the best texture, cook dried beans separately and add the beans and some broth to the stew. Alternatively, use rinsed and drained canned beans.

3 Remove the bay leaf. Stir in 2 tablespoons lemon juice and the tarragon. Adjust lemon and salt to taste (keep in mind that you may want to finish with the flaky sea salt and serve lemon wedges at the table).

4 Serve the stew in individual bowls over a scoop of polenta. Drizzle each with oil and sprinkle with flaky sea salt (if using). Sprinkle generously with garlic breadcrumbs and finish with more minced tarragon. Serve with lemon wedges alongside if you wish.

To store and reheat, see Tips and Takeaways on page 76.

HOW TO PREP BABY ARTICHOKES:

1. Use a serrated knife to remove the base of the stem and one quarter of the top. Snap off the tough outer leaves until you reach the softer, light green leaves.

2. Pare away the tough outer layer of the stem with a paring knife, also smoothing around the base.

3. Cut larger artichokes into quarters; cut smaller ones in half. If there is a choke, use a spoon on a diagonal to remove it. Place the artichokes in lemon water water until ready to use.

MAKES ABOUT 1 CUP

TAKE NOTE: To make 1 cup of coarse fresh breadcrumbs, pulse about 2 ounces of good-quality white or whole-grain bread, torn or cut into cubes, in a food processor until you produce fluffy crumbs, some large and some small for texture.

Crispy Garlic Breadcrumbs

1 tablespoon extra-virgin olive oil

1 cup panko breadcrumbs or coarse fresh breadcrumbs (see Take Note)

1 garlic clove, minced

Fine sea salt

Line a plate with a paper towel. Heat the oil in a medium nonstick skillet over medium-low heat. Add the breadcrumbs and cook, stirring almost constantly, just until they begin to turn golden, about 3 minutes. (Turn the heat down at any time if they start to burn.) Stir in the garlic and cook until the breadcrumbs are golden all over and toasted and the garlic becomes fragrant, another 1 to 2 minutes, or longer for more color and crunch. Season them lightly with salt. Transfer to the prepared plate to cool completely. Use within 4 hours or transfer to an airtight container and store in the refrigerator for up to 4 days. Reheat in a skillet over medium-low heat until warm and crispy. Transfer to a plate to cool.

Butternut and Kale Coconut-Curry Stew

SERVES 6 AS A MAIN

BUTCHER TIP: See page 52 for how to break down butternut squash. See page 25 for how to stem curly kale.

I am almost embarrassed to tell you how often I make this dish in the fall and winter (a lot). A slightly different version of it appeared in my first book, *The Vegetable Butcher*. Feel free to add even more kale than I have suggested here. It adds texture and balances the sweetness of the coconut milk and squash.

FOR THE STEW

2 tablespoons canola oil

1 tablespoon plus 1 teaspoon curry powder

1 large yellow onion, finely diced

1 tablespoon minced garlic

1 tablespoon minced ginger

Fine sea salt

7 cups ¾-inch diced butternut squash (from a 2½- to 3-pound squash)

Freshly ground black pepper

1 can (13½ ounces) coconut milk

7 to 8 cups roughly chopped curly kale

1 cup low-sodium vegetable stock

1 can (15½ ounces) chickpeas, drained and rinsed well (optional)

Steamed brown rice, for serving

TOPPINGS FOR THE TABLE

¾ cup raisins

2 heaping tablespoons shredded unsweetened coconut

¾ cup toasted cashews or peanuts, coarsely chopped

---

1 Make the stew. Heat the oil in a large Dutch oven or heavy-bottomed pot over medium heat. Stir in the curry powder and cook, stirring to break up the powder, until fragrant, about 1 minute. Add the onion, garlic, ginger, and ½ teaspoon salt and cook, stirring, until the onion just begins to sweat, about 2 minutes.

2 Add the squash, 1 teaspoon salt, and ¼ teaspoon pepper and cook, stirring occasionally, allowing the onion mixture to thoroughly coat the squash, about 2 minutes. Stir in the coconut milk, scraping in any cream clinging to the can. Simmer partially covered and stirring occasionally, until the squash is beginning to soften, about 10 minutes. Stir in the kale, vegetable stock, and ½ teaspoon salt. Continue to cook, partially covered and stirring occasionally, until the squash is tender and sweet, another 8 to 10 minutes (or more if you prefer softer squash). Reduce the heat if the liquid is cooking off too quickly.

3 Uncover the pot, reduce the heat, and stir in the chickpeas, if using. Simmer over medium-low heat just until they are warmed through, about 2 minutes. Adjust salt and pepper to taste.

4 Spoon the stew into individual bowls over the brown rice. Offer raisins, shredded coconut, and toasted cashews at the table.

To store and reheat, see Tips and Takeaways on page 76.

Root Vegetable Tagine

SERVES 4 TO 6 AS A MAIN

INGREDIENT INFO:

- Please don't be intimidated by the prep and number of ingredients! Simply wash and peel all the roots at once, then give them a rough chop—¾ inch to 1 inch—just large enough that they will become tender while maintaining some texture. Once the initial work is done, the veggies can simmer along while you prep the rest of the dish.

- Feel free to change up the ratio or variety of vegetables. You'll want 5 to 6 cups of chopped vegetables plus 12 to 16 ounces of potatoes.

EQUIPMENT NOTE:

You don't need the eponymous tagine to make this dish—a Dutch oven or heavy-bottomed pot with a tight-fitting lid will do.

This deeply spiced and subtly sweetened stew is inspired by the Moroccan dish that gets its name from the brilliant cooking vessel traditionally used to make it. There are many ways to build and season a tagine; my take relies on a blend of ginger, turmeric, and saffron to bring it to life, plus just a hint of cinnamon to finish it as well as honey and dried fruit to sweeten it.

---

3 tablespoons extra-virgin olive oil

2 large onions, thinly sliced

4 to 5 garlic cloves, halved and smashed

Fine sea salt

1½ teaspoons ground ginger

1¼ teaspoons ground turmeric

Generous pinch of saffron threads

12 to 16 ounces Yukon gold or red potatoes, peeled and ¾-inch diced (halve or quarter baby potatoes)

10 to 12 ounces turnips, peeled and ¾-inch diced

10 to 12 ounces parsnips, peeled and ¾-inch diced

8 ounces carrot, ¾-inch diced

3 cups low-sodium vegetable stock

½ cup (4 ounces) dried apricots (or dried prunes or raisins), halved

Heaping ½ cup pitted green olives, halved

1 can (15½ ounces) chickpeas, drained and rinsed

1 tablespoon honey (or maple syrup)

Freshly ground black pepper

¼ teaspoon ground cinnamon

2 tablespoons freshly squeezed lemon juice, plus more as needed

Warm couscous, for serving

Chopped fresh cilantro leaves, for serving

⅓ to ½ cup toasted pistachios or sliced almonds, for serving (optional)

---

1 Heat the oil in a large Dutch oven over medium heat, add the onions, and cook until the onions are translucent and softening, about 5 minutes. Stir in the garlic, 1¾ teaspoons of salt, the ginger, turmeric, and saffron and stir until fragrant, about 1 minute. Stir in the potatoes, turnips, parsnips, and carrot. Add the stock—it should almost, but not quite, cover the vegetables (add some water if needed). Bring to a steady simmer, then cover and cook over medium-low heat, uncovering and stirring occasionally, until the vegetables are just tender and the stew has thickened, about 20 minutes.

2 Stir in the apricots, olives, chickpeas, honey, ¼ teaspoon pepper, and the cinnamon. Turn up the heat to medium, return the stew to a simmer, and cook, stirring occasionally, until warmed through, about 3 minutes. Turn off the heat. Stir in the lemon juice. Adjust salt, pepper, and lemon juice to taste.

3 Serve the stew over couscous in individual bowls, with cilantro and toasted pistachios or almonds for topping.

To store and reheat, see Tips and Takeaways on page 76.

SANDWICHES. TACOS. PIZZA. QUESADILLAS.

The Burger

Thoughtfully and unapologetically packed with vegetables, legumes, grains, and a mix of seasonings, these burgers make a ceremonious meal—giving reason to gather and celebrate. Stock the freezer and make them anytime you need to get a meal to the table quickly.

TIPS AND TAKEAWAYS

- A food processor is essential for making veggie burger patties—for speed, ease, and texture.

- Add panko breadcrumbs, oat flour, or your flour of choice if the patties feel extra wet or aren't holding their shape.

- Use a cylindrical ½-cup measure to portion and pack the dough. Tap the side to release the dough and gently reshape if needed to maintain shape and even thickness. Don't be tempted to flatten the burgers. (You can press down gently and flatten slightly when you flip the burgers during the cooking process.)

- The recipes on pages 87 and 93 are designed to yield enough patties to stock your freezer. To freeze uncooked patties, place them on a sheet pan in a single layer in the freezer. Once fully frozen, wrap each patty individually and store in an airtight container for up to 6 months. Pan-fry or bake them straight out of the freezer according to recipe instructions.

- Pan-frying is the technique of choice to give veggie burgers a nice brown crust. Make sure there is plenty of oil to coat the bottom of the pan (and don't overcrowd them; you want at least an inch between them). Tilt the pan as needed throughout cooking to redistribute the oil evenly and crisp up the edges. Reduce the heat if the burgers start to blacken too quickly at any time.

- You can bake burger patties to reduce oil and to eliminate extra hands-on time—a good option when you are making more than 4 patties at once. Set a rack in the middle position. For the beet burgers on page 87 and the sweet potato burgers on page 90, heat the oven to 425°F. For the mushroom burgers on page 93, heat the oven to 375°F. Oil a parchment-lined sheet pan and bake for about 15 minutes (16 to 18 minutes for frozen patties) on each side. This technique produces a crust although not as crispy and without the charred flavor you get from pan-frying. To melt cheese on a baked patty, top with a slice or heaping quarter cup of shredded cheese in the last 2 minutes of baking.

- A variety of toppings makes an already good thing even better.

- From time to time, consider going without a bun. Veggie burger patties are excellent served over dressed greens.

Classic Beet and Black Bean Burgers

MAKES UP TO 8 BURGERS

TAKE NOTE: Chill the burger patty dough ahead for the best texture—at least 2 hours, though 8 to 24 hours is ideal. Shape the chilled dough into patties and freeze ones that you don't plan to cook immediately. Place them on a sheet pan in a single layer in the freezer. Once fully frozen, wrap each patty individually and store in an airtight container for up to 6 months.

SHORTCUTS: Use precooked beets and microwaved frozen rice to speed up the whole process. Stir the cooked rice well and let it stand, continuing to stir occasionally, for at least 5 minutes to release moisture. Or you can make fresh rice and refrigerate it up to 1 day ahead.

This patty never fails to satisfy a craving for the classic. Of the three burgers I offer in this book, this version is a natural fit for summer meals served with crispy potato chips. I've also served these, more than a few times, as a fun, adult birthday dinner—elevated but still easy, even better with a glass of good bubbly. I like to top this burger with chopped kale, pickles, smashed avocado and Dijon mixed with a touch of plant-based mayo or with a slice of tomato, a crisp lettuce leaf, and a generous smear of Secret Sauce (page 95).

FOR THE BURGERS

2 large garlic cloves, peeled

1 cup rolled (old-fashioned) oats

8 ounces cooked peeled beets (see Shortcuts), stem ends trimmed, quartered

½ small onion, peeled and cut into 6 chunks

2 teaspoons smoked sweet paprika

1¾ teaspoons fine sea salt

1 teaspoon ground cumin

¼ teaspoon freshly ground black pepper

1 tablespoon molasses

1 teaspoon unfiltered apple cider vinegar

Thick flaxseed "egg" (see Note on page 88) or 1 large egg, lightly beaten

1 can (15½ ounces) black beans, drained, rinsed well, and patted dry

2 cups cooked and cooled brown rice (see Shortcuts)

Canola oil, for pan-frying

About 8 slices aged Cheddar, Gruyère, or Swiss cheese or 2 to 3 cups shredded cheese, for topping (optional)

About 8 brioche-style burger buns, lightly toasted, for serving

Your favorite burger fixings, for serving

---

1 Process the garlic in the bowl of a food processor with the standard blade attachment on high until it is completely minced and stuck to the bottom and sides of the bowl. Scrape down the side of the bowl and add the oats, beets, and onion. Pulse in five 1-second intervals until the beets and onion are roughly chopped. Add the smoked paprika, salt, cumin, pepper, molasses, and cider vinegar. Pulse in three 1-second intervals to evenly incorporate and further break down the beets and onion. Add the flaxseed "egg," half the beans, and half the rice, and again, pulse 3 times, for 1 second each, to incorporate them without completely breaking down the beans. Scrape down the sides of the bowl. Add the remaining beans and rice and pulse 5 to 7 times, 1 second each, until the beans and rice are evenly combined and coarsely chopped—some beans should remain whole or halved. The mixture will be fairly wet but should hold together loosely.

(recipe continues)

BUTCHER TIP: Place 2 medium beets, scrubbed and trimmed, in a baking dish with 1 cup water and 1 tablespoon oil and cover tightly with foil. Roast at 400°F until tender, 60 to 70 minutes, then drain, let cool, peel, and trim. You can make them up to 4 days in advance and store them in the fridge.

VARIATION: To bake the burgers, see Tips and Takeaways on page 86.

2 Carefully transfer the dough to a large bowl, give it a stir to combine, and wrap it tightly. Refrigerate the dough for 8 to 24 hours. Even a 1- to 2-hour chill will improve the texture of the burgers.

3 To shape the burger patties, line a sheet pan with a piece of parchment. Spoon the chilled mixture into a cylindrical ½-cup measure, packing and leveling it without overfilling it. Tap the measure into your hand or directly onto the parchment until the burger mixture is released. (Gently reshape and pack the patty if needed, but do not flatten it.) Repeat to shape all of the dough. Freeze patties that you don't plan to cook immediately.

4 When ready to cook, heat 4 tablespoons canola oil in a large skillet over medium heat. When the oil begins to shimmer, carefully place the patties in the pan, 3 to 4 at a time, and cook until browned and crisp, 3 to 4 minutes (5 minutes for frozen patties). Carefully flip the patties with a spatula and gently press down to flatten them just slightly (they'll be about 3 inches wide). Cook the other side until well browned and crisp, tilting the pan occasionally to evenly distribute the oil in the pan as well as pooling some oil on the edges of the patty to fry them, another 2 to 3 minutes (4 to 5 minutes for frozen patties). Add more oil if the pan becomes too dry and reduce the heat if the patties start to burn at any point. Transfer the patties to a paper towel-lined sheet pan. Repeat with more patties and oil as desired.

5 If you are adding cheese, heat the broiler with a rack in the top position. Remove the paper towels from the sheet pan and top the patties with cheese. Broil for 45 to 90 seconds until the cheese is melted and bubbling. Transfer the patties to the buns and serve with the fixings of your choice.

NOTE: To make a thick flaxseed "egg," combine 1 tablespoon ground flaxseed with 2 tablespoons water in a small bowl. Stir and let stand until the mixture becomes thick and gelatinous, about 5 minutes. Stir again to evenly combine.

Roasted Sweet Potato–Chickpea Burgers
with Maple-Lime-Chipotle Crema

MAKES 4 BURGERS

BUTCHER TIP: Cutting the sweet potato into large chunks prevents them from drying out while they roast.

VARIATION: To bake the burgers, see Tips and Takeaways on page 86.

I like to pan-fry these burgers for added flavor and a crisp, almost flaky quality to the crust, but baking them is a good hands-off option and uses less oil (see Variation). If you like a burger without a bun, go for it here. Sandwiched or not, it deserves toppings. My favorites are Maple-Lime-Chipotle Crema, smashed avocado, jack cheese, and a handful of arugula or a leaf of butter lettuce.

1 large sweet potato (12 to 14 ounces), peeled and cut into 1-inch chunks

3 garlic cloves, unpeeled

1 tablespoon extra-virgin olive oil

1 teaspoon fine sea salt

1 can (15½ ounces) chickpeas, drained, rinsed, and patted dry

1 teaspoon ground cumin

1 teaspoon smoked sweet paprika

¼ teaspoon freshly ground black pepper

1 cup loosely packed fresh cilantro leaves

⅓ cup chopped scallions

Canola oil, for pan-frying

Freshly grated jack cheese, for topping (optional)

4 burger buns, lightly toasted, for serving

Smashed avocado, for topping

Baby arugula, for topping

Maple-Lime-Chipotle Crema (recipe follows; optional)

1 Heat the oven to 425°F with a rack in the middle position. Place the sweet potato chunks and garlic cloves on an unlined sheet pan and toss with the oil and ¼ teaspoon of salt. Roast until the potatoes and garlic are browning in places and almost tender, about 20 minutes, then turn them and roast until browning (not burnt) all over and tender, about 5 minutes more. Let the sweet potatoes cool completely. Remove the garlic skins and trim the ends of the garlic cloves.

2 Transfer the roasted potatoes and garlic cloves to a large food processor fitted with the standard blade. Add the chickpeas, cumin, smoked paprika, the remaining ¾ teaspoon of salt, the pepper, cilantro, and scallions. Pulse in 1-second intervals, about 15 times, and then scrape down the sides of the bowl and blend on low until the mixture sticks together but remains coarsely chopped, about 5 seconds.

3 To make the burger patties, spoon the mixture into a cylindrical ½-cup measure, packing and leveling it without overfilling it. Tap the cup in your palm until it releases the mixture, then shape it into a 3-inch patty. Place the patty on a parchment-lined plate. Repeat with the remaining mixture to make 4 patties in all. Cook within 30 minutes or refrigerate, tightly covered, for up to 48 hours. Freeze uncooked patties for up to 6 months.

4 When ready to cook, heat 3 tablespoons canola of oil over medium heat in a large skillet until it begins to shimmer. Line a sheet pan with paper towels; set aside. Carefully place the patties in the pan, 3 to 4 at a time, and cook until browned and a crisp crust forms on the bottom, 4 to 5 minutes. Gently flip the patties with a spatula and then press down on the top cooked side of the patties to flatten them slightly (they'll be 3- to 3½ inches wide.) Cook until well browned and crisp, tilting the pan occasionally to evenly distribute the oil in the pan, 4 to 5 minutes more. Add more oil if the pan becomes too dry and reduce the heat and cooking time if the patties start to burn at any point. Transfer the patties to the lined sheet pan.

5 If you are adding cheese, heat the broiler with a rack in the top position. Remove the paper towels from the sheet pan and top the patties with cheese. Broil for 45 to 90 seconds until the cheese is melted and bubbling. Transfer the patties to the buns, top with the avocado, arugula, and/or crema (if using), and serve.

Maple-Lime-Chipotle Crema

MAKES ABOUT 1 CUP

1 cup plain Greek yogurt, coconut yogurt, or sour cream

1 tablespoon freshly squeezed lime juice

2 teaspoons pure maple syrup

1 chipotle pepper in adobo (halved and seeded to temper the heat), finely chopped, plus ½ to 1 teaspoon adobo sauce from the can (optional)

Fine sea salt

Whisk together the yogurt, lime juice, maple syrup, and chipotle pepper in a small bowl. For added heat, whisk in the adobo sauce to taste. Season with a pinch of salt or to taste. The crema will keep in an airtight container in the refrigerator for up to 5 days.

Drive-Through-Style Mushroom-Lentil Cheeseburgers

with Secret Sauce

MAKES 13 PATTIES.
4 FINISHED BURGERS
(PLUS PATTIES TO FREEZE)

TAKE NOTE:

- Many ingredients go into this patty and it requires several steps. To streamline the process, have everything prepped and gathered in advance.

- You can shape and make the burgers straight away, but they will hold together even better if you let the bowl of dough (or patties) chill in the fridge, 1 hour.

- To freeze extra uncooked patties, see Tips and Takeaways on page 86.

- Top the burgers with caramelized onions to really take these over the top.

ALL PLANTS: Sub 2 thick flaxseed eggs for the large eggs (see Note on page 95). Bake the burgers instead of pan-frying them (see Tips and Takeaways on page 86).

This fully loaded cheeseburger totally satisfies that craving for the drive-through variety, although the skillet-fried, lentil–quinoa patty is not trying to be anything it is not. It's an unapologetic plant-powered umami bomb—packed with mushrooms, walnuts, miso, and soy sauce. Layer it with the classics: American cheese, tomato, crisp iceberg lettuce, and a "secret sauce" that combines the best burger condiments into one irresistible mixture.

FOR THE PATTIES

4 cups water

Fine sea salt

1 cup uncooked white quinoa, rinsed well and drained

1 cup uncooked green lentils, sorted, rinsed, and drained

4 to 5 garlic cloves, peeled

1 medium red onion, roughly cut into 2-inch pieces

8 ounces white button or cremini mushrooms, trimmed and quartered

1 cup walnut halves, toasted

1 tablespoon white miso paste

1 tablespoon tamari or soy sauce

¼ teaspoon freshly ground black pepper

1 tablespoon dried oregano (or Italian seasoning)

½ teaspoon crushed red pepper flakes

Finely grated zest of 1 lemon

1¼ cups panko breadcrumbs, plus more as needed

3 tablespoons all-purpose flour

2 large eggs, lightly beaten

Canola oil, for pan-frying

4 slices American cheese

4 brioche or egg buns, lightly toasted

FOR THE FIXINGS

Secret Sauce (recipe follows)

4 burger-size chilled iceberg lettuce leaves

4 tomato slices

4 to 8 pickle slices

(recipe continues)

VARIATION: To bake the burgers, see Tips and Takeaways on page 86.

1 Bring 1¾ cups of water and ½ teaspoon salt to boil in a small saucepan. Add the quinoa and simmer over medium-low heat, covered, until the water is absorbed, about 12 minutes. Remove from heat and let stand, covered, until the quinoa is tender, 10 minutes more. Uncover and fluff the quinoa with a fork. (No water should remain.) Let cool slightly.

2 Meanwhile, use another small saucepan to bring the remaining 2¼ cups of water and ½ teaspoon salt to a boil. Add the lentils and simmer on medium heat, reducing the heat as the water cooks off, until all of the water is absorbed and the lentils are tender, 13 to 15 minutes. Continue to cook if needed—no water should remain. Let cool slightly.

3 Place the garlic in a food processor and process until finely chopped. Add the onion and pulse in five 1-second intervals until roughly chopped. Add the mushrooms and pulse again 5 times, until roughly chopped. Scrape down the sides of the bowl and pulse 3 to 5 times until all of the mushrooms are finely chopped.

4 Add 1 cup each of the quinoa and lentils to the food processor along with the walnuts, miso, and tamari. Pulse in ten 1-second intervals until the lentils and quinoa start to break down and evenly combine. Carefully scrape down the sides of the bowl (it may be very full). Add ½ teaspoon salt, the black pepper, oregano, red pepper flakes, and lemon zest and pulse about 5 times more until the whole mixture is mostly combined. Transfer the mixture to a large bowl and stir well. Add the remaining lentils and quinoa, the breadcrumbs, flour, and the eggs. Stir well until evenly combined. Add up to ¼ cup more breadcrumbs if the dough feels too wet to form a patty and hold together.

5 Carefully transfer the dough to an airtight container or to a large bowl and wrap it tightly. Refrigerate the dough for at least 2 hours, ideally 8 to 24 hours.

6 Line a sheet pan with a piece of parchment paper. To make the burger patties, pack the dough into a cylindrical ½-cup measure, leveling it. Tap the cup into your palm until it releases the mixture, then shape it into a 3-inch patty. Repeat until all of the dough is portioned—you'll have 13 packed patties. Freeze any that you don't plan to cook immediately.

7 Heat 4 tablespoons of oil in a large skillet over medium heat. When the oil starts to shimmer, carefully add 4 patties to the pan, being careful not to crowd them. Cook until the underside is browning, 3 to 4 minutes, then flip the patties and press the cooked side gently with a spatula to flatten slightly. Tilt the pan as needed to evenly distribute the oil. Cook on the second side until evenly browned and a nice crust forms, 2 to 3 minutes. Transfer the patties to a paper towel–lined sheet pan.

8 Heat the broiler with a rack in the top position. Remove the paper towels from the sheet tray and top the patties with cheese. Broil for 45 to 90 seconds until the cheese is melted and bubbling.

9 Smear the buns on both sides with the secret sauce. Add a burger patty to each and layer with the lettuce, tomato, and pickles.

NOTE: To make 2 thick flaxseed "eggs," combine 2 tablespoons ground flaxseed with ¼ cup water in a small bowl. Stir and let stand until the mixture becomes thick and gelatinous, about 5 minutes. Stir again to evenly combine.

MAKES ABOUT 1 CUP

Secret Sauce

½ cup mayonnaise
  (standard or plant-based)

¼ cup ketchup

Heaping 2 tablespoons sweet
  pickle relish, plus more as needed

1 teaspoon white distilled vinegar

1 teaspoon Dijon mustard

¼ teaspoon garlic powder

Stir together the mayonnaise, ketchup, relish, vinegar, mustard, and garlic powder in a small bowl until evenly combined, adding more relish to taste. The sauce will keep in an airtight container in the refrigerator for up to 5 days.

The Deli-Style Sandwich

Imagine a deli case full of gorgeous, colorful vegetables—all different shapes and sizes—ready to be broken down, cooked down, layered together, and piled high between great bread. Take that sandwich, wrap it up in butcher paper, then roll it out when you are ready. Pair it with a bag of chips or a prepared salad. Maybe a fizzy drink, too? This is the vibe that we are going for here. It's the modern deli sandwich stacked with vegetables and made to please.

TIPS AND TAKEAWAYS

- Deli-style sandwiches utilize multiple components to build texture and knock-out flavor.

- To save time, plan ahead and make the various parts and pieces so you can assemble the sandwiches when the mood or need arises. Build a fresh sandwich each day or position the ingredients in an assembly line to quickly make multiple sandwiches at once.

- Source good bread. You decide on your favorite and cut ½-inch slices. Typical soft, sliced sandwich bread will do just fine, too, but you will likely need to toast it so that it can handle layers of filling. Ciabatta, French baguettes, or sourdough rolls are great for veg-heavy sandwiches, but make sure they are soft enough to comply.

Beet and Avocado Sandwich

with Pickled Onions and Chive Goat Cheese

MAKES 4 SANDWICHES

MAKE AHEAD: The beets, chive goat cheese, vinaigrette, and pickled onions will keep well in the fridge for up to 5 days. Prep ahead and assemble the sandwiches throughout the week.

BUTCHER TIP: See page 18 for how to slice the beets on a mandoline.

INGREDIENT INFO:
- Feel free to use 1 pound precooked and peeled beets in a pinch; just be aware that the poaching process infuses the beets with flavor, which you won't get from the precooked ones.

- Use a good-quality multigrain sliced sandwich bread (toasted) or fresh ciabatta or other semi-soft sandwich rolls; the filling will slip out of anything too hard.

This sandwich is one of the best things I've ever created. (A bold statement, I know, but it's true.) I set out to make a deli-style sandwich for my restaurant, Little Eater, that would take the place of the ubiquitous—and often sad—veggie option you find at lots of sandwich shops. It's layer upon layer of all good things—bright, earthy beets over tangy goat cheese whipped with chives, avocado, baby greens dressed in lemony vinaigrette, and sweet-and-sour onions—that bring it all together.

4 to 5 small to medium golden, red, and/or Chioggia beets, stems trimmed to ½ inch and roots gently scrubbed and rinsed (about 1 pound roots)

7 cups water

1 cup apple cider vinegar

2 garlic cloves, halved

1 large bay leaf

Fine sea salt

½ packed cup fresh goat cheese, at room temperature (4 ounces)

2 tablespoons finely chopped fresh chives

1 large avocado

8 slices multigrain sandwich bread or 4 ciabatta rolls (see Ingredient Info)

4 cups baby spring greens mix

House Lemon Vinaigrette (page 21)

Flaky sea salt, such as Maldon, and freshly ground black pepper

Heaping ½ cup Quick-Pickled Onions (recipe follows)

1 Place the beets in a medium saucepan with the water, vinegar, garlic, bay leaf, and 1 teaspoon fine sea salt (add more water if needed to just cover the beets). Bring the liquid to a boil over high heat, then reduce the heat to maintain a steady low boil. Partially cover the pan and continue to cook the beets until they are tender and you can easily pierce the center without resistance, 35 to 40 minutes for smallish beets (40 to 50 minutes for larger ones). Let the beets cool, then peel them using a paring knife to trim the root end and help remove the skins (leave the stem end intact). Grasp the stem end and gently press the root end against a vegetable slicer or mandoline (or use a chef's knife) to cut them into ¹⁄₁₆-inch slices. The beets should be thin with some bite.

2 While the beets cook, stir together the goat cheese and chives in a small bowl until well blended; set aside.

(recipe continues)

ALL PLANTS: Replace the cheese with extra avocado or use a favorite creamy plant-based cheese.

3 When you are ready to assemble the sandwiches, halve and pit the avocado and smash the avocado flesh with the back of a fork in a small bowl until it is coarsely pureed. Season with salt to taste. If you are using sliced sandwich bread, toast it; if using rolls, slice them open.

4 Place the greens in a medium bowl, add a generous pinch of salt and 4 teaspoons of vinaigrette, and toss to coat. The greens should be dressed generously; add more vinaigrette to taste.

5 Spread the chive goat cheese on the bottom half of each sandwich, about 2 tablespoons per sandwich. Evenly spread the smashed avocado on the top half, 2 to 3 tablespoons per sandwich. Layer the beets over the goat cheese, overlapping the slices and spreading them out neatly. Sprinkle the beets with flaky sea salt and a drizzle of the vinaigrette, and pile a quarter of the greens on top of the beets. Place about 2 tablespoons of the pickled onions evenly over the avocado, gently pressing them into the avocado. Place the avocado-smeared half over the bottom half. Close up the sandwiches and carefully cut them in half with a serrated knife.

6 Serve the sandwiches immediately if you are using toasted sandwich bread; if using heartier ciabatta rolls, the sandwiches will keep, wrapped, for about 1 hour (though the beet juices may stain the bread).

Quick-Pickled Onions

ABOUT 3 CUPS

⅓ cup apple cider vinegar (or white wine vinegar or rice wine vinegar or a combination)

1 teaspoon sugar

⅓ cup water

¼ teaspoon fine sea salt

1 large red onion, thinly sliced

Combine the vinegar, sugar, water, and salt in a medium saucepan. Bring to a simmer over medium heat and cook, stirring, until the sugar dissolves. Stir in the onion and cook, stirring occasionally, for 2 to 3 minutes until the onion slices just about begin to soften. Transfer the onion slices to a jar and pour the hot cooking liquid over them. Let stand to cool completely, turning occasionally; cover tightly and refrigerate for up to 1 week.

Cucumber and Pesto Sandwich
with Arugula and Avocado

MAKES 4 SANDWICHES

HOW TO CUT CUCUMBER PLANKS:

Cut the cucumber into thin slices on a sharp diagonal.

TAKE NOTE: If you are not making all four sandwiches, you'll need about 1 cup of arugula tossed with 1 teaspoon vinaigrette for each sandwich.

Crunchy, herbaceous, bright, peppery, and sweet: I could make this sandwich every day. Make sure to cut the cucumbers thin and on a sharp diagonal and get those avocado slices nice and thin to ensure the sandwich filling fits neatly together and stays in place.

---

4 cups loosely packed arugula

About 8 teaspoons House Lemon Vinaigrette (page 21)

Fine sea salt and freshly ground black pepper

8 slices multigrain sandwich bread or pain au levain, or 4 ciabatta rolls

½ cup (4 ounces) fresh goat cheese, at room temperature

2 cucumbers, ends trimmed, ⅛-inch sliced on a sharp diagonal

Flaky sea salt, such as Maldon

½ cup Basil Pesto (page 59) or favorite store-bought pesto

2 medium avocados, sliced lengthwise ⅛ inch thick

---

1 Toss together the arugula and 4 teaspoons of vinaigrette in a medium bowl. Season with fine sea salt and pepper.

2 If you are using sliced sandwich bread, toast it; if using rolls, slice them open.

3 Evenly spread the goat cheese on the bottom half of each sandwich to cover the bread, about 2 tablespoons per sandwich. Top with enough cucumber slices to cover the full surface of the bread (6 to 8 per sandwich), overlapping them in places so they are snugly tucked together and not hanging over the bread. Sprinkle the cucumbers with a generous pinch of flaky sea salt and drizzle with about 1 teaspoon of vinaigrette. Layer the avocado slices over the cucumbers in the opposite direction. For each sandwich, layer 1 cup dressed arugula on top of the avocado. Evenly spread about 2 tablespoons of pesto directly on the top half of each sandwich to coat. Close the sandwiches and use a serrated knife to slice each in half. Serve immediately.

Butternut Squash Steak Sandwich

with Kale, Walnuts, and Apple-Onion Jam

MAKES 4 SANDWICHES

EQUIPMENT TIP: If you are roasting more than 2 pounds of squash, use two sheet pans and space them evenly apart.

TAKE NOTE: Keep leftover dressing around for a simple salad; just add a hint more maple syrup and oil.

ALL PLANTS: Replace the cheese with extra apple-onion jam or use a cream cheese alternative.

TEMP TIP: If you prefer, you can layer in the squash steaks while still warm, or warm the whole sandwich up in a 375°F oven or toaster oven (covered with foil if you have used a crusty roll), for 8 to 10 minutes.

This mighty sandwich offers thick slabs of roasted butternut squash and apple–onion jam spiced with cinnamon and kissed with sage. In between the layers of sweetness, balance and crunch come with kale and walnuts dressed in bright sherry vinaigrette. The prepared squash steaks, jam, and vinaigrette will last for up to 5 days in the refrigerator, stored separately in airtight containers—so you can assemble the sandwiches as desired.

---

2 pounds butternut squash, cut into ½-inch-thick slices

5 tablespoons extra-virgin olive oil

Fine sea salt

2 medium to large onions, ⅛-inch sliced

2 tablespoons water

1 large crisp apple, such as Fuji, peeled and ⅛-inch sliced

4 to 6 large fresh sage leaves

1 tablespoon pure maple syrup

1 tablespoon balsamic vinegar

⅛ teaspoon ground cinnamon

1 tablespoon sherry vinegar

Scant ½ teaspoon Dijon mustard

4 sandwich rolls, such as ciabatta, sliced in half, or 8 slices good-quality, multigrain sandwich bread

About 3 cups chopped curly kale leaves

½ cup toasted walnut halves, coarsely chopped

Freshly cracked black pepper

8 tablespoons (4 ounces) cream cheese or fromage blanc, at room temperature

---

1 Heat the oven to 425°F with a rack in the middle position. Line a sheet pan with parchment paper.

2 Brush the squash pieces evenly all over with oil, about 1 tablespoon total, and sprinkle them on both sides with salt, about a scant ¼ teaspoon total. Spread the slices out in a single layer on the prepared sheet pan, and roast until they begin to soften and turn golden in places, about 20 minutes. Flip and roast until the steaks are lightly browning in places and tender all the way through while keeping their shape, another 15 to 17 minutes.

3 Meanwhile, make the apple-onion jam. Heat 2 tablespoons of oil in a large skillet over medium heat. Add the onions and cook, stirring occasionally with a wooden spoon, until the onions have softened and are turning golden brown in places, about 15 minutes. Turn down the heat if the onions begin to burn at any point. Add the water and stir to incorporate any browned bits at the bottom of the pan. Stir in the apple, sage (torn in halves or thirds), maple syrup, balsamic vinegar, cinnamon, and ¼ teaspoon salt. Continue to cook, stirring more frequently, until the onions are deep brown in color and jammy and all liquid is absorbed, 10 to 12 minutes. Remove from the heat and let cool.

4 Make the sherry vinaigrette. Whisk together the sherry vinegar, mustard, ¼ teaspoon salt, and the remaining 2 tablespoons of oil until emulsified.

5 Lightly toast the bread or leave it untoasted if you prefer. Whisk the dressing again to evenly combine it. Combine the kale and walnuts in a medium bowl and toss with enough dressing to generously and evenly coat, about 2 teaspoons of dressing per cup of kale. Season with pepper to taste.

6 Line up each pair of sliced rolls or bread. Evenly spread the bottom half with cream cheese, about 2 tablespoons per sandwich. Evenly spread the apple–onion jam over the top half, about ¼ cup or more depending on the size of your bread. Top the bottom half with a layer of squash steaks, overlapping them just slightly in places if needed, about 2 full rounds and 2 crescent-moon shapes per sandwich. Top the squash with the kale mixture. Close the sandwiches and use a serrated knife to slice each in half.

HOW TO CUT SQUASH STEAKS:

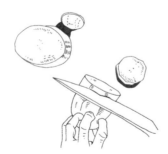 

1. Cut the squash to separate the neck from the bulb, then peel each half (see page 52). Place the neck on its side and cut ½-inch-thick rounds. (If the squash starts to roll on the board, stand the piece vertically and cut a small slice off the side to create a flat surface. Return the squash to that cut side and continue slicing crosswise.)

2. Stand the bulb upright on its flat cut side and halve vertically. Scoop out the seeds and discard them. Place each half scooped-side down on the board, and cut into ½-inch-thick slices. These will mostly be crescent-moon shapes with some half-moons; layer these into the sandwich or dice them for another use.

The Hero Sandwich

These sandwiches are warm, buttery, cheesy, messy, saucy—delicious. Vegetables—braised, grilled, roasted, simmered, pickled, or fried—are the hero. All they need are supporting players in the form of flavorful layers, including something crunchy and bright, maybe a little cheese, and a sauce to bring it all together.

WAYS TO MAKE A HERO SANDWICH OUT OF A HERO DISH

You'll find recipes for some amazing heros on the following pages, but you can easily freestyle your own using leftovers as the "meat." Here are some favorite combos:

- Coconut- and-panko-crusted cauliflower (see page 123) + creamy apple–cabbage slaw (see page 123) + avocado + Quick-Pickled Onions (page 100)

- Cauliflower Steaks (page 199) + Pickled Pepper Relish (page 199) + goat cheese + arugula + vinaigrette

- Celery Root Cutlets (page 200) + Lemon-Cashew Aioli (page 203) + shredded radicchio or arugula

- Chickpea Falafel (page 216) + Tahini Sauce (page 217) + shredded cabbage + Quick-Pickled Onions (page 100) + cucumbers + tomatoes + store-bought hummus or Beet Hummus (page 224)

- Sheet Pan Cauliflower Marbella (page 233) + whipped feta (see page 50) or Red Pepper Pesto (page 230) + shredded radicchio and arugula

- Potato and Spring Pea Frittata (page 269) or Simple Broccoli–Cheddar Frittata (page 271) + Red Pepper Pesto (page 230) or Spicy Tofu "Mayo" (see page 152) + a drizzle of aged balsamic vinegar + arugula

---

TIPS AND TAKEAWAYS

- A hero sandwich doesn't have to be served warm, but heat definitely adds to its allure.

- Don't skimp: These are decadent, special sandwiches. Fill them to the brim.

- Select good bread like soft brioche, French baguette, ciabatta, sesame rolls, or slices of good-quality sourdough or multigrain bread.

- Butter or oil the bread and pan-grill it until crisp and toasty (or toast the whole sandwich).

- Add crisp texture and fresh flavor with something raw like chopped celery, fresh herbs, mild or bitter greens, or shredded cabbage.

- Add something pickle-y and/or something briny like olives, capers, or marinated peppers (see page 41).

- Make it gooey with a layer of melted cheese, sliced avocado, and/or a fried egg.

Saucy Eggplant and Melted Mozzarella Hero

MAKES 6 SANDWICHES

SWAP: Try this sandwich with Italian-style Meatballs (see page 214) in place of the eggplant.

PREP TIPS:

• Make all of the components ahead to allow the flavors in the sauce and pesto to develop, and to save time when you are ready to assemble the sandwiches. Enjoy sandwiches throughout the week or make them all at once. Use a toaster oven to melt the cheese and warm the sandwich if you are making one or two at a time.

• Alternatively, you can serve these sandwiches at room temperature.

• Keep the tomato sauce recipe in your back pocket. It's also fantastic with pasta.

All the layers—pesto, arugula, eggplant, spicy tomato sauce, melted mozzarella, and more sauce—make this sandwich a true hero. Serve this sandwich cold for a summer picnic (if you don't melt the cheese, it travels well), or hot, toasty, and gooey for a late summer or fall dinner with a salad or bowl of soup. It's always a huge, outrageously delicious hit.

FOR THE SAUCE

2 cans (14½ ounces each) diced tomatoes and juice (or 2 pounds fresh tomatoes, cored and diced)

2 tablespoons extra-virgin olive oil

2 to 3 garlic cloves

1 teaspoon sugar

½ teaspoon fine sea salt

¼ teaspoon crushed red pepper flakes

⅓ cup freshly grated Parmesan cheese

½ cup coarsely chopped fresh basil leaves (optional)

FOR THE SANDWICHES

2 medium eggplants (1¾ pounds to 2 pounds total), cut into ⅓-inch-thick rounds

About 4 tablespoons extra-virgin olive oil

½ teaspoon fine sea salt

¼ teaspoon freshly ground black pepper

6 ciabatta rolls, other Italian-style sandwich rolls, or telera rolls (each 4 to 6 inches long), sliced in half lengthwise

½ cup Basil Pesto (page 59) or store-bought pesto

3 cups baby arugula

12 ounces fresh mozzarella cheese, thinly sliced

1 Make the tomato sauce: Combine the tomatoes and juices, oil, garlic, sugar, salt, and crushed red pepper flakes in a high-speed blender (or food processor) and blend until smooth. Transfer the tomato mixture to a medium saucepan, and heat until it just begins to simmer. Reduce the heat to maintain a simmer. Cook, stirring occasionally, until it thickens, 15 to 20 minutes. Stir in the Parmesan and chopped basil (if using). Remove from the heat; set aside.

2 Roast the eggplant: Heat the oven to 400°F with a rack in the middle position. Line a sheet pan with parchment paper. Spread out the eggplant slices, fitting them snugly in a single layer, on the prepared sheet pan. Brush the eggplant on both sides with the oil, adding a little more if needed to generously coat them. Sprinkle both sides with the salt and black pepper. Roast until tender, about 20 minutes. If you plan to serve the sandwiches hot, turn the oven down to 375°F.

(recipe continues)

3 Make the sandwiches: Place the rolls cut side up on a sheet pan. Spread 2 tablespoons pesto over on the bottom half of each roll and top each with ½ cup arugula. Layer eggplant slices on top of the arugula, dividing it evenly. Spread 1 tablespoon of the tomato sauce over the eggplant, then top evenly with the mozzarella slices. Spread 2 tablespoons of the tomato sauce over the top half of each roll. Bake the rolls (still cut side up) until the cheese has melted, 5 to 8 minutes. Assemble the sandwiches, slice each in half, and serve.

Butter-Poached Cauliflower Rolls

MAKES 6 SANDWICH ROLLS

INGREDIENT INFO:

• Celery leaves add delicate flavor and electric green color. Make sure to buy a whole bunch, not precut celery sticks, and look for the leaves on the inner stalks of the bunch, which should yield enough for the recipe. Use 2 tablespoons finely chopped parsley if needed.

• Lettuce leaves are not required and do make for a slightly messy sandwich experience, but they add freshness and texture that I really enjoy. I also think a little mess is part of the fun.

BUTCHER TIP: Cut the cauliflower into small bite-size pieces. Large florets won't fit neatly into the bun. See page 123 for how to break down cauliflower.

There's true romance around the lobster roll. It's the seaside picnic, the summer love, the cold beer, the chips, the salty air, and the briny, buttery goodness that comes wrapped up in a warm bun. But what to do in the off season or if you don't live on the coast—or if you're a veggie eater? Cauliflower happily takes on all the classic lobster roll flavors—it delivers brightness, brine, and butter—ooh, that butter infused in the cauliflower and all over that toasty brioche bun. With a pile of chips (to scoop up florets fallen overboard), it's a sandwich most certainly worthy of a little pomp and circumstance. (The yield for the price is nice, too.)

FOR THE CAULIFLOWER

1 cup water

½ cup whole milk

2 packed teaspoons minced garlic (3 small cloves)

3 tablespoons unsalted butter

1 large head cauliflower (1¾ to 2 pounds), florets cut into small, bite-size pieces (about 7 cups)

¾ teaspoon fine sea salt

FOR THE FILLED ROLLS

5 tablespoons unsalted butter

1 large celery rib with leaves attached, ⅛-inch diced (½ cup), leaves chopped (2 tablespoons tightly packed)

Fine sea salt and freshly ground black pepper

2 large lemons, 1 squeezed (to yield at least 2 tablespoons juice), 1 cut into at least 6 wedges

2 teaspoons packed chopped fresh dill (about ¼ cup loosely packed fronds)

6 top-cut brioche-style hot dog buns

6 large butter lettuce leaves (optional)

Potato chips (or fries, if you have them!), for serving

1 Poach the cauliflower. Bring the water, milk, garlic, and butter to a gentle simmer in a medium saucepan over medium heat. Immediately stir in the cauliflower and salt. Adjust the heat as needed to maintain a steady, but low, boil, and cook, stirring occasionally, until the cauliflower is tender but not overly soft or falling apart, 6 to 8 minutes. Drain the cauliflower immediately.

(recipe continues)

REHEATING LEFTOVERS:

You don't need to make all the rolls at once. To reheat leftover filling: Melt 1 tablespoon butter over medium-high heat in a nonstick or stainless-steel skillet. Stir in the cauliflower and cook, stirring occasionally, until warmed through, 3 to 5 minutes. Taste and add salt if needed.

2 Prepare the filling. Heat 2 tablespoons of butter in a medium nonstick skillet over medium-high heat until it foams. Stir in the diced celery, then the poached cauliflower, ½ teaspoon salt, and ¼ teaspoon pepper and cook until the cauliflower is well coated and hot, about 2 minutes. Turn off the heat and stir in the lemon juice and dill. Adjust salt to taste. Transfer the cauliflower mixture to a bowl and wipe the skillet clean.

3 Toast the rolls. Heat the remaining 3 tablespoons of butter in the skillet over medium heat until it sizzles. (To toast fewer rolls, use at least 1 tablespoon of butter for every 2 rolls.) Place the rolls in the pan on their outsides and cook until golden brown, about 2 minutes per side. Place the rolls cut side up on individual plates or a platter for serving. Line each roll with a piece of lettuce, if using, and add the cauliflower filling—about a heaping ½ cup per roll. Top with the chopped celery leaves and a few twists of pepper. Serve with the lemon wedges and potato chips or fries alongside.

Broccoli Rabe Grilled Cheese
with Olives and Apple

MAKES 4 SANDWICHES

Braised broccoli rabe and apple (or slices of any of fall's fruit) are just right to balance the richness that comes with a traditional grilled cheese (especially one that qualifies as a substantial and nourishing meal on its own). The olives are optional, but their saltiness plays beautifully off the bitterness of the broccoli rabe and the sweetness of the apple—making them difficult to resist.

2 teaspoons extra-virgin olive oil

1 small to medium garlic clove, minced

1 large shallot, thinly sliced (about ½ cup)

1 bunch (12 to 14 ounces) broccoli rabe, trimmed and cut into 1- to 2-inch pieces

½ teaspoon fine sea salt

½ cup water

3 tablespoons currants

2 teaspoons sherry vinegar (or red wine vinegar or apple cider vinegar)

8 slices (¼ inch-thick) sourdough boule

4 tablespoons (½ stick) unsalted butter, at room temperature

8 ounces Asiago fresco or Italian fontina cheese, shredded on the large holes of a box grater (see Take Note)

16 to 24 pitted kalamata olives, halved (optional)

2 Fuji or Honeycrisp apples, ⅛-inch sliced (or pear or Fuyu persimmon)

TAKE NOTE: The key with any grilled sandwich is to butter the bread, not the pan. (Use room-temperature butter.) And make sure that the pan is nice and hot. A medium cast-iron skillet is ideal, but you can also use a nonstick one with excellent results. A flexible spatula to press down and encourage melting is essential. If you are making four or more sandwiches, set a cooling rack into a sheet pan and hold them on the rack in a 200°F oven for up to 15 minutes.

SWAPS:

- In place of fresh fruit, smear a heaping tablespoon of fig jam on the underside of the top piece of buttered bread.

- Gruyère or aged Cheddar also work well here.

1 Heat the oil in a medium sauté pan over medium heat. Add the garlic and shallot and cook, stirring frequently, until fragrant and the shallot is just beginning to turn translucent, about 2 minutes. Add the broccoli rabe, a little at a time if needed to fit the pan, and season with ½ teaspoon of salt. Cook, stirring occasionally, until the broccoli rabe wilts, about another 2 minutes. Add the water and turn the heat up to medium-high. Cook, stirring occasionally, until the broccoli rabe is tender and the liquid has cooked off, about 2 minutes. Stir in the currants, if using, and the sherry vinegar. Cook until the liquid cooks off, about 1 minute. Adjust salt to taste. Remove the pan from the heat to cool.

2 Make the sandwiches. Spread out the bread slices on a sheet pan or work surface, pairing similarly sized pieces. Butter the top of each slice, about 1 tablespoon for every 2 slices depending on their size, and place them buttered side down. Sprinkle about two thirds of the cheese on the bottom slices, being careful to redistribute any cheese that has fallen off the bread. Evenly divide the broccoli rabe among the cheese-topped slices, heaping it up as necessary to fit. Divide the olives, if using, over the top and add the apple slices, about 8 per sandwich, fanning them out evenly. Top the apples with the remaining cheese. Assemble the sandwiches, placing the top pieces of bread buttered side up.

3 Grill the sandwiches. Heat a medium cast-iron or nonstick skillet over medium heat until nice and hot, 60 to 90 seconds. Carefully transfer two sandwiches to the skillet, rounded edges of the bread facing outward. Cook, occasionally pressing down with a flexible spatula to encourage the cheese to melt, until the bread is evenly browned and crisp on one side, about 3 minutes. Flip the sandwiches and let cook until the other side is crisp and the cheese has melted, about 3 minutes more (take care when flipping the sandwiches to keep their filling intact).

4 Transfer the sandwiches to a cutting board and use a sharp chef's knife to cut them into halves or thirds. Serve immediately. If you are making more than two sandwiches, repeat step 3 to make the remaining sandwiches. You can place the just-made sandwiches on a cooling rack set in a sheet pan and hold them in a 200°F oven on the middle rack for up to 15 minutes until ready to serve.

The Toast

A slice of good bread, toasted until golden and crisp, makes a sturdy base on which to show off vegetables in many forms—purees, pesto, pickles, roasted, raw. And without a top piece of bread to cover them up, it's all eyes on the vegetables, which makes this satisfying "sandwich" look prettier than the rest. Here are the basic steps:

Toasted Good Bread + Something Creamy + Vegetables + Extra Goodies + A Drizzle of Oil and a Sprinkle of Flaky Salt to Finish

1. BREAD: Use thick (but not too thick) slices of good bread; you don't want the bread to overwhelm the vegetables. Also, the bread should be dense enough to hold up layered toppings. Toast it.

2. SPREAD ON SOMETHING CREAMY: smashed avocado; hummus, Beet Hummus (page 224), pea puree (see page 112); Basil Pesto (page 59), Broccoli Rabe Pesto (see page 193), Red Pepper Pesto (page 230); Eggplant Caponata Toast (see page 115), Lemon-Beet Sauce (see page 190), butternut squash and jammy onions (see page 141); softened goat cheese, cream cheese, ricotta, or whipped feta (see page 50)

3. LAYER ON 1 TO 2 VEGETABLES: arugula, asparagus, carrot ribbons, cucumber slices, microgreens, pan-roasted mushrooms, sauteed or shredded hearty greens, shaved radishes, summer tomato slices, plus any pickled, fermented, or roasted vegetables (cut into bite-size pieces)

4. ADD EXTRA GOODIES:

- **To Add Crunch:** chopped toasted nuts, seeds, Turmeric Nut-Seed Mix (page 114), pulverized corn nuts, Frico (page 17)

- **To Elevate Flavor:** pickled dried fruit, fresh herbs, scallions, salsa like Avocado–Corn Salsa (page 140)

5. DRIZZLE AND SPRINKLE: good olive oil, herb oil, chili oil or chili crisp, or vinaigrette, and flaky sea salt and black pepper

Sweet Peas on Toast
with Mint and Quick-Pickled Carrots

MAKES 4 TOASTS; SERVES 4
AS A LIGHT MEAL OR
6 TO 8 AS AN APPETIZER

INGREDIENT INFO:

- Use any good-quality bread that has a uniform and dense enough crumb that can hold the puree.

- The carrots can be pickled well in advance. Simply cover and refrigerate for up to 5 days; their flavor will improve with time.

SWAPS:

- Upgrade to French feta for a creamy, salty, and sweet delight; or try shaved Pecorino Romano or Manchego.

- Swap fava beans (shelled, blanched, and skinned) for peas.

BUTCHER TIP: To shave carrot ribbons, trim the ends of the carrot and use a vegetable peeler to peel the outer layer; discard the ends and peels. Then press evenly into the carrot while running the peeler through the whole length of the carrot to produce wide, thin, even ribbons. After about 4 peels turn the carrot and continue peeling, continuing to rotate until you can no longer peel comfortably. Peel short ribbons from the thicker end if it is remaining.

This is modern, grown-up "peas and carrots" served on toast. It's important to use freshly shelled peas to give the puree a stiff and starchy texture that will hold up the other toppings. Bonus: Shelling is a meditative project that you can take on when peas are in season. Alternatively, use bagged shelled fresh peas; they work just as well as long as you rinse them well. (Do not use frozen peas!) For dinner, pair with a simple green salad or Every Season Green Salad (page 18), Parisian-Style Lentil and Crudités Salad (page 39), or Lemony Rainbow Carrot Couscous Salad (page 36).

---

2 tablespoons rice wine vinegar

1 teaspoon sugar

Fine sea salt

¼ cup plus 1 tablespoon water

6 peppercorns (optional)

2 small garlic cloves, smashed

1 large carrot, shaved into ribbons (see Butcher Note)

1 tablespoon unsalted butter

2 small shallots, thinly sliced (about ⅓ cup)

2 cups fresh shelled peas (2 pounds peas in the pod)

About 2 tablespoons chopped fresh mint

Freshly ground black pepper

3 tablespoons extra-virgin olive oil

4 large ½-inch-thick slices good-quality sourdough

½ cup freshly crumbled feta cheese (optional)

2 teaspoons minced fresh chives, for topping (optional)

Best-quality olive oil, for topping

---

1 Whisk together the vinegar, sugar, ¼ teaspoon salt, and the ¼ cup water in a small bowl. Add the peppercorns and 1 smashed garlic clove.

2 Add the carrot ribbons to the vinegar mixture and stir to evenly combine. Let stand at room temperature, stirring occasionally, to infuse them with pickled flavor, at least 30 minutes up to 2 hours (15 minutes if you can't wait). Their flavor will improve with time; refrigerate for up to 5 days.

3 Heat the butter and remaining smashed garlic clove in a large skillet over medium heat until the butter foams. Add the shallots and cook, stirring occasionally, until the shallots begin to soften and turn translucent without browning, 3 to 4 minutes. Stir in the peas, 1 packed tablespoon chopped mint, the remaining tablespoon of water, ½ teaspoon salt, and ¼ teaspoon pepper. Cook, stirring occasionally, until the peas are just slightly tender and no liquid remains in the pan, 2 to 3 minutes. Remove the pan from the heat.

4 Transfer the pea mixture to a food processor and add ½ teaspoon salt. Pulse to coarsely puree the peas. Stream the extra-virgin olive oil through the top feed tube while you blend the mixture on high. Scrape down the sides and process again until the mixture is well blended, but do not overprocess to a smooth paste; a fine texture should remain.

5 Toast the bread until light golden brown and crisp. Spread ¼ cup of the pea puree on each slice. Top with the pickled carrots, twisting and lifting the ribbons to create some height and texture. Sprinkle the toasts generously with feta (if using), coarsely cracked black pepper, the remaining chopped mint, the minced chives, if using, and a very generous drizzle of your best olive oil.

Avocado Toast
with Turmeric Nut-Seed Mix

MAKES 2 TO 3 TOASTS; SERVES 2 TO 3 AS A LIGHT MEAL OR 4 TO 5 AS AN APPETIZER

INGREDIENT INFO:
Depending on the size of your bread, 1 large avocado will make 2 to 3 toasts. If you want to produce more than 2 large toasts, keep extra avocados on hand.

You can elevate an everyday avocado toast to a crunchy, complex, restaurant-worthy meal with a few easy upgrades. The real game changer here is a mix of nuts, seeds, and spices (inspired by the Egyptian spice mix dukkah). Make a batch and keep it on hand for weeks to sprinkle over your daily avocado toast or use it when a dish needs an extra pop of flavor and crunch. A mix of microgreens, Maldon sea salt, and good-quality olive oil make all the difference.

2 large slices (about ½ inch thick) good-quality sourdough or multigrain sandwich bread

1 large avocado (see Ingredient Info)

Flaky sea salt, such as Maldon

2 to 3 teaspoons best-quality olive oil

Turmeric Nut-Seed Mix (recipe follows)

½ cup to 1 cup mixed microgreens (or baby arugula or finely chopped spinach)

1 Toast the bread until golden and crisp on the outside (you want it sturdy enough to hold the toppings) but still slightly soft on the inside.

2 Meanwhile, halve and pit the avocado. Transfer the flesh to a small bowl and use the back of a fork to mash it. Spread the avocado over each toast (about ⅓ cup per large slice of toast) and sprinkle it with flaky sea salt. Drizzle each toast with about ½ teaspoon oil, then evenly sprinkle about 1 tablespoon of the nut-seed mix over the top. Last, top each toast with a generous pinch of microgreens, another pinch of flaky sea salt, and a final drizzle of oil.

(recipe continues)

Turmeric Nut-Seed Mix

MAKES ABOUT ¾ CUP

TAKE NOTE: The recipe for Turmeric Nut-Seed Mix yields enough to make 12 to 14 toasts over several weeks. (And it makes an excellent gift–fill up a jar for a friend!) Store the mix in an airtight container in a cool, dry place or in the refrigerator.

½ cup shelled raw pistachios
  (or sliced almonds)

1 tablespoon plus 2 teaspoons white sesame seeds

2 teaspoons black sesame seeds

1 teaspoon cumin seeds

1 teaspoon fennel seeds

1 teaspoon ground coriander

½ teaspoon ground turmeric

¼ teaspoon fine sea salt

Freshly ground black pepper

1 Heat the oven to 350°F with a rack in the middle position. Line a sheet pan with parchment paper.

2 Combine the pistachios, white sesame seeds, 1 teaspoon of black sesame seeds, the cumin seeds, fennel seeds, coriander, turmeric, salt, and a generous ¼ teaspoon pepper or more as you please in the bowl of a food processor. Pulse and process until the pistachios are finely and evenly ground with a coarse, gravel-like texture. Make sure to stop before the nuts and seeds turn to a paste. Transfer the mix to the prepared sheet pan and spread it out. Bake until fragrant and toasty, 5 to 7 minutes. Remove from the oven, sprinkle the remaining 1 teaspoon of black sesame seeds over the top, and let the mixture cool completely.

Eggplant Caponata Toast

with Arugula and Pickled Raisins

MAKES 8 TO 10 TOASTS;
SERVES 4 TO 6 AS A
MEAL OR UP TO 10 AS
AN APPETIZER

TAKE NOTE: The caponata is a wonderful dip for crudités and crackers, flatbread, or pita chips. It also works as a sauce on pizza or with pasta (thinned with a little pasta water). To make it into a cold pasta salad, toss it with cooked orecchiette or gemelli, plus the arugula, pine nuts, raisins, and olives. (The puree yields 3 to 3½ cups.)

VARIATION: Instead of the arugula salad topping, try thinly sliced cucumbers, flaky sea salt, freshly ground black pepper, a drizzle of oil, crumbled feta, and chopped parsley or basil.

Caponata is a no-fail, Italian-style puree of roasted eggplant, red pepper, tomato, onion, and garlic that is truly irresistible in many applications. Here, you'll smear the sweet-and-sour spread over toasted, crusty olive-studded bread and top it with a simple salad of arugula, quick-pickled raisins, and pine nuts.

---

1 large globe eggplant or 2 to 3 smaller varieties, ¾-inch diced

1 red bell pepper or sweet Italian pepper, ¾-inch diced

1 medium red onion, ¾-inch diced

3 large garlic cloves, smashed or halved

3 roma or small vine tomatoes such as Early Girls (about 5 ounces each), cut into large pieces

4 tablespoons plus 1 teaspoon extra-virgin olive oil

Fine sea salt and freshly ground black pepper

⅓ cup golden raisins (or Thompson raisins)

2 teaspoons warm water

3 teaspoons red wine vinegar

1 tablespoon tomato paste

2 teaspoons balsamic vinegar

Heaping 3 packed cups arugula

3 tablespoons toasted pine nuts

10 pitted Castelvetrano olives, finely chopped (optional)

8 to 10 slices rustic olive bread (or other good-quality bread)

---

1 Heat the oven to 425°F with a rack in the middle position. Line a sheet pan with parchment paper.

2 In a large bowl or directly on the sheet pan, toss the eggplant, bell pepper, onion, garlic, and tomatoes with 3 tablespoons of oil, ¾ teaspoon salt, and ¼ teaspoon black pepper, making sure the vegetables are evenly coated. Spread out the veggies (the pan will be crowded and that's okay). Roast, stirring halfway through, until soft and golden, about 40 minutes. Let cool slightly. (Leave the oven on to toast the bread.)

(recipe continues)

3 Meanwhile, combine the raisins with the warm water, 2 teaspoons of red wine vinegar, and a couple of pinches of salt in a small bowl. Let stand, stirring occasionally.

4 Transfer the roasted vegetables to the bowl of a food processor. Add the tomato paste, 1 tablespoon of oil, 1 teaspoon of balsamic vinegar, the remaining teaspoon of red wine vinegar, and ¼ teaspoon salt and pulse about 12 times, scraping down the sides of the bowl as needed, until a chunky puree forms. Adjust salt and pepper to taste. (You can make the puree up to 4 days in advance and store in the refrigerator; the flavors will continue to develop. Bring the puree to room temperature before using on the toast.)

5 Whisk together the remaining teaspoon of balsamic vinegar and the remaining teaspoon of oil in a medium bowl. Add the arugula, pine nuts, and olives, if using. Briefly drain the raisins and add them, too. Toss gently to combine the salad. Season lightly with salt and pepper to taste.

6 Toast the bread: Spread out the slices in a single layer on a sheet pan and place in the heated oven. Toast until golden and toasty on both sides, 3 to 4 minutes per side. (For fewer slices, use a toaster oven.)

7 Spread about ⅓ cup of the caponata on each toast, adjusting as needed to generously cover each toast. Top with the arugula salad, evenly dividing it, and spoon any raisins and pine nuts (and olives if using) lingering in the bottom of the bowl over the top of each toast. Top with more freshly cracked pepper.

The Seasonal Taco

Given that tacos have their very own day of the week, you almost have to add them to your regular rotation. Let beets, the arrival of sweet corn and peaches, or a beautiful head of cauliflower be your inspiration. From the base to the layered toppings to the salsa to finish the season's best ingredients are ready to shine. The key is to select a seasonal base, then roast, sauté, fry, or grill it, and don't be shy with seasoning, spices, and herbs. Thoughtfully build spicy, sweet, umami, and acidic flavors and creamy and crunchy texture with each additional layer. Get creative with a sauce to top. There are many ways with vegetables for tacos.

GOOD VEGETABLES FOR A TACO BASE:

artichokes, asparagus, beets, broccoli, Brussels sprouts, cabbage, cauliflower, celery root, kohlrabi, mushrooms, onion, peppers, potatoes, radishes, sweet potatoes, turnips, winter squash, zucchini

TIPS AND TAKEAWAYS

- Good-quality small (4½- to 6-inch) tortillas are essential. Choose corn, flour, wheat-corn, or alternative-flour tortillas and keep them stocked in your fridge.

- Tortillas taste and function best (i.e., they're more pliable and less prone to tearing) when warm.

- Toppings bring the fun, so make sure to serve a selection, aiming to hit some key notes: something creamy (like sour cream, avocado, a sauce like Maple-Lime-Chipotle Crema on page 91), something crunchy (like shredded cabbage or toasted pepitas; see Prep Tip, page 26), and something acidic like a fresh salsa and/or a squeeze of lime juice.

HOW TO WARM TORTILLAS FOR TACOS

- **Stovetop:** Spread out tortillas on a griddle or place in a large nonstick skillet (try to space them apart, though slight overlapping is fine) over medium-low heat. Heat the tortillas until they are warm and pliable, about 30 seconds on each side, being careful not to let them burn or crisp.

- **Microwave:** Stack up to 10 small tortillas on a plate and cover with a damp paper towel (or invert a small plate of the same size over the top). Microwave for 30 seconds. Remove the towel (or the plate) and place the tortillas on the bottom half on the top and the top half on the bottom. Cover again and microwave for another 15 seconds.

Wrap warmed tortillas in a clean kitchen towel, then wrap tightly with foil to keep them warm until serving.

Smoky Beet Tacos
with Goat Cheese and Cilantro Salsa

When roasted, beets become sweet and smoky, and an obvious filling for tacos. I recommend building these like this: warm tortilla, smashed avocado, a spoonful of beets, a sprinkling of goat cheese and arugula, and a generous drizzle of cilantro salsa.

---

2 teaspoons ancho chile powder

1 teaspoon ground cumin

1 teaspoon dried oregano

½ teaspoon smoked sweet paprika

Fine sea salt

½ teaspoon freshly ground black pepper

⅓ cup canola oil

1 lime, zest freshly grated, then cut into wedges

4 garlic cloves

2 pounds beets (5 medium), scrubbed, peeled, and ¼-inch diced

1 to 2 avocados, halved and pitted

Cilantro Salsa (recipe follows) or ½ cup fresh cilantro, for topping

4 ounces freshly crumbled goat cheese, for topping

2 to 3 cups baby arugula, for topping

8 to 10 small tortillas, warmed (see page 118), for serving

Cooked black or pinto beans (see page 145 or 65), for serving

---

1 Make the beets. Heat the oven to 375°F with a rack in the middle position. Line a sheet pan with parchment paper. Whisk together the ancho chile powder, cumin, oregano, paprika, 2 teaspoons salt, and the pepper in a large bowl. Whisk in the oil and lime zest. Use a Microplane to finely grate the garlic directly into the bowl. Whisk until blended, then stir in the beets until evenly coated. Transfer to the sheet pan, spreading the beets apart in a single layer. Roast the beets, turning them midway, until tender in the center when pierced, about 30 minutes. Transfer to a platter.

2 Place the avocado in a medium bowl and use the back of a fork to smash it to your desired consistency. Season with salt to taste.

3 Place the warm beets, smashed avocado, and cilantro salsa on the table alongside bowls or plates of the crumbled goat cheese, arugula, lime wedges, and warm tortillas, so people can assemble their own tacos. Serve with the beans alongside.

(recipe continues)

Cilantro Salsa

MAKES ABOUT ½ CUP

TAKE NOTE: To make the salsa by hand, mince or grate the garlic and finely chop the cilantro leaves. Combine and stir together in a small bowl with the remaining ingredients until well blended.

1 garlic clove

1 cup loosely packed fresh cilantro leaves

¼ teaspoon ground cumin

¼ teaspoon fine sea salt

1 teaspoon sherry vinegar (or 2 teaspoons freshly squeezed lime juice)

3 tablespoons extra-virgin olive oil

Combine the garlic, cilantro leaves, cumin, and salt in a small food processor and blend until finely chopped. Add the sherry vinegar and oil and process until well blended. Transfer the salsa to a small bowl and let stand until serving.

Sweet Corn and Black Bean Tacos
with Peach Salsa and Red Cabbage

MAKES 8 TO 10 TACOS; SERVES 4

HOW TO SHAVE CORN OFF THE COB:

Break the cob of corn in half with your hands. Stand each half upright on its flat surface. Use a chef's knife to slice the kernels off the cob. Use the back of your knife to scrape remaining juices off the cob.

These tacos are made in celebration of the beautiful convergence of peach and sweet corn season—from the heart of summer until the end of it—with fresh peach salsa and a sweet corn filling. The peach salsa must be made with in-season, ripe peaches; if those aren't available, skip it and use a favorite tomato salsa instead. The sour cream is key, adding richness and sharp, tart flavor. Look forward to leftovers as a quick lunch for days.

2 tablespoons extra-virgin olive oil

3 garlic cloves, pressed or minced

1 can (15½ ounces) black beans, rinsed and drained

1½ to 2 cups sweet corn kernels (from 2 large ears or frozen)

¾ teaspoon ground cumin

½ teaspoon ground coriander

½ teaspoon fine sea salt

½ cup sour cream

8 to 10 small (5- to 6-inch) flour tortillas, warmed (see page 118)

1 to 2 avocados, diced, for serving (optional)

2 cups finely shredded red cabbage

Peach Salsa (recipe follows)

Lime wedges, for serving (optional)

(recipe continues)

VARIATION: Taco Bowls.
Omit the tortillas. Add
some brown rice or
quinoa to the bottom
of a bowl and layer all
of the ingredients on
top, finishing with sour
cream and salsa.

1 Heat the oil in a large skillet over medium heat until it just begins to shimmer. Add the garlic and cook, stirring frequently and occasionally tilting the pan and pooling the oil to submerge the garlic, until it is golden and tender, about 2 minutes. Be careful not to let it burn.

2 Add the black beans, corn, cumin, coriander, and salt. Cook, stirring occasionally, until the corn is just tender and the black beans are warmed through, about 3 minutes. Taste and adjust salt if needed.

3 To assemble the tacos, spread about 1 tablespoon sour cream over the tortillas, then layer each with about ¼ cup of the corn mixture, diced avocado (if using), a sprinkle of cabbage, and a spoonful of peach salsa. Serve with extra lime wedges.

Peach Salsa

MAKES ABOUT 2½ CUPS

INGREDIENT INFO: Use in-season sweet, floral, juicy peaches. If your peaches are slightly past prime or if you are looking for a more spoonable salsa, pulse all of the ingredients in a small food processor until chunky or completely smooth. Nobody would fault you if you made an additional batch just to enjoy with chips.

Heaping 2 cups ¼-inch diced peaches

Fine sea salt

1½ tablespoons freshly squeezed lime juice, plus more as needed

1 small jalapeño, seeds and ribs removed, finely chopped

¼ cup finely diced sweet onion

½ cup fresh cilantro leaves and thin stems, chopped

Stir together the peaches, ¼ teaspoon salt, lime juice, jalapeño, onion, and cilantro until well combined. Adjust lime juice and salt to taste. Let stand to marinate for at least 30 minutes until serving.

Coconut-Cauliflower Tacos

with Creamy Apple-Cabbage Slaw

HOW TO BREAK DOWN CAULIFLOWER (AND ROMANESCO):

1. Cut the stalk flush with the base of the crown. Stand the crown upright and cut it in half vertically. Halve each piece again lengthwise through the center stalk.

2. Stand each quarter upright. Holding the knife at an angle and turned away from you, slide it between the florets and the core, releasing the florets from the core. Separate the florets and cut them, as needed, into bite-size pieces.

These Baja-style tacos deliver on it all. The cauliflower is coated in a coconut and panko combo that offers crispness and richness without frying. It's a simple technique to coat and roast them to perfection. The apple slaw is a tangy, crunchy, herbaceous, and sweet counterpoint. It adds just the right amount of creaminess, too. Wrapped up in a warm tortilla and topped with a generous squeeze of lime juice and some ripe avocado, this is a beachside-restaurant classic reinvented to enjoy as often as you want at home.

FOR THE CAULIFLOWER

2 tablespoons canola oil

1 can (13½ ounces) coconut milk, well stirred

2 teaspoons garlic powder

1 teaspoon ground cumin

1¼ teaspoons fine sea salt

1½ cups panko breadcrumbs

1 cup unsweetened shredded coconut

1½ teaspoons chili powder

⅛ teaspoon ground cayenne pepper (optional)

1 large head (about 2 pounds) cauliflower, cut into ¾-inch florets

FOR THE APPLE-CABBAGE SLAW

⅓ cup full-fat sour cream (or yogurt)

2 tablespoons freshly squeezed lime juice

1 tablespoon canola oil

1 teaspoon honey

Fine sea salt

4 heaping cups thinly sliced green and/or red cabbage

1 large Honeycrisp or Fuji apple, ¼-inch diced

1 jalapeño, seeds and ribs removed, minced

1 cup loosely packed fresh cilantro, chopped, plus more for topping

12 small (4½- to 6-inch) corn or flour tortillas, warmed (see page 118), for serving

1 to 2 avocados, pitted and diced, for serving

8 lime wedges (1 large lime), for serving

(recipe continues)

INGREDIENT INFO: The breading on leftovers can appear soggy but actually it reheats beautifully when done right. Store leftover cauliflower in an airtight container. (Don't overpack it.) To reheat, heat the oven to 450°F with a rack in the middle position. Evenly coat a sheet pan with 1 tablespoon of canola oil, spread the cauliflower florets out in a single layer, and roast for 8 minutes. Carefully turn and roast for another 2 minutes until hot and crispy.

PREP TIP: Put aside about half of the panko–coconut mixture before you begin to dip the cauliflower. Replenish as needed throughout the dredging process.

1 Heat the oven to 450°F with two racks positioned in the upper and lower thirds. Drizzle two sheet pans with 1 tablespoon of canola oil each, then use a brush or your fingers to evenly coat each pan.

2 Assemble your coating station: Whisk together the coconut milk, garlic powder, cumin, and salt in a medium bowl; set it to one side. In a large shallow plate or bowl (a pie plate works well), combine the panko, coconut, and chili powder and stir together evenly; set it beside the coconut milk mixture.

3 Working in 3 batches, prepare the cauliflower: Add about a third of the cauliflower pieces to the coconut milk mixture and toss gently to coat. Use a slotted spoon to lift the cauliflower florets (a few at a time) and gently shake to drain excess coconut milk back into the bowl. Transfer these pieces to the panko mixture, spreading them apart so there is room to toss and coat each floret individually (don't overcrowd them). Gently turn the florets to coat them in the panko mixture, using your fingers to sprinkle more on top and pressing gently to adhere. Gently lift and transfer the cauliflower florets to the sheet pans, spacing them apart. Repeat this process to dip and coat the remaining cauliflower.

4 Roast the cauliflower until almost tender and the panko coating is turning golden and crisp on one side, about 15 minutes. Flip with a metal spatula, carefully and swiftly sliding it under the florets to prevent the crust from separating. Gently spread the florets out again so they are spaced evenly. Rotate the pans between racks. Roast until the cauliflower is just tender and the crust is golden and crisp all over, another 7 to 10 minutes.

5 Meanwhile, make the slaw: Whisk together the sour cream, lime juice, canola oil, honey, and ¼ teaspoon salt. Add the cabbage, apple, jalapeño, and cilantro, and toss well to combine and coat. Adjust salt to taste. Cover, and chill until ready to serve.

6 Serve the cauliflower hot out of the oven, with warm tortillas, the chilled slaw, diced avocado, lime wedges, and extra cilantro for topping.

The Pizza

This isn't red-sauce pizza loaded with "the veggie" toppings and an indiscriminate amount of cheese. (There's a time and a place for that.) Vegetable-inspired pizza performs with all varieties of produce and lets many toppings get involved. We are making pizza here with sautéed Swiss chard and olives in the spring; ribbons of zucchini, shaved red onion, and sweet bell peppers in the summer; and thinly sliced pears and arugula in the fall. With good dough on standby there's no combination that we can't explore.

GOOD SAUCES FOR PIZZA: Simple Tomato Sauce (page 242), spicy tomato sauce (see page 105), Basil Pesto (page 59), Red Pepper Pesto (page 230), Lemon-Beet Sauce (see page 190), butternut squash sauce (see page 244), fennel Alfredo sauce (see page 188), smashed-mozzarella white sauce (see page 128)

GOOD PRODUCE FOR PIZZA: apples, artichokes, raw arugula, asparagus, broccoli, Brussels sprouts, cauliflower, corn, eggplant, garlic, greens (sautéed collards, broccoli rabe, kale, mustard greens, spinach, Swiss chard), herbs, mushrooms, olives, onions, nuts, peaches, pears, sweet and spicy peppers, potato, ramps, tomatoes, zucchini

TIPS FOR STRETCHING PIZZA DOUGH:

- Bring the dough to room temperature. Lightly flour your board and turn the dough out of the bowl and onto the board. Use your fingers to gently press down and out to flatten and shape it (without pushing down all the way to the board). If you are making pizza with a defined, airy crust, don't push down on the outer edge, just push out toward it (keeping the air in the dough).

- Pick up the dough. Make a fist and place the dough on top. Now use gravity to stretch the dough, turning it and shaping it as you go. Alternatively, simply push and shape it in a sheet pan. For thin-crust flatbreads you can use a floured rolling pin to gently roll out the dough.

- If the dough gets tough or tight at any time, give it a couple of minutes for the gluten to rest.

TIPS AND TAKEAWAYS

- Keep a disc of fresh or frozen store-bought dough to use when you don't have time to make fresh dough. (All of these recipes can be made with store-bought dough.) My homemade doughs (see pages 129 and 135) will keep, well wrapped, in the refrigerator for up to 2 days or in the freezer for up to 6 months. Bring to room temperature before using.

- Double-zero flour, or 00 flour, is a very finely ground Italian flour that is known for producing pizza with excellent texture and chew. You can use this specialty flour in place of bread flour in these dough recipes to give them an extra-special quality. The fine grind requires less hydration, which means you don't need to add quite as much water, so start with a couple of tablespoons less than called for and add more as needed.

- For a thin-crust pizza, stretch the dough with a rolling pin. For a crusty dough, press and stretch it into a round (or rectangle) with your fingers.

- A pizza stone harnesses and holds the heat in a hot oven, creating near restaurant-quality crust and improving texture overall. If you have one, preheat it with the oven, then use a well-floured pizza peel to transfer the topped dough to the hot stone. (First, give the dough a gentle shake on the peel to make sure it isn't sticking. Add more flour if needed. Semolina flour is a great option if you have it on hand.) If you haven't built confidence with a peel or don't have one, carefully transfer the dough by hand and let it parbake on the hot stone until firm enough to easily remove with tongs, about 2 minutes. Transfer it back to your work surface for topping, then transfer back to the stone for baking. Be sure to watch the pizza closely as it will cook faster, and turn it if it is cooking unevenly in places.

- Don't fret if you don't have a stone. A sheet pan works well. Oil the sheet pan and place the stretched dough on it. Top the pizza and then bake.

- Pizza made on a grill is magic. Try it! I like the char and excellent texture that comes from grilling directly over a hot fire. Small (8-ounce) discs of dough are easiest to work with for this method. Stretch the dough, then carefully place it across a well-oiled grill. Cook until bubbling and firm enough to flip. Top the grilled side and continue cooking until the toppings are cooked and the cheese is melted. If the crust starts to burn before the pizza finishes, turn off the heat or move the pizza away from hot spots and cover to finish cooking. You can also use a stone on a grill or use a grill like an oven and cook, covered, with indirect high heat.

Garlicky Swiss Chard Flatbread

with Mozzarella, Olives, and Pine Nuts

MAKES 2 THIN-CRUST,
12-INCH FLATBREADS;
SERVES 2 TO 4 AS A MAIN

ABOUT THE YIELD:
The recipe for Classic
Pizza Dough yields
about 32 ounces of
dough, which you can
divide into four or two.
This recipe calls for
dividing the dough into
four, using two of the
8-ounce discs of dough
to make two thin-crust,
12-inch flatbreads, and
freezing the other two
discs of dough.

SWAPS:
• Use ¾ cup whole-milk
ricotta in place of the
3 ounces of pulverized
mozzarella in the sauce.

• Try asparagus, broccoli,
or broccoli rabe in place
of Swiss chard—just toss
with olive oil, salt, and
pepper, then pan-roast
or roast in the oven until
crisp-tender.

BUTCHER TIP: See page
164 for how to prep Swiss
chard.

Swiss chard sautéed in olive oil with garlic and red pepper flakes, then finished with a splash of sherry vinegar, is a no-fail, classic combination. With a creamy (and easy) smashed-mozzarella white sauce, Castelvetrano olives, and pine nuts on a crispy, thin-crust flatbread, the result is obviously delicious.

Extra-virgin olive oil

4 garlic cloves, thinly sliced

¼ to ½ teaspoon crushed red pepper flakes

About 11 packed cups shredded Swiss chard leaves and 1 to 1½ cups ⅛-inch diced stems (from 2 to 3 bunches)

Fine sea salt

2 teaspoons sherry vinegar

8 ounces fresh mozzarella cheese, ⅓-inch diced

¼ cup plus 1 tablespoon heavy cream

¼ cup plus 1 tablespoon well-shaken buttermilk

½ cup finely grated Parmesan cheese

¼ teaspoon freshly ground black pepper

2 discs (8 ounces each) Classic Pizza Dough (recipe follows) or store-bought dough

2 tablespoons pine nuts

½ cup pitted Castelvetrano olives, briefly rinsed and drained, in half

Best-quality olive oil (optional)

---

1 Heat 3 tablespoons extra-virgin olive oil and the garlic in a large skillet over medium-low heat. As soon as small bubbles form around the garlic, stir almost constantly until it becomes golden and translucent, about 90 seconds. Do not let the garlic burn. Stir in the red pepper flakes and cook for another 30 seconds, then stir in the chard stems and a scant ½ teaspoon salt. Cook, stirring occasionally, until the stems just begin to soften, about 2 minutes. Turn the heat up to medium-high and add the chard leaves, a little at a time to fit the pan. Cook, stirring occasionally, until the chard is wilted and the pan is almost completely dry, 7 to 9 minutes. Add the sherry vinegar and stir constantly until the vinegar is incorporated and any remaining liquid has fully cooked off, 1 to 3 minutes. Remove the pan from the heat.

2 Place half of the diced mozzarella on a cutting board. Working against the board, use the side of a chef's knife to push down and slide it across the mozzarella, smashing it into a chunky paste; transfer to a medium bowl. Stir in the cream, buttermilk, ¼ cup of Parmesan, a scant ¼ teaspoon salt, and the black pepper until evenly incorporated.

VARIATION: Thick-Crust Pizza: You can make larger (14-inch) pizzas with thicker crust using all of the dough. Divide the dough into two 16-ounce discs and shape the dough by hand to produce two roughly 14-inch thicker-crust pizzas, shaped to fit the sheet pan. Add some extra olives and pine nuts. Bake the larger pizzas for 14 to 17 minutes.

3 Heat the oven to 450°F with a rack in the middle position. Coat a sheet pan with oil. Roll out one disc of dough evenly and thinly with a rolling pin (including the outer edge that will become the crust) to about 10 inches in diameter. Transfer the dough carefully to the oiled sheet pan, gently repositioning it if it shrank during transfer and stretching and pushing the dough to 11½ to 12 inches.

4 Spread half of the white sauce (about ½ cup) all over the dough, leaving about a 1-inch border. Top with an even layer of half of the chard, then sprinkle with 1 tablespoon of the pine nuts, half the olives, and half of the remaining Parmesan. Evenly scatter half of the reserved diced mozzarella over the top. Bake until the crust is golden on the edges, 12 to 14 minutes.

5 Meanwhile roll out and top the remaining dough as directed to make a second flatbread.

6 Remove the baked flatbread from the oven and brush the crust with your best olive oil, if using, before slicing and serving. Bake, finish, and serve the remaining pizza in the same fashion.

Classic Pizza Dough

MAKES ENOUGH
FOR 4 SMALL OR
2 MEDIUM PIZZAS

SHORTCUT: If you are short on time, you can forgo the second rise altogether; just let the dough rest briefly after dividing it and shaping it into discs.

INGREDIENT INFO: You can use all-purpose flour instead of bread flour in a pinch.

1½ cups warm water (105°F to 115°F), plus up to 2 teaspoons more if needed

1 teaspoon active dry yeast

4¼ cups stirred, spooned, and leveled (19.2 ounces) bread flour (4 cups if scooped and leveled), plus more as needed

1 teaspoon fine sea salt

2 teaspoons sugar

3 tablespoons extra-virgin olive oil, plus extra to oil the bowl

1 In a 2-cup liquid measure, combine ¼ cup of warm water and the yeast. Let the mixture swell for 5 minutes. Lightly flour a work surface, pizza peel, or cutting board.

2 Place the flour, salt, and sugar in the bowl of a food processor and pulse a few times to combine.

3 Add the remaining 1¼ cups of warm water to the yeast mixture and stir to combine. Pulse the dry ingredients again, then gradually pour the yeast mixture through the top feed tube, followed by the oil. Continue to pulse the dough until it pulls away from the sides of the bowl and forms a ball. (Add up to 2 teaspoons more warm water, one at a time, and pulse if it is not coming together.)

(recipe continues)

TAKE NOTE: The longer the dough rests, the more easily it will stretch. It will keep, well wrapped, in the refrigerator for up to 2 days or in the freezer for up to 6 months. Bring to room temperature before proceeding.

4 Use a silicone spatula to scrape the dough out onto the prepared work surface. Knead it briefly until it is slightly sticky and smooth. (If your dough feels too sticky, sprinkle on a few more pinches of flour and knead it for about 1 minute until it comes together.) Coat a large bowl with oil. Shape the dough into a ball and place it in the bowl, cover with plastic wrap or a dish towel, and set it aside in a warm place to rise until it doubles in size, about 1½ hours (at least 30 minutes if you can't wait).

5 Flour the work surface again. Punch down the dough and scrape it onto the work surface. Divide the dough into two to four pieces and knead each briefly into a smooth ball. Flatten the balls into thick discs, wrap individually in plastic wrap, and let rest for at least 20 minutes or up to 2 hours at room temperature.

Summer Vegetable Grilled Pizza
with Burrata

MAKES TWO 12 × 7-INCH PIZZAS; SERVES 2 TO 4 AS A MAIN

BUTCHER TIP: To shave zucchini ribbons, trim the ends of the zucchini and peel it with a standard vegetable peeler to produce wide, thin ribbons. Turn the zucchini between every couple of strokes. Peel as much as you can, including any short bits on the ends. Stop peeling when you reach the seeds and core and can no longer peel comfortably.

When pizza dough bubbles up on the grill, it feels like a little miracle. Crisp at the edges and soft and chewy in the middle, this fresh pizza is loaded with raw summer squash, ribbons of zucchini, sliced sweet peppers, onion, and creamy burrata. Make sure to gather the toppings and tools before you head to the grill.

Good-quality extra-virgin olive oil

2 discs (8 ounces each) Classic Pizza Dough (page 129) or 1 pound store-bought pizza dough, at room temperature

1 medium zucchini, shaved into ribbons (see Butcher Tip)

1 small to medium yellow summer squash, sliced into ⅛-inch rounds or half-moons

1 small red onion, halved and thinly sliced

1 small red bell pepper, thinly sliced

8 to 10 fresh basil leaves, torn

8 ounces burrata cheese

Flaky sea salt, such as Maldon, and freshly ground black pepper, for finishing

(recipe continues)

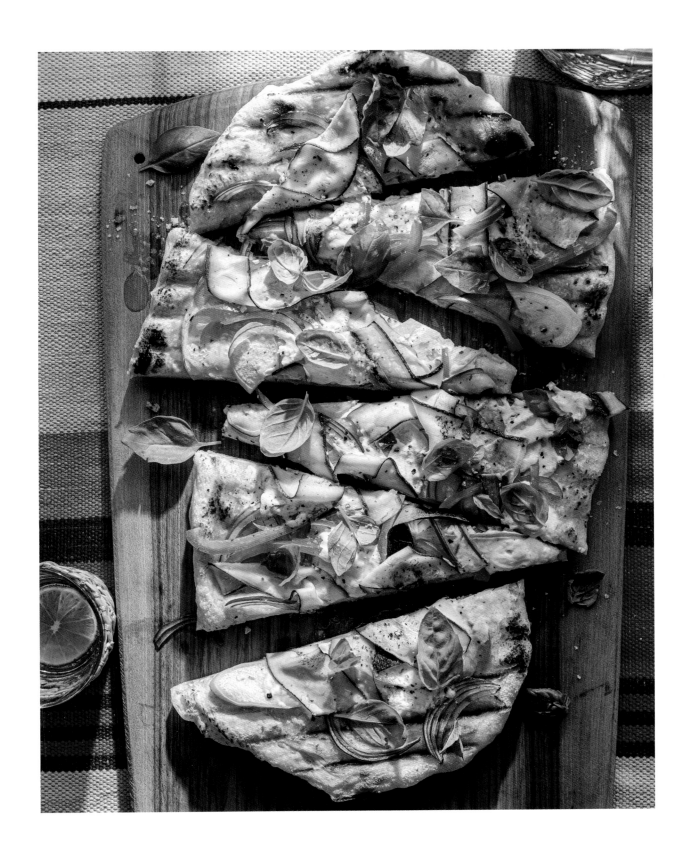

- This pizza is designed
  for an outdoor grill.
  Alternatively, you can
  bake the pizzas, one at
  a time, in a 550°F oven.
  First, stretch the dough
  and place it on a well-
  oiled sheet pan. Brush
  the stretched dough
  lightly with olive oil, then
  top as directed. You can
  use two 8-ounce discs
  of dough stretched to
  roughly 12 × 7 inches and
  bake for 6 to 7 minutes,
  or use two 16-ounce
  discs of dough stretched
  to roughly 13 × 11 inches.

- The larger pie will
  produce a thicker,
  chewy crust and
  naturally be lighter
  on the cheese. You will
  have plenty of other
  toppings to top the
  larger pies.

- Use leftover dough and
  this grilling technique to
  make simple flatbreads
  for dipping; see About
  the Yield, page 128.
  Brush with olive oil and
  sprinkle with flaky sea
  salt and herbs, then
  serve as a side to salads,
  stews, and grain bowls or
  dips (like Beet Hummus,
  page 224; Red Pepper
  Pesto, page 230; Pine
  Nut–Chili Yogurt,
  page 156; Cucumber-
  Dill Yogurt, page 219).

1 Generously oil two sheet pans. Gently stretch each disc of dough by hand to form a rectangular shape, roughly 12 inches long and 7 to 9 inches wide; place on the pans. (Don't stretch it too thin in the middle! You can stretch the dough directly on the oiled sheet pan if helpful.)

2 Place the zucchini ribbons, yellow squash, red onion, bell pepper, and basil in individual small bowls on a tray to transport to the grill. Blot the whole ball of burrata with a towel to absorb excess moisture, and set it in a small bowl on the tray. You will also need the flaky sea salt and black pepper, a small bowlful of oil, and tongs or a spatula, a silicone brush, a kitchen towel, and a pizza cutter.

3 Preheat a grill to medium-high heat (375°F to 450°F). When ready to cook, clean the grill with a grill brush and oil the grates.

4 Using both hands, gently lift one of the stretched dough rectangles and transfer it to the grill, carefully draping it onto the grates oiled side down. Grill, covered, until the underside is golden and crisp and grill marks appear, 1½ to 3 minutes. Using tongs or a spatula, return the crust, grilled side down, to the sheet pan or slide it over to a cooler part of the grill.

5 Brush the uncooked top of the crust with oil, then flip it so the grilled side faces up. Evenly scatter about half of the summer squash, red onion, and bell pepper over the crust. Sprinkle lightly with flaky sea salt. Tear half the burrata into pieces and evenly scatter it over the crust and between the vegetables. Sprinkle a little basil over the top, reserving most to top the pizza before serving. Place about half of the zucchini ribbons on top of the crust, curling and twisting them. Brush or drizzle the ribbons with oil and season lightly with flaky sea salt and black pepper. Lift the sheet pan, if using, and use tongs or a spatula to slide the pizza to the hottest part of the grill. Grill, covered, until the underside is golden brown, crisp, and firm; the cheese should be melted, the zucchini charred in places, and the outer crust golden and crisp, 2½ to 4½ minutes more.

6 Slide the pizza back onto the sheet pan or a platter for serving. Drizzle lightly with more oil all over, top with fresh basil, and season with more flaky sea salt and black pepper to taste. Slice and serve immediately (ideally) or let it stand while you make the second pizza in the same way.

Pear and Arugula Pizza
with Gorgonzola, Honey, and Hazelnuts

MAKES TWO 10- TO 11-INCH
PIZZAS; SERVES 2 TO 3
AS A MAIN

ABOUT THE YIELD:

The dough recipe will yield twice as much dough as you need for these pizzas, so wrap two discs of dough in plastic wrap and freeze them to use another time. Alternatively, you can double the toppings if you'd like to make four 10- to 11-inch pizzas or two 13-inch pizzas (using all the dough).

Sweet, spicy, nutty, creamy—the toppings for this fall–winter pizza are sublime and require very little preparation. The wheat crust comes together easily and is just right to deliver the pears, creamy cheeses, honey, hazelnuts, and arugula (though you can absolutely make this pizza with Classic Pizza Dough (page 129) or a store-bought dough). A pizza stone adds to everything this pie already has going for it by producing an even, crisp underside and crust. If you have one, use it, but don't worry if you don't. If you are using a sheet pan and want to make both pizzas at one time for ease, you can stretch the dough into a rectangular shape to fit.

This pizza makes a wonderful meal on its own or with a bowl of soup. It is also a hit at a party cut into smaller pieces and served as an hors d'oeuvre with a glass of sparkling wine.

Extra-virgin olive oil

4 ounces fresh mozzarella cheese

½ cup shaken heavy cream

Fine sea salt and freshly ground black pepper

2 discs (8 ounces each) Sweet Wheat Pizza Dough (recipe follows) or store-bought dough

1 large ripe Bartlett pear (or 2 small to medium), thinly sliced

3-ounce piece of Gorgonzola cheese (avoid pre-crumbled)

2 tablespoons honey

Flaky sea salt, such as Maldon, for finishing

¼ cup toasted and skinned hazelnuts (see Prep Tip, page 134) or pecans, finely chopped

2 to 4 cups baby arugula (see Ingredient Info, page 134)

Best-quality olive oil, for topping

2 teaspoons aged balsamic vinegar (optional)

---

1 If you are using a pizza stone, position it on the center rack and heat the oven to 480°F. If you don't have a pizza stone, heat the oven to 550°F with a rack in the middle position. Lightly oil a sheet pan with about 1 teaspoon extra-virgin olive oil and set it aside.

2 Place the mozzarella in a medium bowl and use the back of a fork to break it down into a coarse, chunky paste. (It's fine for some big pieces to remain.) Stir in the cream and season with ¼ teaspoon each fine sea salt and pepper. Set aside.

(recipe continues)

PREP TIP: Toast the hazelnuts on a small sheet pan in a toaster oven for 4 to 5 minutes or roast them in a 375°F oven for about 10 minutes, until the skins are pulling away from the nuts and the nuts are golden brown. Transfer the nuts to a clean dish towel and wrap them up. Let them cool for a minute, then rub the nuts together in the towel to remove the skins. Transfer the nuts, leaving the skins behind, to a cutting board. Let cool completely and finely chop the nuts.

INGREDIENT INFO: 1 cup of arugula per pizza will just garnish the top; 2 cups per pizza will make for more of a salad-topped pizza. Both ways are wonderful.

3 Lightly flour a pizza peel or cutting board. Use your hands and fingertips to pull and stretch one of the discs of dough over the peel or board to form a 10- to 11-inch round. (Try not to pull or push air out of the crust. You want to push and stretch the dough evenly out toward the sides, allowing excess dough along the edges to form a rim.)

4 If you are using a pizza stone, carefully transfer the dough to the stone, carefully repositioning and stretching as needed. Parbake it until the dough is bubbling and appears dry enough all over to remove it easily from the oven, about 2 minutes; transfer it back to your board with tongs or a spatula.

If you are using the oiled sheet pan, transfer the dough carefully to the sheet pan, gently stretching the dough and repositioning it if it shrank during transfer.

5 Spread half the white sauce mixture all over the crust (or dough), leaving about a ½-inch border. Evenly spread out about half the pears, generously covering the pizza. Sprinkle half the Gorgonzola evenly over the pears. Return the topped crust to the stone or place the sheet pan in the oven.

6 If using a pizza stone, bake for 5 minutes, then slide a metal spatula between the crust and stone to rotate the pizza, and continue baking until the crust is golden brown and the cheese is bubbling and golden brown all over, 3 minutes more.

If using a sheet pan, bake, rotating the pan halfway through, until the crust is golden brown and the cheese is bubbling and golden brown all over, 8 minutes.

7 Transfer the pizza to a cutting board, sheet pan, or wooden board for serving. Drizzle the pizza with 1 tablespoon of the honey, holding your hand high above the pizza to get good coverage, and avoiding the crust as much as possible. Sprinkle evenly with flaky sea salt, a couple of twists of pepper, and half the chopped hazelnuts. Top the pizza with half the arugula, and lightly drizzle with your best olive oil and, if using, the aged balsamic vinegar.

8 Slice and serve immediately, or let stand while you make the second pizza in the same way.

Sweet Wheat Pizza Dough

MAKES FOUR 10- TO 11-INCH PIZZAS OR TWO 13-INCH PIZZAS

INGREDIENT INFO: I like to use Italian 00 flour (very finely ground flour) in this pizza crust to balance the density of the whole wheat flour. The combination of high-protein whole wheat flour and lower-protein 00 flour produces a light and crispy crust that is also sturdy with good chew. Bread flour will work, too (as will all-purpose flour), although it will produce a slightly denser, chewy crust.

TAKE NOTE: The longer the dough rests, the more easily it will stretch. It will keep, well wrapped, in the refrigerator for up to 2 days or in the freezer for up to 6 months. Bring to room temperature before proceeding.

1½ cups warm water (105°F to 115°F), plus up to 2 teaspoons more if needed

1 tablespoon honey

1 teaspoon active dry yeast

2 cups wheat flour

2 cups 00 flour or bread flour (or all-purpose flour in a pinch), plus more as needed

1 teaspoon fine sea salt

1 teaspoon sugar

2 tablespoons extra-virgin olive oil, plus extra to oil the bowl

1 In a 2-cup liquid measure, whisk together ¼ cup of warm water and the honey, then stir in the yeast. Let the mixture swell for 5 minutes. Lightly flour a work surface, pizza peel, or cutting board.

2 Add the wheat and 00 flours, the salt, and sugar to the bowl of a food processor and pulse a few times to combine.

3 Add the remaining 1¼ cups of warm water to the yeast mixture and stir to combine. Pulse the dry ingredients again, then gradually, while pulsing, pour the yeast mixture through the top feed tube, followed by the oil. Continue to pulse the dough until it pulls away from the sides of the bowl and forms a ball. (Add up to 2 teaspoons more of warm water, one teaspoon at a time, and pulse if it is not coming together.)

4 Use a silicone spatula to scrape the dough out onto the prepared work surface. Knead it briefly until it is slightly sticky and smooth. (If your dough feels too wet and sticky, sprinkle on a few more pinches of flour and knead for about 1 minute until it comes together.) Coat a large bowl with oil. Shape the dough into a ball and place it in the bowl, cover with plastic wrap or a dish towel, and set it aside in a warm part of the kitchen to rise until it doubles in size, about 1 hour 30 minutes (at least 30 minutes if you can't wait).

5 Flour the work surface again. Punch down the dough and scrape it onto the work surface. Divide the dough into 4 equal-size pieces, about 8 ounces each. (For 13-inch pizzas, divide the dough into 2 equal-size pieces, about 16 ounces each. See About the Yield on page 133.) Very briefly knead and shape each into a smooth ball. Flatten the balls into thick discs, wrap individually in plastic wrap, and let rest for at least 20 minutes (if you can wait) or up to 2 hours at room temperature. (The longer it rests, the more easily it will stretch.)

The Quesadilla

These produce-inspired quesadillas are not really about the cheese. Stuffed full of vegetables plus fresh seasonal salsa, they offer a variety of flavors and textures all in one bite.

TO FOLD (FOR 8- TO 10-INCH TORTILLAS):
In the pan, sprinkle half the surface of the tortilla with cheese, leaving a ¼-inch border. Top with vegetable filling, then more cheese. Fold the untopped half over the filling to create a half moon shape, pressing down gently with the back of a spatula to flatten.

TO STACK (FOR 5- TO 6-INCH TORTILLAS):
In the pan (or out of the pan), sprinkle the full surface of the tortilla with a sprinkle of cheese, leaving a ¼-inch border. Top with vegetable filling, then more cheese. Place another tortilla on top and press down gently with the back of a spatula to flatten (in the pan).

GOOD VEGETABLES FOR FILLING (CUT SMALL OR SHREDDED IF RAW):
asparagus, beans, beets, broccoli, broccoli rabe, Brussels sprouts, cabbage, cauliflower, hearty greens, corn, eggplant, fennel, fresh herbs, leeks, mushrooms, onions, peas, peppers, potatoes, radishes, ramps, scallions, spinach, sweet potatoes, winter squash, zucchini

GOOD SALSAS FOR SERVING:
Fresh Strawberry Salsa (page 138), Avocado–Corn Salsa (page 140), Cilantro Salsa (page 120), Salsa Verde (page 252)

TIPS AND TAKEAWAYS

- Finely chop vegetables destined for filling. Add them raw, or quickly sauté or grill them over high heat (or roast starchy roots and tubers) for more robust flavor. Leftover cooked veggies are great, too.

- Add something unexpected like Basil Pesto (page 59), pea puree (see page 112), eggplant caponata (see page 115), Beet Hummus (page 224), or Red Pepper Pesto (page 230).

- Use a nonstick pan to make wiping the pan clean between quesadillas a breeze. You can also use a cast-iron skillet or stainless-steel skillet, adjusting the heat as needed to prevent burning, with good results.

- Give each quesadilla your attention and cook them one at a time or use multiple pans to make more than one at once.

- These quesadillas are packed full of vegetables—which can make them a little tricky to flip without spilling their contents—so give special care as you flip them.

- Keep quesadillas warm in a 200°F oven for up to 20 minutes.

- Serve these quesadillas hot, but give them a moment to set before slicing.

- Serve quesadillas with a fresh salsa and a spoonful of something creamy like smashed avocado, guacamole, or sour cream. Add black beans or pinto beans (see pages 65 and 145) as a side or filling.

Asparagus-Leek Quesadillas
with Fresh Strawberry Salsa

MAKES 4 TO 6
QUESADILLAS;
SERVES 4 AS A MAIN

ABOUT THE YIELD: Use 8-inch tortillas to yield 6 quesadillas or 10-inch (burrito-size) tortillas to yield 4 quesadillas—dividing the filling evenly among them. (You can stretch the filling and add a bit more cheese to produce 6 quesadillas with 10-inch tortillas.)

SHORTCUT: Use one large red or yellow onion, halved and thinly sliced, in place of the leeks. Follow the same cooking instructions for the leeks, cooking until the onion is tender before adding the asparagus.

BUTCHER TIP: See page 47 for how to clean leeks.

SWAP: The queso fresco adds a mild salty-sour kick to the quesadillas, but you can replace it with an additional cup (4 ounces) of freshly shredded jack cheese.

This quesadilla, stacked with asparagus and leeks and topped with a fresh strawberry salsa, makes an everyday kind of meal with a weekend-meal kind of feel. You can shake up the asparagus–leek combination with freshly shelled peas instead of asparagus or red onion in place of the leeks (see Shortcut). Use other spring herbs like chives or cilantro or no herbs at all. Add a dollop of smashed avocado or guacamole. The strawberry salsa is an ode to spring with its headlining fruit bringing unexpected, but welcome, sweetness and vibrant color. There's jalapeño, cilantro, and lime to round it out with traditional notes of acid, herbs, and heat. It's a real treat, but the quesadilla is also wonderful with your favorite tomato salsa.

---

2 tablespoons extra-virgin olive oil

2 garlic cloves, thinly sliced

3 large leeks, white and light green parts only, trimmed, halved lengthwise, cleaned well, and thinly sliced (4 to 4½ cups)

Fine sea salt and freshly ground black pepper

8 ounces asparagus, ¼-inch sliced leaving tips intact (1½ cups)

2 tablespoons water

2 tablespoons loosely packed chopped fresh mint

4 tablespoons canola oil

4 to 6 medium (8- to 10-inch) flour tortillas

1 cup freshly crumbled queso fresco (4 ounces)

1 cup coarsely grated jack cheese (4 ounces)

Fresh Strawberry Salsa (recipe follows), for serving

Smashed avocado, for serving (optional, but recommended)

---

1 Heat the oven to 200°F and place a sheet pan on the middle rack to preheat.

2 Heat the olive oil and garlic in a large skillet over medium heat. When the garlic just begins to simmer in the oil, cook, stirring, until fragrant and just turning golden in places, about 90 seconds. Add the leeks, ½ teaspoon salt, and ¼ teaspoon pepper. Cook, stirring occasionally, until the leeks are tender and golden, about 5 minutes. Stir in the asparagus, water, ¼ teaspoon salt, and the mint. Cook, stirring, for about 2 minutes, until the asparagus is crisp-tender and no liquid remains. Remove the pan from the heat to cool briefly. Adjust salt and pepper to taste.

(recipe continues)

3 Heat 2 teaspoons of the canola oil in a large nonstick skillet over medium-high heat. When it is very hot, add one tortilla, then reduce the heat to medium. Sprinkle half of the surface of the tortilla with queso fresco and jack cheese (⅓ to ½ cup total), leaving about a ¼-inch border so the cheese doesn't melt into the pan. Top the cheese with about ½ cup of the asparagus–leek mixture, enough to generously cover. Gently fold the untopped half of the tortilla over the filling to make a crescent shape, pressing down gently with the back of a spatula to flatten slightly. Move the quesadilla to the center of the pan. Cook until the bottom is golden brown and crisp, about 1 minute. Carefully flip the quesadilla and cook until the other side is golden brown and crisp all over, another minute or so. Remove the pan from the heat and transfer the quesadilla to a sheet pan and keep warm in the oven.

4 Wipe the skillet clean and repeat 3 more times, with the remaining ingredients, using 2 teaspoons of oil for each tortilla and dividing the filling and cheese evenly. Reduce the heat and cooking time as needed to prevent burning. Transfer the quesadillas to the oven as you make them to keep warm (they can rest there comfortably for up to 20 minutes).

5 When ready to serve, transfer the quesadillas to a cutting board and use a sharp chef's knife to cut each into 4 wedges. Serve immediately with the salsa and smashed avocado, if using, alongside.

Fresh Strawberry Salsa

MAKES 2 CUPS

TAKE NOTE: Try to dice the onion and jalapeño as fine as possible, about ⅛ inch.

2 cups ¼-inch diced strawberries (1 pint/about 8 ounces)

½ cup finely diced sweet onion (about ½ medium onion)

¼ cup finely diced jalapeños (3 small jalapeños, seeds and ribs removed)

3 tablespoons freshly squeezed lime juice

½ cup finely chopped fresh cilantro leaves

Fine sea salt

Combine the strawberries, onion, and jalapeños in a medium bowl. Stir in the lime juice and then the cilantro. Add ¼ teaspoon salt, taste, and add more if needed. Set aside at room temperature to let the flavors meld, ideally at least 30 minutes. Or cover and refrigerate for 1 hour or up to 8 hours. Serve chilled or at room temperature.

Zucchini and Black Bean Quesadillas
with Avocado-Corn Salsa

MAKES 4 QUESADILLAS:
SERVES 4 AS A MAIN

Summer quesadillas should be unfussy and extra fast, so raw zucchini shredded on a box grater is a natural choice to fill them—a technique that saves time and breaks down the zucchini to blend seamlessly with the shredded cheese. Simply toss the zucchini and cheese with scallions, ancho chile powder, and black beans, then stuff the tortilla and pan-fry it. The result resembles the average homemade cheese variety on the outside, but the inside proves that it is so much more. With a must-make Avocado–Corn Salsa, this meal is really out of this world. Quite an accomplishment, I'd say, for how uncomplicated it is to pull together.

---

1 medium zucchini (8 to 10 ounces)

2 large scallions, thinly sliced

¾ teaspoon ancho chile powder (or standard chili powder)

½ teaspoon ground cumin

1 cup drained and rinsed canned black beans

2 packed cups Monterey Jack cheese (5 ounces)

¼ teaspoon fine sea salt

⅛ teaspoon freshly ground black pepper

4 tablespoons canola oil

4 burrito-size (10– to 12–inch) flour tortillas

Avocado–Corn Salsa (recipe follows), for serving

Sour cream, for serving

---

1 Heat the oven to 200°F and place a sheet pan on a rack in the middle position to preheat.

2 Shred the zucchini against the large holes of a box grater over a clean kitchen towel or paper towels to absorb moisture. Let the shredded zucchini stand for a couple of minutes, then gently pat the top of the pile to absorb excess moisture there.

3 Gently stir together the zucchini, scallions, ancho chile powder, cumin, and black beans in a large bowl to combine. Stir in the cheese and season with the salt and pepper.

(recipe continues)

4 Make the quesadillas. Heat about 2 teaspoons of oil in a large nonstick skillet over medium-high heat. When it begins to shimmer, use a heat-safe brush to quickly and evenly brush the oil over the surface of the pan. Place a tortilla in the pan and reduce the heat to medium. Top half of the surface of the tortilla with about ¾ cup of the filling, spreading it evenly but leaving a ¼-inch border so the cheese doesn't melt into the pan. Gently fold the untopped tortilla half over the filling to create a crescent shape, pressing down gently with the back of a spatula to flatten slightly. Move to the center of the pan, cover, and cook until the bottom is golden and crisp and the cheese is starting to melt, 1½ minutes. Carefully flip the quesadilla, cover, and cook until the other side is golden brown and the cheese has melted, about 1 minute more. Uncover, cook for another 30 seconds, then flip and cook for another 30 seconds. Remove the pan from the heat and transfer the quesadilla to the sheet pan in the oven to keep warm.

5 Wipe the skillet clean and repeat the process 3 more times, using 2 teaspoons of oil for each tortilla and dividing the filling evenly among them. Reduce the heat and cooking time as needed to prevent burning. Transfer the quesadillas to the oven as you make them to keep warm (they can rest there comfortably for up to 20 minutes).

6 When ready to serve, transfer the quesadillas to a cutting board and use a sharp chef's knife to cut each into 4 wedges. Serve the quesadillas immediately with Avocado–Corn Salsa and sour cream.

Avocado-Corn Salsa

MAKES 2 TO 2½ CUPS

INGREDIENT INFO: Thawed frozen corn is just fine in the salsa but when sweet corn is in season, use it. Grill the corn until tender for a dynamic smoky, charred flavor, or boil it briefly until tender. Alternatively, if your corn is extra fresh and juicy, shave it straight off the cob, raw, directly into the salsa (see page 120).

1 large avocado, diced

1½ to 2 cups sweet corn kernels (from 2 large ears or frozen)

1 jalapeño, seeds and ribs removed, ⅛-inch diced

2 scallions, dark greens finely chopped, whites and light greens sliced lengthwise and finely chopped

½ cup packed fresh cilantro leaves and thin stems, roughly chopped

Fine sea salt

Freshly squeezed juice of 1 lime

Gently stir together the avocado, corn, jalapeños, scallions, cilantro, ¼ teaspoon salt, and 1½ tablespoons lime juice in a medium bowl. Adjust salt and lime juice to taste. This salsa is best enjoyed immediately. The avocado will oxidize, but you can store leftovers in an airtight container and still use it for up to 1 day later.

Browned-Butter Quesadillas
with Butternut Squash and Jammy Onions

MAKES UP TO 8 SMALL
QUESADILLAS; SERVES 4
AS A MAIN

INGREDIENT INFO:

- I suggest a combination of queso fresco and Monterey Jack. Alternatively, use Monterey Jack or a mild white Cheddar on its own.

- Increase filling, skillet size, and cooking time for larger tortillas and ensure cheese is melted and tortillas are nicely browned and crisp.

SHORTCUT: Instead of breaking down a whole butternut squash, use 2 pounds of precut squash.

This fall–winter quesadilla is a knockout combination of sweet, sour, and spicy butternut squash, jammy onion, spinach, and tangy cheese on the inside—with a browned butter–fried tortilla on the outside. Pair it with smashed avocado or a dollop of sour cream and your favorite salsa. Serve it with a side of black or pinto beans or a simple salad. This quesadilla takes more time than the others in this section, thanks to the butternut squash prep, but I promise your efforts will be worth it. (And you can certainly use precut squash if you'd like.)

FOR THE QUESADILLAS

7 cups (about 2 pounds) ½-inch diced butternut squash (from a 3½-pound squash; see Shortcut)

4 tablespoons extra-virgin olive oil

Fine sea salt

¼ teaspoon crushed red pepper flakes

1 small yellow onion or ½ large onion, thinly sliced

2 tablespoons apple cider vinegar

2 tablespoons pure maple syrup

3 cups packed baby spinach (or trimmed and thinly sliced spinach leaves)

16 small (5- to 6-inch) corn-wheat or flour tortillas

About 1½ cups crumbled queso fresco (6 ounces)

About 3 cups shredded Monterey Jack cheese (6 ounces)

4 tablespoons unsalted butter

FOR SERVING (OPTIONAL)

Smashed avocado or guacamole

Favorite salsa

Sour cream

Quick Black Beans or Pinto Beans (recipe follows)

1 Heat the oven to 450°F with a rack in the middle position. Line a sheet pan with parchment paper.

2 Prep the butternut squash. Toss the butternut squash directly on the prepared sheet pan with 3 tablespoons of oil, 1½ teaspoons salt, and the red pepper flakes to coat evenly. Spread the squash out in a single layer and roast until tender and browning on the edges, turning the butternut squash with a spatula halfway through cooking, 30 to 35 minutes.

(recipe continues)

ABOUT THE YIELD:
The recipe will yield up to 8 small quesadillas; plan on one to two per eater (they are quite filling). If cooking for one or two, halve the recipe or don't assemble all of the quesadillas at once. Store unused filling and shredded cheeses for up to 5 days in the fridge and you will be ready to make fresh quesadillas throughout the week.

3 Meanwhile, heat the remaining tablespoon of oil in a medium skillet over medium heat. Add the onion and ¼ teaspoon salt and cook, stirring frequently, until the onion is tender and browning, about 8 minutes, adding up to 2 tablespoons of water if the pan is too dry at any point. Add the vinegar and maple syrup and stir constantly, deglazing the pan and cooking the onion until the liquid has absorbed and the pan is mostly dry. Stir in the spinach, a little at a time if needed to fit the pan, and cook until it just wilts and any liquid has cooked off, 1 to 2 minutes. (If you are using more mature spinach, this may take an extra 2 minutes until the leaves are wilted and tender.) Remove the pan from the heat. Stir in the butternut squash and use a potato masher or the back of a fork to mash the butternut squash into a chunky puree and stir it into the onion–spinach mixture.

4 Assemble the quesadillas. Discard the parchment paper from the sheet pan and place 8 tortillas directly on the sheet pan, stacking the remaining 8 tortillas nearby. Combine the cheeses in a small bowl. Evenly sprinkle about ¼ cup of the cheese on each tortilla, spread out about ¼ cup of the squash mixture on top of the cheese, sprinkle each with 1 to 2 heaping tablespoons of cheese, then top with a reserved tortilla.

5 Cook the quesadillas. Heat the oven to 200°F. Melt ½ tablespoon of butter in a nonstick skillet over medium heat until it foams. Carefully transfer one of the quesadillas to the pan. Cook until a crisp crust forms on the bottom tortilla, 1½ to 2 minutes. Gently press down on the top tortilla to ensure it has attached to the cheesy filling, then carefully flip the quesadilla. Carefully swirl the pan to redistribute any remaining butter to the middle of the pan. Cook, pressing down gently to evenly distribute and melt the cheese, until a golden-brown crust forms and the cheese is melting out the sides just slightly, about 1 minute. Remove the pan from the heat and transfer the quesadilla to the sheet pan in the oven to keep warm.

6 Wipe the skillet clean and repeat the process with the remaining tortillas and butter, adjusting the heat as needed to prevent burning. Transfer the quesadillas to the oven as you make them to keep warm (they can rest there comfortably for up to 20 minutes).

7 When ready to serve, transfer the quesadillas to a cutting board and use a sharp chef's knife to cut. Serve hot or at room temperature with the accompaniments of your choice.

Quick Black Beans or Pinto Beans

MAKES ABOUT 3½ CUPS

2 tablespoons extra-virgin olive oil

1 medium onion, ¼-inch diced

2 garlic cloves, minced

1 teaspoon chili powder

1 teaspoon dried oregano

½ teaspoon fine sea salt, plus more as needed

½ teaspoon ground cumin

2 cans (15½ ounces each) black beans or pinto beans, drained and rinsed well

⅓ cup low-sodium vegetable stock

1 tablespoon freshly squeezed lime juice or orange juice (or 2 teaspoons apple cider vinegar)

Lime wedges, for serving (optional)

Heat the oil in a medium saucepan or medium sauté pan over medium heat. Add the onion and cook, stirring frequently, until it begins to soften, about 4 minutes. Add the garlic, chili powder, oregano, salt, and cumin and cook, stirring, until well incorporated, another 30 to 60 seconds. Gently stir in the beans and the vegetable stock, gently scraping and incorporating any browned bits from the bottom of the pan. Bring the beans to a low simmer, reduce the heat to medium-low, and cook, stirring occasionally, until the liquid mostly evaporates, 4 to 6 minutes. Stir in the lime or orange juice. Adjust salt to taste. Serve with lime wedges if you wish. Refrigerate leftovers in an airtight container for up to 4 days.

GRAIN BOWLS. NOODLE BOWLS.

4

The Grain Bowl

With a cooked grain, a veggie, something crunchy, and a sauce on top, a bowl can be simple to prepare, extremely satisfying, and a useful make-ahead meal. You can pull together assorted components at least a couple of days ahead and then assemble them when it's time to eat.

Whole Grain or Pseudograin Base + Star Vegetable + Legumes/Nuts/Seeds/Tofu + Sauce

GRAIN BOWL BASICS

SELECT A WHOLE GRAIN OR PSEUDOGRAIN BASE: amaranth, barley, bulgur, couscous, farro, fonio, freekeh, millet, quinoa, rice, spelt berries, wheat berries. Turn to precooked grains when you are short on time.

CHOOSE A STAR VEGETABLE—OR SEVERAL: A variety of vegetables and preparations (e.g., roasted, sautéed, steamed, pickled and/or raw) will make a bowl tastier and more interesting.

ADD LEGUMES, NUTS, SEEDS, OR TOFU: These protein-rich additions bulk up grain bowls and balance the starchy base.

TOP WITH A PESTO, SAUCE, OR VINAIGRETTE: These add a pop of concentrated sweet, salty, spicy, tangy, herby, and/or umami flavor to every bite.

GREAT GRAIN BOWL COMBINATIONS

Start with a sauce or spread and compose a bowl around it using a selection of choose-your-own ingredients. Here are some ideas to get you started:

BASIL PESTO (PAGE 59) OR BASIL VINAIGRETTE (PAGE 22): farro; sautéed zucchini and cannellini beans; fresh corn and tomatoes tossed with fresh basil, olive oil, and balsamic; arugula

BEET HUMMUS (PAGE 224): freekeh; sautéed, blanched, or grilled snow peas and sugar snap peas; sautéed mushrooms; raw radishes; chives; avocado; sesame seeds

MAPLE-LIME-CHIPOTLE CREMA (PAGE 91): brown rice and quinoa; roasted sweet potatoes; sautéed peppers and onions; scallions; romaine; black beans; pepitas

GREEN GODDESS DIP (PAGE 224): black rice; steamed broccoli and/or roasted cauliflower and/or roasted sweet potatoes; shredded red cabbage or baby arugula; store-bought fermented vegetables, kimchi, or pickled onions (see pages 66 and 100); Turmeric Nut-Seed Mix (page 114)

LEMON-BEET SAUCE (PAGE 190): farro, black rice, or quinoa; roasted butternut squash and Brussels sprouts; raw or pickled red onion; walnuts; dried cranberries; thyme; arugula or kale

ORANGE-SESAME VINAIGRETTE (SEE PAGE 33) OR PEANUT SAUCE (SEE PAGE 151): brown rice, quinoa, or fonio; napa cabbage or red cabbage; carrots; cucumber; scallions; tofu; peanuts

CUCUMBER-DILL YOGURT (PAGE 219): bulgur; tomato, roasted eggplant, blanched green beans, chickpeas; pickled red onion; avocado; chopped spinach or romaine; crumbled toasted pita; pine nuts

RED PEPPER PESTO (PAGE 230): couscous; roasted cauliflower, romanesco, broccoli, or Brussels sprouts; pickled currants; olives; pistachios; arugula

---

TIPS AND TAKEAWAYS

- Make a big batch of grains and a sauce or vinaigrette at the beginning of the week so that your bowl base and topping is always ready to go. (Or keep a frozen grain like rice or a store-bought hummus or pesto around as sauce.)

- Greens add a fresh raw component. Keep prewashed baby arugula on hand, or wash, dry, and chop kale ahead (it will store for up to 5 days).

- Keep a batch of Quick Pickled Onions (page 100) or other pickled or fermented produce in the fridge.

- Toast nuts and/or seeds ahead, up to 5 days in advance.

- Roast or sauté vegetables ahead and warm them ahead of serving or cut the vegetables ahead, keep them raw, and then cook them just before serving. Broccoli, Brussels sprouts, cauliflower, carrots, cabbage, and sweet potatoes are good ones to keep around for off-the-cuff bowl making. Keep a package of precooked beets in stock and broil them briefly to concentrate their flavor (see Shortcut on page 21).

- Keep canned beans and tofu on hand.

- When there is time, give more attention to the grain: Toast the grain by sautéing it with garlic and oil (and perhaps herbs and spices) to bring out a deep nutty aroma, then add water to steam or boil it. Try mixing a variety of grains together for added texture and nutrients.

Brassicas and Brown Rice Bowls
with Peanut Sauce and Crispy Tofu

MAKES 4 BOWLS:
SERVES 4 AS AN ENTRÉE

SHORTCUT: Frozen and microwavable brown rice is a timesaver.

TAKE NOTE: Refrigerate leftover coconut milk for up to 1 week and make Sheet Pan Smoky Coconut Greens and Sweet Potatoes. You can also freeze coconut milk for up to 1 month. Defrost then whip it in a blender or with an immersion blender before using.

SWAP: A combo of broccoli and cauliflower is recommended, but you can use 6 to 7 cups of one or the other.

This classic grain bowl hits the spot all throughout the year. (And with well-timed choreography, it's a breeze.) When I don't have time to make the tofu, I'll use avocado in its place and add chopped peanuts or sesame seeds. Memorize the simple anatomy of this dish; it's a perfect template to riff on.

FOR THE TOFU

14 to 15 ounces extra-firm tofu

⅓ cup cornstarch

½ teaspoon coarsely ground black pepper

2 tablespoons canola oil

Fine sea salt

FOR THE SAUCE

½ cup well-stirred unsweetened coconut milk

¼ cup plus 1 tablespoon smooth natural (unsweetened) peanut butter

2 tablespoons tamari or soy sauce

2 teaspoons sugar (or maple syrup), plus more as needed

1 to 3 teaspoons red curry paste (depending on heat level, add to taste)

1 tablespoon plus 2 teaspoons freshly squeezed lime juice, plus more as needed

FOR THE BOWLS

4 cups broccoli florets and peeled stems (1 large head)

2 to 3 cups cauliflower florets (½ small head)

2 carrots, peeled and ⅛-inch sliced on a diagonal (optional)

Cooked brown rice, white rice, quinoa, or other grain, for serving

2 cups shredded red cabbage

¼ cup sliced scallions

1 Drain the tofu and place it on a few paper towels or a folded kitchen towel to continue to drain until the towels are saturated, at least 20 minutes.

2 Meanwhile, make the sauce. In a medium bowl or 4-cup liquid measure, whisk together the coconut milk, peanut butter, tamari, sugar, red curry paste, and lime juice. Taste and add another splash of lime juice and/or sugar if needed; set aside.

3 Cut the tofu into ¾-inch cubes. Place another towel over the top to remove any remaining liquid. In a medium bowl, whisk together the cornstarch and pepper. Carefully toss the tofu in the mixture to evenly coat.

4 Place a steamer basket into a pot. Fill with water until it reaches just below the basket. Cover and bring to a boil.

(recipe continues)

5 While the water comes to a boil, make the tofu. Line a plate with a paper towel. In a medium or large nonstick pan, heat the canola oil over medium heat until warm but not shimmering, about 60 seconds. Carefully add the tofu, stir and separate the pieces, then let them cook undisturbed until lightly golden and crisp on one side, about 5 minutes. Turn the tofu and continue to cook and turn the tofu so it crisps and a golden-brown crust forms all over, another 5 to 7 minutes. Transfer the tofu to the prepared plate to absorb excess oil. Sprinkle lightly with salt.

6 Return to the steamer. Evenly scatter the broccoli, cauliflower, and carrots, if using, around the basket, cover, and steam until tender but with some bite, 3 to 5 minutes (up to 8 minutes if you like them softer).

7 Evenly divide the grains among 4 bowls. Top with the steamed veggies, red cabbage, and tofu. Sprinkle the scallions over the top and serve with the peanut sauce.

Asparagus Sushi Rice Bowls
with Spicy Tofu "Mayo"

MAKES 4 BOWLS;
SERVES 4 AS AN ENTRÉE

SWAPS:

- For the spicy mayo, I love tofu for the creaminess and plant protein it adds, but you can use a scant cup of standard or plant-based mayo instead.

- Replace the asparagus with blanched or steamed broccoli florets, then follow the same steps to quickly stir-fry the broccoli with tamari, toasted sesame oil, and sesame seeds. In the fall, try a combination of broccoli and roasted sweet potato.

I love these big, deconstructed sushi-inspired bowls, which are packed with the best parts of the roll, but easier to throw together. Serve these with tamari and wasabi, pickled ginger, and sesame seeds at the table—they're not only so fun to eat, but they're extremely delicious, bursting with acid, salt, and heat.

FOR THE SUSHI RICE

2 cups uncooked sushi rice

3 cups water

2 tablespoons rice wine vinegar

1 tablespoon plus 1½ teaspoons sugar

¾ teaspoon fine sea salt

FOR THE SPICY TOFU "MAYO"

7 ounces extra-firm or soft tofu

2 tablespoons sriracha

1 tablespoon plus 1 teaspoon freshly squeezed lemon juice, plus more as needed

¾ teaspoon fine sea salt

2 to 3 tablespoons water

2 tablespoons canola oil

FOR THE ASPARAGUS

1 tablespoon canola oil

1 pound asparagus, 1½-inch sliced on a diagonal, leaving tips intact (3½ to 4 cups)

1½ teaspoons toasted sesame oil

1 tablespoon tamari or soy sauce

1¼ teaspoons white and/or black sesame seeds, plus more for serving

FOR TOPPING AND SERVING

1 large avocado, pitted and very thinly sliced lengthwise

1 cucumber, quartered lengthwise and cut into ⅛-inch slices on a diagonal

4 to 6 red or Easter egg radishes, ¹⁄₁₆-inch sliced into coins or half moons

1 to 2 sheets of sushi nori, roughly chopped into small flakes or sliced into thin strips, plus extra for serving

Tamari or soy sauce, for serving

Wasabi paste, for serving

Pickled ginger, for serving

---

1 Cook the rice. Place the sushi rice in a fine sieve and rinse with cold water until the water runs clear. Transfer the rice to a medium saucepan and combine it with the water. Bring to a boil over high heat, then immediately cover the pan. Reduce the heat to low and simmer for 20 minutes, or until the water has fully absorbed. Remove the pan from the heat and let stand, covered, to steam for another 10 minutes.

2 Make the mayo. Combine the tofu, sriracha, lemon juice, salt, and 2 tablespoons of water in a high-speed blender and process on high speed until creamy. With the blender running, stream in the canola oil through the top feed tube. Add another tablespoon of water to loosen the sauce if needed, and more lemon juice to taste. Transfer to a small serving bowl and set aside for serving at the table.

3 Stir-fry the asparagus. Heat a large skillet over high heat until a drop of water immediately disappears. Add the canola oil, then the asparagus, and cook, stirring almost constantly, for 2 minutes. Add the sesame oil, then the tamari, and stir to combine. Sprinkle in the sesame seeds and continue to cook, stirring constantly, until the asparagus is crisp-tender, 1 minute more. Do not overcook the asparagus—it should be just tender with some bite remaining. Remove the pan from the heat and transfer the asparagus and any liquid to a bowl.

4 Return to the rice. Whisk together the vinegar, sugar, and salt in a large bowl. Uncover the rice and fluff it with a fork, then add it to the bowl and use two spoons to toss it gently with the vinegar mixture.

5 Compose each bowl (or place all of the components at the table for eaters to compose on their own). Place about 1 cup of sushi rice at the bottom of each bowl, then layer and spread out on top: one quarter of the sliced avocado, about ¼ cup of sliced cucumbers, 1 sliced radish, and one quarter of the asparagus. Top each with a sprinkling of sesame seeds and nori. For serving, set the table with tamari, wasabi, pickled ginger, and the spicy "mayo" along with more nori and sesame seeds.

Tomato-Cucumber Freekeh Bowls
with Spiced Chickpeas and Pine Nut–Chili Yogurt

MAKES 4 BOWLS:
SERVES 4 AS A MAIN

TAKE NOTE: Leftovers make an excellent salad tossed with or without a few handfuls of arugula or chopped romaine.

Many years ago, I became obsessed with a recipe in Yotam Ottolenghi's *Jerusalem* cookbook: a fresh take on the classic summer salad of tomato, cucumber, and fresh herbs paired with spiced chickpeas. My obsession inspired this fresh and hearty bowl that I make at least once a week for dinner in the summer. The luscious, simple pine nut yogurt is absolutely delicious, made of pine nuts fried in olive oil with Aleppo pepper flakes and garlic. That recipe alone deserves a place in your repertoire.

FOR THE FREEKEH

Fine sea salt

1¼ cups freekeh, rinsed well and drained

½ cup dried currants

FOR THE TOMATO-CUCUMBER SALAD

2 tablespoons freshly squeezed lemon juice

1 tablespoon sherry vinegar

½ teaspoon sugar

¼ teaspoon fine sea salt, plus more as needed

¼ teaspoon freshly ground black pepper, plus more as needed

3 tablespoons extra-virgin olive oil

1 pint cherry tomatoes, halved or quartered depending on their size

1 large cucumber, ¾-inch diced (3 to 4 cups)

½ cup loosely packed fresh flat-leaf parsley leaves

½ cup loosely packed fresh cilantro leaves

FOR THE CHICKPEAS

1 tablespoon extra-virgin olive oil

1 teaspoon ground cumin

½ teaspoon ground cardamom

½ teaspoon ground allspice

¼ teaspoon fine sea salt

1 can (15½ ounces) chickpeas, drained, rinsed, and patted dry

FOR SERVING

Pine Nut–Chili Yogurt (page 156) or other sauces (see Variations)

---

1 Make the freekeh. Bring a medium saucepan of water to a boil and add 1¼ teaspoons salt. Add the freekeh, stir, and boil until tender and chewy, 20 to 25 minutes. Drain the freekeh and transfer it to a medium bowl. Immediately stir in the currants and keep warm, covering if needed, until ready to serve.

(recipe continues)

VARIATIONS:

- Try rice, bulgur, or couscous in place of the freekeh. Add olives, feta, avocado, red onion or pickled red onion.

- Instead of the Pine Nut–Chili Yogurt, try a spoonful of Lemon-Feta Vinaigrette (see page 34) or simply Greek yogurt and a drizzle of oil and a pinch of red pepper flakes.

- Try a dollop of Lemon-Beet Sauce (see page 190), or Beet Hummus (page 224), or hold the sauce and top the bowl with toasted pine nuts or pistachios.

2 Make the salad. In a 1-cup liquid measuring cup or small bowl, whisk together the lemon juice, sherry vinegar, sugar, salt, and pepper, then stream in the oil while whisking until emulsified. (This can be made up to 5 days in advance and stored in an airtight container in the fridge.) Gently combine the tomatoes, cucumber, parsley, and cilantro in a large bowl. Add the dressing and toss gently to coat. Adjust the salt and pepper.

3 Make the chickpeas. Heat the oil with the cumin, cardamom, allspice, and salt in a medium skillet over medium heat, stirring to combine the spices. Add the chickpeas and cook, gently stirring or shaking the pan occasionally, until the spices evenly coat the chickpeas and the chickpeas are warmed through, about 5 minutes. Turn off the heat and leave the chickpeas to stay warm, stirring if needed to prevent sticking to the pan.

4 Assemble individual bowls or let eaters make their own. Place about 1 cup of freekeh in the bottom of each bowl and top with a heaping ½ cup of the tomato-cucumber salad, a generous spoonful of warm chickpeas, and a dollop of the Pine Nut–Chili Yogurt. Top the yogurt with a generous drizzle of the reserved oil and pine nuts. Serve immediately.

Pine Nut–Chili Yogurt

MAKES ABOUT 1¼ CUPS

⅓ cup pine nuts

⅓ cup extra-virgin olive oil

1 teaspoon Aleppo pepper or ½ teaspoon crushed red pepper flakes

1 garlic clove, grated with a Microplane (you can do this directly into the pan)

1 cup full-fat Greek yogurt

¼ teaspoon fine sea salt, plus more as needed

Dry-toast the pine nuts in a small skillet over medium heat, shaking the pan occasionally, until they just begin to turn golden in color, about 3 minutes. Add the oil, then the Aleppo pepper and garlic, and let sizzle until the pine nuts turn more deeply golden in color, being careful not to burn them, about 30 seconds. Remove the pan from the heat and let cool briefly. Stir about half of the pine nuts and oil into the yogurt until evenly combined. Stir in ¼ teaspoon of salt then adjust salt to taste. Reserve the remaining pine nuts and oil for serving. (This can be made and refrigerated up to 3 days in advance. If you would like, return the reserved oil and pine nuts to a skillet and warm them over medium heat before serving.)

The Comforting Bowl of Rice

Rice is personal. The many beloved regional rice dishes around the world—drawing fierce and passionate opinions about the "right" way or the best way to make them—is proof enough. We are going to explore a few of these dishes and, with a vegetable-forward spin, discover how rice, sauéed and simmered, lifts up all types of vegetables as an all-in-one meal in a bowl. And to be clear, this isn't a typical grain-base bowl that relies on a punchy sauce and multiple components to bring all the flavor (like the ones we cover on pages 148 to 156). The rice here is front and center, cooked with focus and care and infused with flavor from aromatics, spices, and herbs. In equal partnership with beautiful vegetables, it brings us comfort in every bite.

TIPS AND TAKEAWAYS

- These rice dishes need plenty of vegetables, so don't skimp on them.

- Make sure to prep all ingredients in advance. The steps for these rice dishes move quickly and timing is everything.

- For paella (see page 158) and risotto (see page 163), make sure to gently simmer the stock before adding it. (Don't add it cold.) This may seem fussy and you may be tempted to skip it, but it's essential to maintaining the rice's correct cooking time and texture. And just barely simmer it (do not boil it) to minimize evaporation.

- This is not set-it-and-forget-it cooking. Use your senses to make adjustments to heat level. The heat should never be so high that the liquid evaporates before the rice cooks through.

- We are going for rice that is just cooked through (no hint of crunch) with just the slightest bite.

- Store leftovers in an airtight container for up to 3 days. To reheat, warm the rice in a saucepan over medium heat, adding some water or vegetable stock to loosen to your desired consistency or to hydrate as needed, 5 to 8 minutes depending on portion size. Adjust salt to taste.

Asparagus and Artichoke Paella

SERVES 6 AS A MAIN

BUTCHER TIP: To use fresh baby artichokes, trim and peel 1 to 1½ pounds baby artichokes to reveal their tender, light green-yellowish leaves and heart. Halve or quarter them into bite-size pieces (see page 79) In step 1, add the artichokes to the skillet with 2 tablespoons olive oil and a generous pinch of salt. Sauté until they begin to soften, about 4 minutes, then add the asparagus and radishes, and sauté until all the vegetables are tender, 4 minutes more.

INGREDIENT INFO:
- Avoid pencil-thin asparagus. Standard-size asparagus should be cut in ½-inch pieces. If using thicker asparagus, cut it on a diagonal into 1-inch slices. Cut jumbo asparagus into thin (¼-inch) rounds.

- Spanish paella rice is short-grained rice that soaks up liquid (flavor) gradually without becoming overly soft and sticky. Seek out Calasparra or bomba rice, or use Arborio rice in a pinch.

You can make paella, the famous and beloved Spanish-born, saffron-scented rice, at home with all kinds of vegetables. (And you don't need a special paella pan to do it—just a large skillet.) This version is a springtime treat featuring asparagus and artichokes. You can use jarred or frozen artichoke hearts, but fresh baby artichokes are extra delicious when you can procure them. Fava beans or English peas make fine additions, too. I highly recommend the summer and fall variations as well.

¼ cup plus 1 tablespoon extra-virgin olive oil

1 pound asparagus, stalks cut into ½-inch pieces, tips intact (see Ingredient Info)

12 baby red radishes, halved or quartered, or 6 red radishes, cut into small bite-size wedges (heaping 1 cup)

Fine sea salt and freshly ground black pepper

Heaping 1 cup grilled marinated baby artichokes (7 to 9 ounces), drained and cut into bite-size pieces (see Butcher Tip)

½ cup pitted and halved green olives or kalamata olives

4 cups low-sodium vegetable stock

1 medium onion, ¼-inch diced (2 cups)

1 medium fennel bulb (12 ounces), cored and thinly sliced (2 cups)

4 garlic cloves, minced

1¼ teaspoons smoked sweet paprika

2 tablespoons tomato paste

1½ cups paella rice (see Ingredient Info)

⅓ cup plus a splash of sherry or dry white wine

Scant ½ teaspoon saffron threads

2 bay leaves

½ cup loosely packed fresh flat-leaf parsley leaves and thin stems, finely chopped (or 2 tablespoons minced chives)

Lemon wedges, for serving

---

1 Heat 1 tablespoon of oil in a large skillet over medium-high heat. Add the asparagus, radishes, ¼ teaspoon salt, and a few twists of black pepper. Cook, stirring occasionally, for 2 minutes. Add the artichokes and olives and continue to cook, stirring occasionally, until the asparagus and radishes are crisp-tender and the artichokes and olives are warmed through, another 2 minutes. Transfer the mixture to a bowl and set aside. Return the pan to the stovetop (off the heat).

2 In a medium saucepan, bring the stock to a gentle simmer and leave to barely simmer on the lowest setting.

(recipe continues)

3 Heat the remaining ¼ cup of oil in the just-used skillet over medium heat. Add the onion, fennel, and ½ teaspoon salt and cook, stirring occasionally, until they soften and become golden in places, 6 to 8 minutes. Stir in the garlic and cook, stirring, for about 30 seconds until fragrant. Stir in the smoked paprika until evenly combined, then stir in the tomato paste and cook, stirring, until broken up and evenly incorporated, about 1 minute.

4 Stir in the rice and ½ teaspoon salt and continue stirring to coat and briefly toast the rice, about 1 minute. Carefully add the wine plus a small splash more, briefly stirring and scraping the bottom of the pan to deglaze it. Crumble the saffron with your fingers and stir it in. If the wine needs to cook off further, continue to cook, stirring, for another minute. Carefully pour in the hot stock, add the bay leaves, and stir, scraping up any browned bits on the bottom of the pan. Use the spoon to evenly spread out the rice in the pan. Once the stock begins to simmer, reduce the heat to low and simmer very gently, without stirring, until much of the stock is absorbed, about 15 minutes.

5 Scatter the reserved vegetables evenly over the top without disturbing the rice. Continue to cook the rice for about another 3 minutes on low heat until almost all of the liquid has been absorbed and the rice is al dente. (If the rice needs a little more time to cook, cover with foil and cook for a couple of minutes more.) As soon as the rice is done, turn up the heat to medium and cook, rotating the pan to ensure even heat and prevent burning, to cook off any excess liquid and to lightly brown and crisp (not burn) the rice stuck on the bottom of the pan, another 2 to 7 minutes. You should hear some sizzling as the last of the liquid cooks off and the socarrat forms. This is the prized browned crust at the bottom of the pan. Stop when you slip a spoon beneath the rice in places and it catches on rice (and before it burns!). Cover with foil and let rest for 5 to 10 minutes.

6 Uncover the paella, adjust salt to taste, and top with parsley (or chives). Serve the paella directly out of the pan with lemon wedges around the edges or on the side.

To store and reheat, see Tips and Takeaways on page 157.

VARIATIONS

This recipe can be adapted for other seasons. For each variation, keep the onion, fennel, and garlic base and replace the artichokes, asparagus, and radishes with 4 to 5 cups chopped vegetables.

SUMMER PAELLA: Saute a small, thinly sliced red and yellow bell pepper with the onion and fennel. Add 1 medium zucchini, cut into ¼-inch half-moons, as a substitute for the asparagus, and cook off excess liquid. Add 1 cup diced fresh tomatoes and the olives to the almost cooked rice at the end.

FALL PAELLA: Add 3 to 4 cups roasted cauliflower or Romanesco (a medium to large head cut into small, bite-size pieces) along with ½ cup peas and the olives to the top of the rice just before it finishes cooking.

Spiced Lentil Pilaf
with Spinach-Currant Salad

SERVES 4 AS A MAIN

SWAP: You can use whole baby arugula leaves instead of the chopped spinach.

This is a simple and delicious spiced lentil and rice bowl inspired by the Middle Eastern dish mujadara, with a tangy spinach and currant salad to serve on top. The dressing is explosively bright, with lemon, sherry, and a touch of yogurt to balance the earthy notes in the pilaf.

FOR THE PILAF

1 cup green or brown lentils, picked through and rinsed

3 tablespoons extra-virgin olive oil

2 medium onions, thinly sliced

Fine sea salt

1½ teaspoons ground coriander

1 teaspoon ground cumin

¾ teaspoon ground turmeric

½ teaspoon ground cinnamon

½ teaspoon ground allspice

Freshly ground black pepper

1 cup white basmati rice

2 cups water

FOR THE SALAD

1 tablespoon freshly squeezed lemon juice

½ teaspoon sherry vinegar

Heaping 1 tablespoon Greek yogurt

2 tablespoons extra-virgin olive oil

Fine sea salt

4 packed cups baby spinach, chopped

¼ cup dried currants

Freshly ground black pepper

1 Make the pilaf. Place the lentils in a medium pot and add water to cover by a depth of about 2 inches. Bring to a boil and cook until the lentils are just tender in places with some bite, 8 to 10 minutes. Drain the lentils.

2 Heat the oil in a Dutch oven or large, deep sauté pan (with lid) over medium-high heat. Add the onions and ½ teaspoon salt and cook, stirring frequently, until tender and browning, 8 to 10 minutes. Reduce the heat to medium and stir in the coriander, cumin, turmeric, cinnamon, allspice, ¾ teaspoon salt, and ¼ teaspoon pepper. Stir in the rice and cook, stirring, until the spices are fragrant and the rice is evenly coated, about 1 minute. Add the water and stir in the parcooked lentils, stirring up any browned bits from the bottom of the pan. Bring the water to a boil, then reduce the heat to low. Cover and simmer until the water has been absorbed and the lentils and rice are tender, but not mushy, 15 to 18 minutes. Remove the pan from the heat and adjust salt and pepper to taste.

3 Meanwhile, make the salad. Whisk together the lemon juice, sherry vinegar, yogurt, and oil in a medium bowl until well blended. Season with salt to taste. Add the spinach and currants and toss to thoroughly combine. Adjust salt and add pepper to taste.

4 Serve the pilaf in a large shallow bowl, topped with the salad.

Swiss Chard Risotto

SERVES 4 AS A MAIN

INGREDIENT INFO:

- I recommend the wine for the flavor it imparts, but you can omit it and add a squeeze of lemon juice or a couple of pinches of lemon zest at the end.

- Italian risotto rice is a starchy short-grain rice that cooks slowly and evenly to produce the perfect, classic risotto texture. Look for Arborio, carnaroli, and vialone nano varieties.

This risotto is simple with a classic base of onion and the addition of garlic, Swiss chard (leaves and stems), and Italian herbs to give you a feel for the technique and ways you might riff on it throughout the seasons. It's difficult to find a vegetable that risotto wouldn't take beautifully, so I urge you to run wild with the possibilities. (See the Variations for some ideas to get you started.)

At least 7 cups low-sodium vegetable stock

3 tablespoons unsalted butter

1 tablespoon extra-virgin olive oil

1 medium yellow onion, ¼-inch diced

1 bunch Swiss chard, stems ¼-inch diced (½ cup to 1 cup), leaves chopped (5 to 6 cups) (see How to Prep Swiss Chard on page 164)

Fine sea salt

3 large garlic cloves, minced

1 tablespoon Italian seasoning

¼ teaspoon ground nutmeg

1¾ cups risotto rice (see Ingredient Info)

1 cup dry white wine (optional; see Ingredient Info)

1½ cups finely grated Parmesan cheese, plus more for serving

Freshly ground black pepper

Best-quality olive oil, for topping

1 Bring the stock to a gentle simmer in a medium saucepan over medium-low heat. Rest the base of a ladle in a bowl or measuring cup large enough to fit it; place it next to the saucepan. (You will use this ladle to spoon the stock into the risotto and the bowl to catch drips upon transfer.)

2 In a Dutch oven or heavy-bottomed pan, melt 2 tablespoons of butter with the extra-virgin olive oil over medium heat. Stir in the onion, chard stems, and ¾ teaspoon salt and cook, stirring occasionally, for about 5 minutes until the onion is just soft and translucent. Add the garlic, Italian seasoning, and nutmeg and cook, stirring, for about 30 seconds until fragrant. Add the rice and cook, stirring frequently, to toast and evenly coat it in the butter–onion mixture, 1½ to 2 minutes. Add the wine, if using, and cook, stirring occasionally, until it is absorbed (the pan should be mostly dry), about another 2 minutes or so. Stir in half the chard leaves and 2 cups warm stock and bring to a simmer.

3 Reduce the heat to medium low and set a timer for 18 minutes. Stir the rice frequently and add more stock, 1 to 2 ladles at a time, as each addition is absorbed. (Try to evenly pace the additions of the stock throughout the 18 minutes and reserve some for adding as needed later.)

(recipe continues)

HOW TO PREP SWISS CHARD:

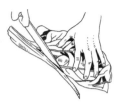

1. Fold each leaf in half lengthwise to expose the stem. Run your knife along the stem to remove it.

2. Wash the stems well to remove any dirt. Wash the leaves separately (see Dunk-and-Shake Method on page 11).

3. Stack several leaves at once and fold them over lengthwise. Roll the folded leaves from side to side, tucking in the bottom to make a tight cigar shape.

4. Slice crosswise through the roll to shred the greens into thin ribbons. (When chopped leaves are called for, go back through the pile in the other direction to break them down further.)

5. Trim the stems and cut them lengthwise then crosswise into fine dice.

4 After the timer goes off, stir in the remaining chard leaves until they are evenly incorporated and just wilted. Taste the rice to check for doneness: It should be creamy with a slight "bite"; it should not be crunchy at all! If needed, add another cup of stock (plus more as needed) and continue to stir for another 1 to 2 minutes, until the rice is cooked through and the risotto has reached the right consistency. Turn the heat down to low and stir in the remaining 1 tablespoon of butter and the Parmesan until incorporated. Turn off the heat and adjust salt and add pepper to taste.

5 Serve immediately with more Parmesan, black pepper, and a drizzle of good olive oil for topping if you wish.

To store and reheat, see Tips and Takeaways on page 157.

VARIATIONS

HANDS-OFF RISOTTO: In step 1, bring 6 cups of stock to a simmer (not 7 cups). Follow step 2. In step 3, instead of adding a couple of ladles of stock to start, add 5 cups of the warm stock, half of the chard, and the nutmeg at the beginning. Stir, reduce the heat to medium low, and cover the Dutch oven with its lid. Set the timer for 16 minutes and simmer, uncovering and stirring a few times throughout, until the rice is tender, about 16 minutes. Taste the rice for doneness; it should be tender with some "bite." Simmer for about another 2 minutes if it's crunchy, or, conversely if by chance it seems there's a lot of excess liquid in the pot. Uncover and stir in the remaining chard and 1 cup of stock, and simmer for about another 2 minutes, stirring frequently, until the rice is creamy and the chard is wilted. Over low heat, stir in the butter and Parmesan. Adjust salt and add pepper to taste. Serve immediately with more Parmesan, black pepper, and a drizzle of good olive oil for topping if you wish.

CLASSIC RISOTTO: With the garlic, add ¾ to 1 pound mixed mushrooms (cleaned and sliced or torn) and sauté them for a few minutes before adding the rice. Or omit the chard altogether and add 1 pound to 1¼ pounds mixed mushrooms with the garlic, including some rehydrated porcini mushrooms. (Strain the hydrating liquid through a piece of cheesecloth or a fine double mesh strainer. Add the strained liquid to the risotto for rich mushroom flavor.)

SPRING RISOTTO: Add fresh peas or sliced asparagus and chives toward the end of cooking with about 4 minutes remaining. Top with fresh herbs and lemon zest.

SUMMER RISOTTO: Add 2 cups raw corn kernels (and milky pulp left on the cob), a big handful of freshly torn basil, and halved cherry tomatoes toward the end of cooking.

FALL RISOTTO: Add 2 to 3 cups bite-size pieces of roasted butternut squash toward the end of cooking. Throw in 2 tablespoons chopped fresh sage to cook throughout, or top with fried sage leaves.

The Stir-Fry

A hot pan and oil, maybe some garlic and ginger, plus colorful vegetables make good things happen every time. There's no getting around it: prep all the ingredients for the stir-fry in advance. This is high-heat, fast cooking. As soon as your wok or skillet is smoking hot, it's time to go, go, go.

GOOD VEGETABLES TO STIR-FRY:
asparagus, bok choy, broccoli, Brussels sprouts, cabbage, carrots, cauliflower, celery, edamame, eggplant, garlic, ginger, green beans, kale, kohlrabi, sweet and hot peppers, mushrooms, okra, onions, radishes, romanesco, scallions, snow peas, spinach, sugar snap peas, Swiss chard, turnips, zucchini

STIR-FRY PANTRY ESSENTIALS: vegetable stock, tamari or soy sauce, stir-fry sauce or hoisin, tortillas, rice, noodles, nuts, toasted sesame oil, neutral vegetable oil like canola oil

TIPS AND TAKEAWAYS

- Stir-fries come together fast. Prep everything in advance and place it near the stovetop.

- Pat vegetables dry after washing to remove excess water. Too much water will cause the vegetables to steam and lose their signature, crisp-tender stir-fry texture.

- Use a 14-inch flat-bottomed wok (if you have one). Without overcrowding, you will produce comfortable, even movement, which translates to good texture, even cooking, and the best chance for browning and producing smoky flavor. A large skillet also will work fine.

- Get your pan smoking hot. Cook the vegetables over high or medium-high heat, frequently moving all ingredients around in the pan until they are crisp-tender.

- If the vegetables are sticking before they become tender, carefully add splashes of water to help with movement, but don't add so much that the vegetables steam and lose their crisp texture. (You can use a small drizzle of oil, but be careful, you can quickly end up with an oily stir-fry if you get too loose with multiple additions.)

- Resist the temptation to add tamari during the cooking process, unless it is called for in a stir-fry sauce. Reserve the solo addition of tamari, if using, to season a stir-fry toward the end of cooking and use it sparingly or you may produce an overly salty stir-fry.

- Serve vegetable stir-fries over rice or any whole grain. Or add grains or noodles to the pan and fry the veggies and grains or noodles together. To bulk up the meal and add some protein, gently toss in some crispy fried tofu (see page 151).

Once-a-Week Broccoli Stir-Fry

SERVES 4 AS A MAIN

HOW TO PREP BROCCOLI:

1. Separate the florets from the stalk by cutting just under the crown with a chef's knife. Cut the florets into even, bite-size pieces.

2. Trim the dry end of the stalk and any small leaves and stems attached. Use a vegetable peeler (see illustration) to remove the tough, fibrous outer layer of the stalk—until you reach the lighter green, more tender center.

3. Cut the stalk into bite-size pieces. (If it is extra-wide, first cut it in half lengthwise.)

SHORTCUT: You can use precut broccoli and forgo the addition of the stalks. Make sure to trim the broccoli and cut it into bite-size pieces. You'll need about 8 cups of florets to account for the missing stalks.

This is the stir-fry for your weekly rotation. Consider adding or substituting halved Brussels sprouts, bok choy and mushrooms, cabbage and cauliflower, asparagus, or green beans and eggplant. (Just make sure they are all cut in bite-size pieces so that they cook evenly.)

¾ cup low-sodium vegetable stock

1 teaspoon toasted sesame oil

1 teaspoon sugar

3 tablespoons canola oil

2 tablespoons minced garlic

1 tablespoon minced ginger (1-inch piece fresh ginger, peeled)

1 jalapeño, seeds and ribs removed, minced

½ cup thinly sliced scallions

1¾ pounds broccoli (2 large stalks), florets cut into bite-size pieces, stalk trimmed, peeled, and cut into bite-size pieces

3 tablespoons tamari or soy sauce

1 cup shelled frozen edamame, thawed

2 teaspoons lightly toasted sesame seeds, plus more for topping

½ to ¾ cup toasted cashews (or other nuts), coarsely chopped or left whole (optional)

Steamed brown or black rice, for serving

---

1 Whisk together the stock, sesame oil, and sugar in a small bowl. Set aside.

2 Heat a large stainless-steel skillet or 14-inch wok over medium-high heat until a drop of water evaporates in 2 seconds. Swirl the canola oil around in the pan, then add the garlic, ginger, jalapeño, and half the scallions and cook, stirring constantly, for 1 minute. Add the broccoli and cook, stirring frequently and carefully (the pan will be very full), until becoming tender in places, about 2 minutes. Add the tamari and cook until it is mostly absorbed, about 1 minute.

3 Stir in the edamame, then add the stock mixture. Turn up the heat to high and let simmer, stirring occasionally, until the broccoli is crisp-tender, much of the liquid has been absorbed, and a thin sauce remains, 2 to 3 minutes. Turn off the heat and stir in the remaining scallions, the sesame seeds, and the cashews if using. Serve immediately over rice with some sauce and a sprinkle of sesame seeds.

Weeknight Stir-Fry Wraps

SERVES 4 AS A MAIN

TAKE NOTE:

• Heat the tortillas in a toaster oven or microwave between two plates until they are warm and pliable.

• Red cabbage will bleed color onto the eggs; you can use all green cabbage if the discoloration bothers you. (I don't mind it.)

SWAPS:

• Serve the stir-fried vegetables over rice or add noodles to the stir-fry.

• Top with crushed peanuts and fresh cilantro.

• Try strips of tofu—pan-seared in sesame oil and drizzled with tamari—in place of the egg.

• Imagine new combinations with snow peas, broccoli, bok choy, napa cabbage, celery, or onions. Just stick to 9 to 10 cups of vegetables to maintain the right ratio of seasoning and sauce.

This must-know, make-anytime recipe is a produce-inspired, moo shu–style stir-fry made with a base of vegetable-drawer mainstays like cabbage and carrots, seasoned with pantry staples, then drizzled with store-bought hoisin sauce and wrapped up in flour tortillas.

---

2 tablespoons plus 1 teaspoon tamari or soy sauce

2 teaspoons toasted sesame oil

2 teaspoons sugar (or honey or agave)

2 teaspoons minced ginger (½-inch piece fresh ginger, peeled)

½ teaspoon garlic powder

½ cup low-sodium vegetable stock

3 large eggs

1 tablespoon plus 1½ teaspoons canola oil, plus more as needed

2 large scallions, thinly sliced on a diagonal, whites and green parts separated

1 cup thinly sliced shiitake mushroom caps (about 2 ounces shiitake mushrooms)

1 large red bell pepper, thinly sliced

2 carrots, cut into thin coins (about 1 cup)

Heaping 3 cups shredded red cabbage

Heaping 3 cups shredded green cabbage

1 teaspoon toasted white sesame seeds (optional)

Warm flour or cassava tortillas, for serving

Hoisin sauce, for serving

---

1 In a 1-cup liquid measure, whisk the 2 tablespoons of tamari, 1 teaspoon of sesame oil, the sugar, 1 teaspoon of ginger, the garlic powder, and vegetable stock; set aside.

2 In a small bowl, whisk together the eggs and the remaining 1 teaspoon each of tamari and sesame oil. Heat the 1½ teaspoons of canola oil over medium heat in a large nonstick skillet. (Cook the eggs in a smaller skillet if you don't have a large nonstick.) Add the egg mixture and swirl to spread it out over the pan. Let it cook, undisturbed to set, about 1 minute 30 seconds. Use a rubber spatula to flip it and cook until it sets on the other side and is no longer runny, about 1 minute. Slide the egg to a cutting board and cut it in thin strips; set aside.

3 Wipe the skillet clean or set another large skillet or a wok on the stove. Heat the remaining 1 tablespoon of canola oil over medium-high heat. Add the whites of the scallions and the remaining 1 teaspoon of ginger and cook for about 1 minute, until lightly browned. Add the mushrooms and cook, stirring, another minute. Add the bell pepper and carrots and cook, stirring occasionally, until just tender, about another 2 minutes. Add another small splash of canola oil if needed. Add the cabbages a little at a time to fit the pan, and cook to just wilt them, stirring frequently, about another 2 minutes. Whisk the sauce again and add it around the perimeter of the pan. Cook the vegetables, stirring, until they are tender and almost all of the liquid has been absorbed, 4 to 6 minutes. Stir in the remaining green parts of the scallions and the egg strips just to incorporate them. Add the sesame seeds if you wish and serve immediately with warm tortillas and hoisin sauce.

Fried Rice
with Brussels Sprouts and Cashews

TAKE NOTE: The pan will be quite full here. If you have a 14-inch wok, use it. The Brussels sprouts will get more brown, crisp, and flavorful if they have room to move around.

BUTCHER TIP: To keep the cut vegetables relatively uniform in size, extra-small Brussels sprouts should be halved, extra-large ones cut into eighths.

SWAPS: Swap broccoli for the Brussels sprouts and cook the same way. Or try bok choy: Reduce the added water to ¼ cup and cook uncovered until the bok choy is tender and the water has cooked off. Then continue with the recipe as is.

This fried rice is all about the stir-fried Brussels sprouts. The ratio of rice to sprouts is generously tilted in the latter direction with a feel-good effect that a rice-heavy version just doesn't create. With shallots, garlic, a handful of cilantro, and a squeeze of lime juice, it's a warm and hearty dish with a welcome hint of freshness and brightness.

3 tablespoons tamari or soy sauce, plus more as needed

2 tablespoons brown sugar

2 teaspoons toasted sesame oil

½ teaspoon crushed red pepper flakes (or 1 to 2 teaspoons chili oil, chili paste, or chili–garlic sauce)

3 eggs

Fine sea salt

3 tablespoons plus 2 teaspoons canola oil

1 medium-large shallot, thinly sliced (about ½ cup)

3 small to medium garlic cloves, minced

1½ pounds Brussels sprouts, quartered

½ cup water

4 cups cooked and chilled (overnight) long-grain white rice or jasmine rice

½ cup thinly sliced scallions

½ cup toasted cashews, plus more for serving

½ cup fresh cilantro leaves and thin stems, coarsely chopped, plus more for topping

1 teaspoon white and/or black sesame seeds (optional)

Lime wedges, for serving

1 In a small bowl, whisk together 2 tablespoons of tamari, 1 tablespoon of brown sugar, the sesame oil, and the red pepper flakes. Set aside.

2 In a medium-size bowl, whisk the eggs with a couple of pinches of salt. Heat 2 teaspoons of canola oil in a nonstick skillet over medium heat and tilt the pan to evenly distribute it. Add the eggs and cook, stirring, until softly scrambled with no browning, about 1 minute. Transfer the scrambled eggs to a small bowl or plate and set aside.

3 Heat the remaining 3 tablespoons of canola oil in a large skillet or 14-inch wok over medium heat. Add the shallot and garlic and cook, stirring, until fragrant, about 1 minute, and the shallot is becoming translucent. Turn the heat up to medium high. Stir in the Brussels sprouts and cook, stirring, for about 1 minute until well coated and incorporated. Add the water, gently shake the pan to evenly distribute, cover, and cook, undisturbed, for about 4 minutes until all of the water has evaporated and the sprouts start to sizzle. Uncover and stir, moving the sprouts around in the pan. Sprinkle with the remaining 1 tablespoon of brown sugar and the remaining 1 tablespoon of tamari. Continue to stir for about 1 minute until browning in places.

(recipe continues)

4 Carefully stir in the rice, eggs, and ¼ cup of scallions until well combined. Pour the sauce evenly around the perimeter of the pan. Stir to incorporate, then scrape and incorporate any browned bits from the bottom of the pan. Continue carefully stirring to break up any clumps of rice and evenly combine all of the ingredients, about 1 minute. Add more tamari to taste, if needed. Stir in the cashews, the remaining ¼ cup of scallions, and the cilantro.

5 Transfer to individual bowls or a serving bowl and sprinkle with sesame seeds and/or more cashews if you would like. Serve with lime wedges.

The Saucy Noodle Bowl

Saucy, savory, and maybe even a little sweet and spicy—served hot or cold—there is something about a tangle of long noodles plus sauce that is irresistible to us all. Add vegetables. Turn them up, and really let them get loud, and a bowl of saucy noodles becomes a can't-get-enough-of-it meal that will turn you wild.

SAUCY NOODLE PANTRY ESSENTIALS

- **NOODLES:** udon, ramen, rice, soba, or spaghetti noodles

- **A BASE FOR SAUCE (ADDS BODY AND RICHNESS):** peanut butter, almond butter, tahini, hoisin, miso, coconut milk, stir-fry sauce

- **AROMATICS TO ENHANCE THE SAUCE (AND/OR TO TOSS WITH THE COOKED NOODLES):** ginger, garlic, scallions, chilies

- **SEASONING THAT ADDS POP TO THE SAUCE:** toasted sesame oil, rice wine vinegar, citrus juice and zest, tamari/soy sauce/shoyu, red curry paste, chili paste such as sambal oelek, harissa, ponzu

- **SEEDS AND NUTS TO TOP THE FINISHED NOODLES:** sesame seeds, peanuts, cashews, almonds

- **TOPPINGS THAT ADD ANOTHER PUNCH OF FLAVOR:** chili oil, chili crisp, fresh herbs

GOOD VEGETABLES FOR SAUCY NOODLE BOWLS: asparagus, bok choy, broccoli, Brussels sprouts, cabbage, carrots, cauliflower, celery, edamame, eggplant, garlic, ginger, green beans, kale, kohlrabi, sweet and hot peppers, mushrooms, onions, radishes, romanesco, scallions, snow peas, spinach, sugar snap peas, turnips, Swiss chard, zucchini

TIPS AND TAKEAWAYS

- Make a saucy noodle bowl with boiled noodles, a creamy sauce (think peanut butter, tahini, almond butter, coconut milk, miso), and raw or crisp-tender vegetables. Or stir-fry the vegetables, add the noodles, and toss and cook to allow the noodles to soak up and deliver a flavorful sauce.

- Prevent sticky noodles: Don't overcook them and don't let them stand! Follow package instructions closely and taste them for doneness well before the finish time. Keep tasting until al dente. Drain, rinse to cool, and transfer immediately to the sauce or toss with a teaspoon of vegetable oil or toasted sesame oil if they must wait.

- To bulk up noodle bowls, gently toss in some crispy tofu (see page 151).

Saucy Garlic-Ginger Noodles

with All the Green Things

SERVES 3 TO 4 AS A MAIN

PREP TIP: Make sure to rinse out the base of the bok choy stalks where dirt gathers.

EQUIPMENT TIP: Use the largest pan you can find—you'll need plenty of space to turn all of the ingredients.

VARIATIONS:: Cabbage, asparagus, julienned kohlrabi, and spinach are great additions or substitutes. After sautéeing the garlic, ginger, and mushrooms in step 3, add 1½ to 2 pounds of vegetables. When riffing, use that quantity as your guide; cook the vegetables to crisp-tender or until just wilted.

BUTCHER TIP: See page 167 for how to prep broccoli stems, page 223 for how to string pea pods.

This is what happens when you stir-fry lots of good green things, then toss them with noodles and a flavorful sauce. I like a good mix of broccoli, sugar snap and/or snow peas, and bok choy, but you could easily select just one or two to reduce prep time and simplify the ingredient list.

FOR THE SAUCE

¼ cup low-sodium vegetable stock

¼ cup vegetarian hoisin or stir-fry sauce

2 to 3 tablespoons tamari or soy sauce

1 tablespoon toasted sesame oil

2 teaspoons rice wine vinegar

2 to 3 teaspoons brown sugar or maple syrup

2 teaspoons cornstarch

2 teaspoons chili paste, such as sambal oelek (or ¼ teaspoon crushed red pepper flakes)

FOR THE NOODLES

About 10 ounces udon noodles or spaghetti

3 tablespoons canola oil

4 ounces shiitake mushrooms, stemmed, caps thinly sliced

3 large garlic cloves, minced

1 tablespoon minced ginger

12 ounces broccoli, florets and peeled stems cut into small bite-size pieces (about 5 cups)

8 ounces snow peas and/or sugar snap peas, trimmed, strings removed, and halved on a sharp diagonal

1 to 2 bunches baby bok choy or ½ large bunch bok choy, trimmed and ½-inch sliced

3 large scallions, thinly sliced

Finely chopped toasted peanuts or cashews, for serving (optional)

1 Make the sauce. Whisk together the stock, hoisin, tamari, sesame oil, vinegar, brown sugar, cornstarch, and chili paste in a 1-cup liquid measure; let stand.

2 Make the noodles. Bring a large pot of water to a boil. Add the noodles and cook according to the package directions until al dente. If the noodles finish before you are ready to add them to the vegetables, rinse them under cold water.

3 Meanwhile, heat 2 tablespoons of canola oil in a 14-inch wok or large skillet over medium-high heat. Add the mushrooms and cook, stirring occasionally, until browned and tender, 3 to 4 minutes. Add the remaining 1 tablespoon of canola oil, the garlic, and ginger. Cook, stirring, until fragrant, about 30 seconds. Add the broccoli and snow peas and cook for 3 minutes, stirring almost constantly. Add a couple of tablespoons of water if the vegetables stick to the pan. Add the bok choy and carefully stir it in and cook until the greens begin to wilt and the other vegetables are crisp-tender, about 2 minutes.

4 Add the cooked noodles. Briefly whisk the sauce again, then pour it mostly around the perimeter of the pan with some evenly over the top. Stir and toss briefly to incorporate. Sprinkle in the scallions. Cook, stirring evenly to combine the noodles, sauce, and vegetables, until the mixture is well coated and has absorbed much of the sauce, another 1 to 2 minutes. Top with chopped peanuts or cashews if you wish and serve.

Sesame-Peanut Noodles
with Crunchy Vegetables and Garlic-Scallion Chili Oil

SERVES 4 TO 5 AS A MAIN

MAKE AHEAD: You can make the sauce and noodles ahead, but do not combine them until you are ready to serve. As soon as the noodles are drained, rinsed, and drained again, toss them with a couple of teaspoons of toasted sesame oil. Store separately.

Crunchy, saucy, spicy—cold sesame noodles are a must for every vegetable-forward rotation. This recipe spotlights cucumbers, raw shredded cabbage, and spinach. The garlic, sesame, and scallion oil brings the whole dish to life with a kick of heat (it wakes up tired leftovers, too). You can use a store-bought chili oil, no problem, just add some sliced scallions to the noodles.

FOR THE SAUCE

1½ tablespoons sugar

¼ cup plus 1 tablespoon well-stirred tahini

¼ cup plus ½ tablespoon rice wine vinegar

3 tablespoons toasted sesame oil

3 tablespoons tamari or soy sauce

2 tablespoons natural smooth unsalted peanut butter

FOR THE NOODLES

8 to 10 ounces dry ramen or soba noodles (or spaghetti or linguine fini; see Note on page 177)

3 to 4 mini seedless cucumbers (such as Persian), thinly sliced in rounds or half-moons, or 1 medium to large cucumber, peeled, seeded, and cut into thin 2-inch sticks

2 to 3 cups finely shredded red cabbage or napa cabbage

2 packed cups baby spinach, roughly chopped or shredded into thin ribbons

½ cup shelled frozen edamame, thawed (optional)

1½ teaspoons black and/or white sesame seeds (optional)

2 to 3 tablespoons Garlic-Scallion Chili Oil (page 177), plus more as needed

⅓ cup unsalted dry roasted peanuts, very finely chopped or processed in a small food processor

(recipe continues)

- This recipe can handle up to 7 cups of veggies.

- **In spring:** blanched, sautéed, or steamed sugar snap or snow peas (strings removed and halved or cut into thirds) and asparagus (cut into 1-inch pieces on a diagonal), raw or sautéed celery (thinly sliced on a diagonal), raw radish (thinly sliced).

- **In summer:** raw red bell pepper (thinly sliced).

- **In fall/winter:** blanched, roasted, or raw broccoli and/or cauliflower florets.

1 Make the sauce. Whisk together the sugar, tahini, vinegar, sesame oil, tamari, and peanut butter in a large bowl until evenly combined. Pour half the sauce in a 1-cup liquid measure or a small bowl; set both aside.

2 Cook the noodles. Bring a medium pot of water to a boil, add the noodles, and cook according to the package directions until al dente (they should retain some bite and chewiness), tasting often for doneness to avoid overcooking. Drain and rinse under cold water, turning, until they are cold. Drain the noodles again. Immediately transfer to the large bowl with the sauce and toss to coat evenly.

3 Add the cucumbers, cabbage, spinach, and edamame (if using) to the top of the noodles, drizzle with about half of the remaining sauce, and sprinkle with the sesame seeds (if using). Lightly toss the vegetables in sauce without fully incorporating them into the noodles at first. Now, combine the vegetables and noodles, tossing, then add more of the remaining sauce to taste. Drizzle in 1 to 2 tablespoons of the Garlic-Scallion Chili Oil and toss until evenly incorporated.

4 Serve, topping with more chili oil to taste and a generous sprinkle of peanuts.

NOTE: Some types of noodles, such as ramen noodles, may need to be rehydrated in hot water rather than boiled. Follow the package instructions and add them directly to the bowl of sauce in step 2.

Garlic-Scallion Chili Oil

MAKES ABOUT ⅓ CUP

TAKE NOTE: If you want to reserve the dark green parts of the scallions, you can chop them and add them to the noodles.

¼ cup plus 1 tablespoon canola oil

2 scallions (white and light green parts only), finely chopped

1 teaspoon white sesame seeds

1 to 1½ teaspoons crushed red pepper flakes

1 large garlic clove, grated

Combine the oil, scallions, sesame seeds, and red pepper flakes and bring to a very low simmer over low heat. Very gently simmer, stirring occasionally, until the scallions are golden and just barely sizzling and the oil has a pale reddish tint, about 10 minutes. Add the garlic and cook until fragrant, another minute. Carefully transfer to a heat-safe bowl. If making ahead, cool to room temperature and refrigerate in an airtight container. The oil will keep for 7 days.

Orange-Miso Soba Noodle Bowl

with Broccoli and Carrot Ribbons

SERVES 4 AS A MAIN

BUTCHER TIP: See page 112 for how to shave carrots into ribbons.

VARIATIONS:

- **Spring Soba Noodle Bowl:** asparagus, snap peas, snow peas, carrots, radishes or any mild or spicy greens

- **Summer Noodle Bowl:** eggplant, cucumber, and/or green beans

- **Fall/Winter Soba Noodle Bowl:** sweet potato, winter squash, broccoli, cauliflower, romanesco, bok choy, Brussels sprouts

- **Peanut Soba Noodle Bowl:** Replace the orange-miso sauce with peanut sauce (see page 151) made with coconut milk and lime. Top with crushed peanuts.

This is a lunchtime or weeknight noodle bowl that is built for speed. Its bold and bright citrus-miso sauce does the heavy lifting, offering high-impact flavor.

---

4 tablespoons white miso paste

2 tablespoons tamari or soy sauce

1 tablespoon pure maple syrup

2 teaspoons toasted sesame oil

2 teaspoons sambal oelek or other chili paste

1 teaspoon freshly grated orange zest

3 tablespoons freshly squeezed orange juice

8 to 9 ounces soba noodles

1 pound broccoli, florets and peeled stems cut into small bite-size pieces (about 6 cups)

2 carrots, shaved into ribbons with a vegetable peeler (see Butcher Tip)

1 large scallion, thinly sliced (optional)

1 tablespoon toasted sesame seeds, plus more for topping

A handful of fresh cilantro, roughly chopped

---

1 Bring a large pot of water to a boil.

2 Meanwhile, whisk together the miso, tamari, maple syrup, sesame oil, sambal oelek, orange zest, and orange juice in a large bowl. (Add 1 to 2 tablespoons of warm water as needed to smooth out the miso.) Use a measuring cup to remove a scant ⅓ cup of the sauce and reserve it.

3 Cook the soba noodles according to the package instructions, making sure not to overcook them. Use a large spider or tongs to transfer the noodles to a colander to drain briefly. Immediately transfer them to the large bowl with the sauce and toss briefly.

4 Add the broccoli to the boiling water and cook until bright green and just crisp-tender, about 2 minutes. Drain well, then toss it into the noodles with the carrot ribbons, scallion if you are adding it, and the sesame seeds. Add some of the reserved sauce to taste, tossing again.

5 Top with the cilantro and more sesame seeds and serve.

The Vegetable-Packed Pasta

Turn down the pasta and turn up the vegetables (way up) and you have the Vegetable-Packed Pasta. There are still carby noodles, just enough not to overwhelm the veggies but to support them and deliver all the comfort that you expect to find here. The Vegetable-Packed Pasta gives you permission to enjoy pasta as often as you'd like.

GOOD VEGETABLES FOR VEGETABLE-PACKED PASTA: artichokes, arugula, asparagus, broccoli, broccolini, broccoli rabe, cabbage, corn, Brussels sprouts, cauliflower, eggplant, green beans, kale, mushrooms, peas, radicchio, spinach, Swiss chard, tomatoes, winter squash, zucchini

VEGETABLE-PACKED PASTA PANTRY ESSENTIALS: pasta, salt, good-quality olive oil, garlic, Parmesan

ADDED LIFTS: aged balsamic vinegar, chili oil, fresh herbs, lemon, red pepper or Calabrian chili flakes, wine

EXTRA ADD-INS: beans such as chickpeas or cannellini beans; nuts such as pine nuts, pistachios, or walnuts

TIPS AND TAKEAWAYS

- Salt pasta water generously until it tastes like the sea. Without a big, rich sauce these pastas must be seasoned properly, and you will use reserved pasta cooking water—at least 1 cup—to coat the pasta and make a simple sauce.

- For pastas with larger cuts of vegetables like broccoli or cauliflower, consider using tube-shaped or other shorter pastas that are closer in size and shape to the cut vegetables. This way you'll get a bit of pasta and vegetable in every bite. Penne, gemelli, cavatappi, casarecce, strozzapreti, and campanelle are good choices.

- Pine nuts or chopped pistachios, hazelnuts, or walnuts add crunch and extra protein to balance the carbohydrate-rich pasta. Dry-toast nuts in a pan over medium heat, stirring frequently, until golden and fragrant.

- Remember this: If you increase the pasta, add more vegetables. As a general rule, start with at least double the weight of raw vegetables to dry pasta.

Cacio e Pepe
with Roasted Cauliflower and Spinach

SERVES 4 AS A MAIN

ALL PLANTS: Warm up 1½ to 2 cups of creamy fennel Alfredo sauce (see page 188) in a microwave or in a saucepan, stirring frequently, over medium heat. Add it in place of the Pecorino with lots of pepper. Hold back on pasta cooking water additions; you won't need quite as much.

BUTCHER TIP: See page 123 for how to break down cauliflower.

This super simple veggie-packed pasta is the kind of dish that's perfect when you don't know what else to make. The ratio of veggies to pasta is weighted heavily in the veggie direction, so it feels more balanced and satisfying than a standard bowl of pasta, especially for a creamy one like this. File away this technique for roasting the cauliflower, which allows it to brown and crisp. It's a winner.

Fine sea salt

1 medium to large cauliflower, cut into bite-size florets

Extra-virgin olive oil

Freshly ground black pepper

3 ounces Pecorino Romano cheese, finely grated on a Microplane

12 ounces penne lisce or other smooth tubular pasta

2 packed cups baby spinach, chopped

Heaping 1 cup thinly sliced radicchio (optional)

Lemon wedges, for serving (optional)

1 Heat the oven to 475°F with a rack in the bottom position. Bring a large pot of water to a boil and generously salt the water until it tastes like the sea.

2 Meanwhile, combine the cauliflower, about 2 tablespoons of oil, ¼ teaspoon salt, and a few twists of pepper on a sheet pan and toss together until well combined. Spread out the cauliflower in the pan, then roast it until browning on the bottom and mostly tender, about 15 minutes. Carefully shake the pan and turn the florets. Continue to roast until tender, crisp in places, and nicely browning all over, about 5 minutes.

3 Stir together 2 tablespoons of oil, 1½ teaspoons of pepper, and 1 cup of cheese in a large, shallow serving bowl (large enough to toss the pasta in it) until a paste forms. Spread it around the bowl.

4 Add the pasta to the boiling water and cook according to the package directions until al dente (taste it about 2 minutes shy of the shortest cook time). Reserve 1 cup of pasta cooking water, then drain the pasta in a colander and immediately transfer it to the mixture in the serving bowl, stir vigorously.

5 Stir in ¼ cup of the hot reserved water. Gradually sprinkle in the cheese while stirring and adding more cooking water between cheese additions to loosen the "sauce" that is forming (another ¼ to ½ cup of water). Stir in the spinach and radicchio (if using), and a splash of hot cooking water if needed. The sauce should be thin and creamy, not watery. Stir in the cauliflower to combine.

6 Serve immediately. Offer lemon wedges on the side if you wish.

Tomato, Sweet Corn, and Zucchini Pasta
with Fresh Basil

SERVES 4 AS A MAIN

TAKE NOTE:
- Drizzle Chili Oil (page 6) made with crushed red pepper flakes or crushed Calabrian chilies over the top to finish.
- Try serving with a dollop of ricotta cheese on top.
- Try a variety of pasta shapes. Use thin long noodles like linguine, spaghetti, or bucatini, or short pastas like penne, gemelli, or radiatori.

INGREDIENT INFO: Use any in-season tomatoes (halving or quartering any large ones), such as Sungolds, mixed baby heirlooms, or Early Girls.

This recipe is my first thought and my final thought when it's time to decide what's for dinner in the summer months. It lives in my back pocket, and I pull it out weekly until the last of the corn and sweetest tomatoes are gone. It's *simple* simple, but the star ingredients must be in their prime. To mix things up, stir in a few dollops of Basil Pesto (page 59) in place of the butter and fresh basil leaves.

Fine sea salt

¾ pound linguine fini or any favorite pasta

3 tablespoons extra-virgin olive oil

3 very large garlic cloves, thinly sliced or smashed

A pinch to ¼ teaspoon crushed red pepper flakes, adjust to personal taste

2 medium zucchini, sliced into ⅛-inch half-moons or quarter moons

2 large ears raw sweet corn, freshly shaved off the cob

Heaping 2 cups cherry tomatoes (see Ingredient Info)

1 tablespoon unsalted butter

½ cup packed fresh basil leaves, chopped or torn

¼ cup pine nuts, toasted (optional)

½ cup finely grated Parmesan cheese, plus more for serving

Freshly ground black pepper

Best-quality olive oil

1 Bring a large pot of water to a boil and salt it generously until it tastes like the sea. Add the pasta and cook according to the package instructions until al dente.

2 In a large skillet, heat the extra-virgin olive oil with the garlic and red pepper flakes (if using) over medium heat. When the garlic just begins to simmer, cook for about 2 minutes, stirring frequently, until the garlic becomes fragrant and turns golden. Add the zucchini, turn up the heat to medium high, and cook, stirring occasionally, for 3 to 4 minutes until al dente and just beginning to brown in places. Stir in the corn, tomatoes, and ½ teaspoon salt. Sauté for about another 2 minutes until the corn is warmed and until the halved or quartered tomatoes are just beginning to melt and whole ones are just about to burst.

3 Carefully reserve about 1 cup of the pasta cooking water. Drain the pasta briefly and immediately transfer it to the skillet to keep it from drying out. Toss the pasta with the vegetable mixture and add the butter (or an extra tablespoon of olive oil) and a couple of tablespoons of the reserved pasta water, to help encourage a light sauce to form. Add more pasta water, a little at a time, as needed to loosen further. (Reserve the remaining pasta water to help freshen any leftovers.) Toss in most of the fresh basil (reserving some to finish), pine nuts (if using), and the ½ cup Parmesan and salt and pepper to taste. Top with more Parmesan, a drizzle of your best olive oil, and the remaining freshly chopped or torn basil.

Creamy Eggplant and Tomato Sauce
with Rigatoni and Ricotta Salata

SERVES 4 AS A MAIN

MAKE AHEAD: This sauce will develop deeper flavors as it stands. Let it sit out for up to a couple of hours until ready to make and serve the pasta. (Refrigerate the sauce overnight.)

TAKE NOTE:

- Make sure to reserve the pasta cooking water. Before serving, bring the sauce back to a simmer, loosen with cooking water, and toss with the pasta.

- Adjust the cream, up or down, depending on how rich you want to go.

INGREDIENT INFO:

- Buy eggplant in season and use it as soon as possible. It becomes more bitter as it ages. Eggplants also vary in size. For this recipe use a few small eggplants or 1 large eggplant (7 to 8 cups diced); no need to be exact.

- You can use ½ pound pasta to serve 4 or up to ¾ pound to serve up to 6. The sauce works either way; you will get a smaller yield but more eggplant per serving if you go with less pasta.

My grandmother perfected this eggplant-rich creamy tomato sauce. It's full of sophisticated flavor, which is impressive given how easy it is to make. My grandmother made it with fresh pasta, but I tend to make it with dry pasta for ease, and I top it with shavings of ricotta salata. You could also finish the pasta with coarsely grated Parmesan or stir in diced fresh or smoked mozzarella.

Fine sea salt

2 tablespoons extra-virgin olive oil

2 tablespoons unsalted butter

1 cup finely diced shallot (1 to 2 shallots)

3 to 4 large garlic cloves, minced

1½ to 1¾ pounds eggplant, ¾-inch diced (see Ingredient Info)

1 teaspoon Italian seasoning (optional)

¼ teaspoon crushed red pepper flakes

Freshly ground black pepper

⅓ cup dry white wine

1 can (15 ounces) tomato sauce

½ cup shaken heavy cream

1 cup fresh basil leaves, chopped

½ pound to ¾ pound rigatoni or other tube-shaped pasta

1 cup coarsely grated ricotta salata cheese (about 3 ounces)

---

1 Bring a large pot of water to a boil and generously salt it until it tastes like the sea.

2 Meanwhile, heat the oil and butter in a large, deep sauté pan or Dutch oven over medium heat until the butter is just about melted. Add the shallot and garlic and cook, stirring frequently, until translucent, about 2 minutes. Add the eggplant, Italian seasoning, if using, ½ teaspoon salt, the red pepper flakes, and ¼ teaspoon black pepper. Cook, stirring occasionally, for about 5 minutes until the eggplant is just tender and lightly browning, but not soft. Carefully add the wine, stirring and scraping any browned bits from the bottom of the pan. Turn the heat up to medium high and continue to cook, stirring occasionally, until the liquid evaporates, about 2 minutes. Add the tomato sauce and simmer, stirring often, until warmed through and well incorporated, 2 to 3 minutes more. Turn off the heat and stir in the cream, then three quarters of the basil, reserving the remaining basil for topping.

3 Add the pasta to the boiling water and cook according to the package instructions until al dente. Reserve 1 cup of the pasta cooking water, then briefly drain the pasta. Immediately, while it is still very wet, transfer the pasta to the sauce and stir to combine evenly. If you'd like to loosen the sauce, add pasta cooking water, a little at a time, to reach your desired consistency. Adjust salt to taste.

4 Transfer the pasta to a serving bowl. Top with the ricotta salata, more pepper, and the remaining basil.

The Tomato-Less Pasta

Cooked down and blended, vegetables turn into a creamy, irresistibly delicious, nutrient-rich sauce—a fresh alternative to the standard tomato sauce. Make any of these vegetable-based sauces to serve immediately; or freeze them and they're ready to turn everyday pasta into an elevated meal.

SMOOTH AND CREAMY TOMATO-LESS PASTA SAUCE

The base of this tomato-less sauce is made with braised, stewed, or roasted vegetables blended with liquid in a high-speed blender (essential to create a smooth, glossy sauce).

GOOD VEGETABLES FOR TOMATO-LESS SAUCE: artichokes, asparagus, beets, butternut squash (and other winter squashes like pumpkin, kabocha, and acorn), carrots, cauliflower, celery root, corn, eggplant, fennel, mushrooms, parsnips, peas, romanesco, sunchokes, zucchini

- To braise, start by sautéing aromatics like onion and garlic in oil or butter. Then add the star vegetable to pan-fry a bit and get some color. Add stock or water (or coconut milk) to soften it as well as to create a loose, sauce-like texture.

- To stew, no initial sautéing is required; just combine the aromatics and selected vegetable in liquid and simmer until soft.

- To make sauce with roasted vegetables, roast the vegetable until very soft, then puree it. Add liquid and blend to loosen.

- When it comes time to blend, consider adding cream, a soft spoonable cheese, yogurt, or nut milk or nut-based cheese (or a combination) for added richness and silkiness.

PESTO

Pesto is made with raw or cooked vegetables, garlic, nuts or seeds, cheese (or not), and good olive oil. It's blended in a food processor until well combined and creamy, but not completely smooth.

GOOD VEGETABLES FOR PESTO: Cooked first until tender: artichoke hearts and tender inner leaves, broccolini, broccoli rabe (see page 193), cardoons, corn, nettles, sweet peppers (see page 230)

Raw or briefly blanched: asparagus, garlic scapes, hearty greens (collards, kale, Swiss chard), green root tops (carrot, beet, radish), fresh herbs (e.g. basil (see page 59), mint, and parsley), ramps, spinach

GOOD NUTS AND SEEDS FOR PESTO: almonds, hazelnuts, pecans, pine nuts, pepitas, pistachios, walnuts

TIPS AND TAKEAWAYS

- These sauces can thicken up and become stiff once combined with pasta. Reserve the cooking water to loosen them.

- Don't overcook your pasta! You want a little tension between the super-creamy sauce and the pasta. Cook the pasta just shy of al dente.

- Use tomato-less sauce for pasta salad. For ¾ pound of pasta, use at least ¾ cup of vegetable pesto and 1 to 2 cups of a smooth vegetable sauce.

- You can spoon these sauces over grain bowls, dip into them with crackers and crudités, layer them into a sandwich, or use them on vegetable steaks and flatbreads.

- Store these sauces in an airtight, freezer-safe container and freeze them for up to 3 months. Thaw in the refrigerator for 24 hours before reheating.

Creamy (No-Cream) Fennel Alfredo Sauce
with Bucatini

MAKES ABOUT 2 CUPS
SAUCE; SERVES 4 WITH
PASTA AS A MAIN

EQUIPMENT TIP: This recipe requires a high-speed blender that will completely pulverize the nuts to produce sauce with a smooth and creamy consistency. A regular blender will likely produce an uneven, grainy sauce, fine in a pinch.

ADD SOME GREEN: Add a handful of fresh arugula on top of the finished pasta. Throw fresh or frozen peas into the pasta cooking water, about 90 seconds before the pasta finishes, then drain them with the pasta and toss together.

ABOUT THE YIELD: The sauce will yield about 2 cups, which is enough to make one saucy ¾- to 1-pound batch of pasta.

MAKE AHEAD: Refrigerate the sauce for up to 3 days or freeze it for up to 3 months in an airtight container. To defrost, thaw in the refrigerator overnight.

Raw fennel's bold, sometimes polarizing, licorice-like flavor mellows when you cook the vegetable until tender and sweet. I absolutely love fennel prepared in this way (I think you will, too), so it got me thinking about turning it into a vegetable sauce. This one looks like a creamy Alfredo sauce, but with fennel cooked down in that special way and whipped with shallot, garlic, and cashews, it makes a sauce that's far more interesting than any Alfredo (without any "real" cream at all). With subtle and surprising sweet notes of anise and richness that comes from plant-protein cream, this dreamy sauce can and should be enjoyed on weeknights and special occasions alike.

---

1 to 1¼ pounds fennel bulb with 10 to 12 inches of stalks and fronds

2 tablespoons extra-virgin olive oil

⅓ cup minced shallot

1 small garlic clove

Fine sea salt

1 cup raw cashews

1 tablespoon freshly squeezed lemon juice

¾ pound dried bucatini or other favorite pasta

Freshly ground black pepper

2 tablespoons chopped fresh flat-leaf parsley leaves (optional)

---

1 Wash the fennel. Cut the tubular stalks and feathery fronds to separate them from the bulb. Pull 1 to 2 tablespoons of fronds from the stalks, roughly chop them, and reserve them to garnish the pasta later. Trim the base of the fennel (see page 40) and discard any brown spots or badly bruised bits. Cut the bulb in half lengthwise through the core, then lengthwise again to quarter it. Rinse the bulb again if you see dirt between the layers.

2 Place the quartered bulb and stalks in a medium-size pot (trim the fronds, if needed, to fit). Fill the pot with enough water to just cover the fennel. Cover and bring the water to a boil. Uncover the pot and boil over medium-high heat until the fennel is completely soft, about 15 minutes. Carefully remove the fennel with tongs, allowing liquid to drain back into the pot; transfer the bulbs to a cutting board, discard the stalks. Reserve the fennel cooking water. (If it's full of leaves or grit you can strain it through a fine-mesh sieve, but I don't usually bother.)

3 Meanwhile, heat 1 tablespoon of oil in a small skillet over medium heat. Add the shallot, garlic, and ¼ teaspoon salt, and cook, stirring frequently, until the shallot has softened and is translucent, 2 to 3 minutes.

4 Combine the cashews and ½ cup of the fennel cooking water in a high-speed blender. Blend until well combined and mostly smooth. (It will still appear a bit grainy.) Add the shallot-garlic mixture, the fennel bulb, and any layers that came apart—you can leave out any tough outer pieces. Add another ¼ cup of the fennel cooking water, the remaining 1 tablespoon of olive oil, the lemon juice, and ¼ teaspoon salt. Blend again on high until completely smooth. Add more fennel cooking water to thin the sauce to reach your desired consistency. Adjust salt to taste.

5 When ready to make the pasta, bring a pot of water, including any remaining fennel cooking water, to a boil and generously salt it until it tastes like the sea. Add the pasta and cook, stirring a couple of times throughout, according to the package directions until just shy of al dente. Reserve about 1 cup of the pasta cooking water. Drain the pasta and put the empty pot back on the stove.

6 Put the fennel sauce in the now empty pot and warm it over medium-low heat stirring often. Add the pasta and toss to evenly coat. Add ¼ cup of the reserved pasta cooking water to loosen the sauce; add more by the teaspoonful as needed. The sauce should cling to the pasta but should not be watery. Adjust salt and add pepper to taste.

7 Transfer the pasta to a serving bowl or individual bowls and top with the reserved chopped fennel fronds or, if using, the chopped parsley. Finish with a couple of twists of pepper and serve immediately.

Lemon-Beet Sauce and Fusilli

with Peas and Poppy Seeds

MAKES ABOUT 2½ CUPS SAUCE; SERVES 4 AS A MAIN WITH AN EXTRA BATCH OF SAUCE TO FREEZE

INGREDIENT INFO: Try to avoid overgrown (extra-large) beets. They can be less sweet and take a long time to cook (up to 90 minutes). Trim the stems to 1 inch above the root. Reserve the greens for another use. If you're concerned about stained fingers, you can wear food-safe gloves when you peel the beets; otherwise, don't worry—a beet stain on your hands will disappear after a couple of washes. If you're short on time, use 1 to 1¼ pounds precooked and peeled beets. Just don't skip the roasted garlic!

EQUIPMENT TIP: You'll need a blender or food processor to puree the cooked beets. A blender—particularly a high-speed blender—yields a creamier texture and is ideal.

TAKE NOTE: You will only use half of the sauce for this recipe. To freeze the extra sauce, let it cool and then transfer it to an airtight container; it will keep for up to 3 months.

This recipe is an homage to the celebrated beet- and ricotta-stuffed ravioli with butter sauce and poppy seeds from the venerable Al Di La Trattoria in Park Slope, Brooklyn. The dish is simply unforgettable. I've used the flavors that stand in my mind to develop this velvety beet-based pasta sauce with lemon and ricotta. It is easy to prepare and the result is strikingly beautiful and bright.

FOR THE SAUCE

About 1¾ pounds beets, scrubbed and trimmed (see Ingredient Info)

6 garlic cloves, unpeeled

3 tablespoons olive oil

1 teaspoon fine sea salt

2 tablespoons freshly squeezed lemon juice plus 1 teaspoon finely grated lemon zest

1 cup whole-milk or cashew-milk ricotta cheese

FOR THE PASTA

2 to 3 tablespoons unsalted butter

1 teaspoon poppy seeds

¾ pound fusilli or other twisty or tube-shaped pasta

¾ to 1 cup frozen or fresh shelled peas (optional)

2 tablespoons minced fresh chives

2 packed cups baby arugula (about 2 ounces)

Finely grated Parmesan or Pecorino Romano cheese, for topping (optional)

Freshly ground black pepper (optional)

1 Roast the beets. Heat the oven to 400°F with a rack in the center. Wrap like-size beets in foil packets (wrap extra-large beets individually). Place the unpeeled garlic and 1 tablespoon of oil in the center of a small piece of foil, and fold up the foil to seal it. Place the beets and garlic on a sheet pan and roast until the garlic is soft, light golden, and fragrant, about 15 minutes. Remove the garlic packet from the oven and allow the garlic and oil to cool. Continue to roast the beets until they are tender through the middle—a paring knife should pierce the center without resistance—60 to 75 minutes for medium to large beets, up to 90 minutes for extra-large beets.

(recipe continues)

2 Make the sauce. When the beets are cool enough to handle, trim the tops off and use your hands to rub off the skins. Quarter the beets and place them in a high-speed blender (preferred to produce the smoothest texture) or a food processor. Peel and trim the roasted garlic cloves and add them along with the garlic oil to the blender. Pulse or process the beets until they are coarsely broken down, about 8 times. Add the 2 remaining tablespoons of oil, the salt, and the lemon juice and blend until smooth, about 30 seconds. Add the ricotta and blend again until well incorporated and completely smooth, another 20 seconds. Divide the sauce into two equal portions and set one aside (see Take Note).

3 To make the pasta: Bring a pot of water to a boil and generously salt it so it tastes like the sea.

4 Meanwhile, melt the butter over medium heat until it foams. Add the poppy seeds and lemon zest and cook, carefully tilting and swirling the pan to toast the poppy seeds and ever so slightly lightly brown the butter in places, 30 seconds to 1 minute. Set aside on the stove but off the heat.

5 Set a colander inside a serving bowl (or a mixing bowl). Cook the pasta until about 2 minutes under al dente according to the package instructions—you want it to retain some toothsomeness. (Do not overcook the pasta!) Use a spider to drain the pasta into the colander and continue to boil the water. Reserve 1 cup of the pasta cooking water. Add the peas, if using, to the boiling water and cook for 60 to 90 seconds until warmed through. Use the spider to transfer the peas to a small bowl.

6 Drain the pot and return it to the stove over medium-low heat. Put the pasta in the pot with ¼ cup of the reserved cooking water and stir to combine. Add the beet sauce and stir until evenly combined and warmed through. Add more pasta water to loosen the sauce if you wish and stir in half the peas and 1 tablespoon of chives.

7 Dry the serving bowl, if necessary, and transfer the pasta to it. Top the pasta with the remaining peas. Drizzle the melted butter mixture over the pasta and top with the remaining chives, then the arugula. Top with the Parmesan and pepper if you wish. Serve immediately.

Broccoli Rabe Pesto
with Fettuccine and Chickpeas

MAKES ABOUT 1¼ CUPS
PESTO; SERVES 4 AS A MAIN

TAKE NOTE: Use this recipe as a guide to make pestos with other types of greens, mixing and matching as you wish. Kale, spinach, and Swiss chard are perfect contenders.

SWAP: No walnuts? Use pistachios or almonds instead.

BUTCHER TIP: Trim ½ inch off the ends of short bunches of broccoli rabe. At farmers markets you may find extra-large bunches with thicker and longer stems; trim off 1 to 2 inches.

Leafy broccoli rabe functions like basil here to make a rich and complex pesto-like sauce. Please don't let broccoli rabe's "bitter, spicy" reputation deter you. Blanching it mellows its profile and all the hallmarks of traditional pesto make this a crowd-pleaser.

Fine sea salt

8 ounces broccoli rabe, thick stems trimmed and leaves and stems cut into 2- to 3-inch pieces (see Butcher Tip)

¾ pound fettuccine or other long pasta

1 medium garlic clove

⅓ cup plus ¼ cup walnut halves, toasted, ¼ cup chopped and reserved for topping

⅛ teaspoon crushed red pepper flakes

⅓ cup to ½ cup extra-virgin olive oil

2 ounces finely grated Parmesan or Pecorino Romano cheese

Freshly ground black pepper

1 cup canned chickpeas, drained and rinsed

---

1 Set a colander in the sink. Bring a large pot of water to a boil and generously salt it until it tastes like the sea. Carefully add the broccoli rabe and boil until just tender, 2 to 3 minutes, then transfer it with a spider to the colander. (Keep the water boiling for the pasta.) Rinse the broccoli rabe under cold water and drain, then squeeze to release excess water and let stand.

2 Add the pasta to the boiling water and cook it until just shy of al dente, according to the package instructions.

3 Meanwhile, add the garlic to a large food processor and process on high until it is completely broken down. Add ⅓ cup of walnuts and the red pepper flakes and pulse until finely chopped. Add the drained broccoli rabe and pulse about 5 times until roughly chopped. Add ⅓ cup of oil and process until the broccoli rabe is very finely chopped and the whole mixture is well blended. Scrape down the sides of the bowl. Add all but a couple of generous tablespoons of the Parmesan, then blend until just combined. Adjust salt and add black pepper to taste, then add another 1 or 2 tablespoons of oil to taste and to reach your preferred texture. Place 1 cup of the pesto in a large shallow pasta bowl, reserving about ¼ cup.

4 Reserve 1 cup of the pasta cooking water. Drop the chickpeas in the boiling water. After 15 seconds, drain the pasta and chickpeas. Immediately add the pasta and chickpeas to the pesto in the large bowl and toss to combine. Add ¼ cup of the pasta water to start, then more if needed, to loosen the pesto and coat the pasta well. Top with the reserved Parmesan, the reserved chopped walnuts, some black pepper, and more pesto if you like.

5

STEAKS. FRITTERS. MEATBALLS. SHEET PAN MEALS.

The Steak

A thick or thin cut of vegetable, roasted or grilled or breaded and pan-fried, the Steak is a classic entrée made modern that you can dig into with a fork and knife.

GOOD VEGETABLES FOR STEAKS: beets, broccoli, cauliflower, celery root, eggplant, kohlrabi, romanesco, rutabaga, tomatoes, butternut squash (see the Butternut Squash Steak Sandwich on page 102)

BEST TECHNIQUES FOR VEGETABLE STEAKS: Peel and/or trim fibrous, dry parts and skin with a vegetable peeler or sharp chef's knife. Use a sharp chef's knife to cut the steaks into thick slabs.

For broccoli, cauliflower, and romanesco: Cut ¾- to 1-inch slabs lengthwise through the crown and stem. For eggplant (¾ pound to 1 pound each), halve lengthwise through the stem end and make several deep slashes ½ inch apart diagonally across the flesh, going two-thirds down. For butternut squash, peel and cut ½-inch-thick slabs out of the neck of the squash (reserve the bulb for another use). Brush these thick cuts with oil and roast until tender at a high temperature to get nice browning.

For roots and kohlrabi: Peel and cut ½-inch-thick rounds. Brush with oil and roast at 400°F until just tender, then grill or dredge in a crisp breading and pan-fry until crispy.

For tomatoes: Who says a steak has to be cooked? Cut thick slabs of big height-of-season heirloom or beefsteak varieties with a serrated knife and serve raw with your best olive oil, herb oil, or House Lemon Vinaigrette (page 21), Lemon-Feta Vinaigrette (see page 34), or Basil Pesto (see page 59). Add flaky sea salt and Crispy Garlic Breadcrumbs or a salad of delicate greens on top.

TIPS AND TAKEAWAYS

- Serve steaks with a salad or sauce on top or pair them with something starchy like potatoes, rice, or your favorite whole grain.

- Steaks love sauces with body and bold flavor. Try Basil Pesto (page 59), Red Pepper Pesto (page 230), Broccoli Rabe and Walnut Pesto (see page 193), or other vegetable pestos (see page 186); salsas such as Avocado-Corn Salsa (page 140), Salsa Verde (page 252) and Peach Salsa (page 122); and vegetable sauces such as Lemon-Beet Sauce (see page 190) and Cucumber-Dill Yogurt (page 219). See also the sauces shared in this section: Orange Beurre Blanc (page 197) and Lemon-Cashew Aioli (page 203)

- Vegetables steaks are extra-tender, so make sure to add a crunchy, crisp component—like nuts, seeds, toasted breadcrumbs (page 79), or Frico (page 17)—or a raw component like arugula, cabbage, frisee, hearty or micro greens, chopped lettuces, or radicchio—to the dish for balance.

- To reheat steaks, place them on a sheet pan in a 425°F oven for 10 to 12 minutes until crisp on the outside and hot through the center.

Macadamia-Crusted Kohlrabi
with Orange Beurre Blanc

MAKES 12 TO 14 STEAKS:
SERVES 4 AS A MAIN

**HOW TO CUT
KOHLRABI STEAKS:**

1. Snap off and trim any stems attached to the bulb. Cut a thin slice from the top and bottom of the bulb to create a flat surface on each end.

2. Rest the kohlrabi on its broadest cut end. Working from top to bottom and following the curve of the bulb, slide your knife under the skin to peel it and remove any fibrous underlying flesh. If it still seems tough in places, shave it with a vegetable peeler until you reach the pale, crisp flesh.

3. Place the kohlrabi upright on its widest cut surface and slice vertically into ½-inch thick rounds (see illustration).

Kohlrabi doesn't get the attention it deserves, I think, because it doesn't come with instructions for what to do with it. Cut into rounds, roasted, then breaded with a macadamia nut crust and pan-fried, it is sweet with subtle brininess almost like a fillet of something that came from the sea (a revelation, for sure). This vegetable steak is delicious with steamed jasmine rice and a tangy orange butter sauce to top it off. For the sauce, it's best to prep all of the ingredients in advance. Keep everything but the butter by the stove so it's within reach; store the butter pieces in the fridge until the last second.

FOR THE KOHLRABI STEAKS

1¾ pounds kohlrabi bulbs, trimmed, peeled, and cut into ½-inch-thick rounds

Extra-virgin olive oil, for coating and pan-frying

Fine sea salt

Scant 1 cup salted macadamia nuts

¾ cup panko breadcrumbs

½ cup finely grated Parmesan cheese

1 cup all-purpose flour

2 large eggs

¼ teaspoon freshly ground black pepper

FOR THE ORANGE BEURRE BLANC

1 small shallot, minced

3 tablespoons dry white wine

2 tablespoons white wine vinegar

2 tablespoons shaken heavy cream

8 tablespoons (1 stick) unsalted butter, cut into 8 to 10 pieces and chilled

1 teaspoon orange zest

Fine sea salt

FOR SERVING

Steamed jasmine rice

Chopped fresh parsley, chives, or cilantro (optional)

1 Heat the oven to 400°F and set a rack in the middle position. Place a wire rack topped with a couple of paper towels (or a clean dish towel) near the stovetop.

2 Make the kohlrabi steaks. Brush both sides of the kohlrabi steaks evenly with about 1½ tablespoons oil and season lightly with salt. Spread the steaks out in an even layer on a sheet pan or two. (If using two pans, evenly space the racks in the upper and lower parts of the oven.) Roast the steaks for about

(recipe continues)

15 minutes until just about tender. Flip the steaks with a spatula and cook for another 3 to 5 minutes until they are browning and tender but not overly soft. Remove the steaks from the oven. If they appear oily, transfer them to the towel-lined rack and flip them as necessary to blot some oil; let stand until they are cool enough to handle. Move the oven rack to the lower-middle position and reduce the oven temperature to 200°F.

3 Pulse and process the macadamia nuts in a food processor until they break down into a fine crumble. (Don't overprocess them into a paste.) Transfer them to a shallow bowl and stir in the panko breadcrumbs and Parmesan.

4 Set up an assembly line to dredge and coat the steaks: Pour the flour onto a plate. Crack the eggs into a shallow bowl, add ¼ teaspoon pepper, then beat with a fork. Set the shallow bowl with the nut–panko mixture beside the eggs. Place an empty plate at the end of the line.

5 Working one at a time, dip a steak into the flour to coat both sides, gently shaking to release excess, then dip into the egg to coat, allowing excess to drip off. Gently drop the steak into the nut–panko mixture, sprinkling and pressing the crumbs on both sides to evenly coat and adhere. Carefully lift the fully coated steak and transfer it to the empty plate. Repeat to dredge the remaining steaks.

6 Fry the steaks. Replace the towels on the wire rack if needed. Heat a scant ½ cup oil in a large skillet over medium-high heat until it just begins to shimmer. Add enough steaks to fit comfortably without crowding, and cook until both sides are golden brown, about 2 minutes per side. (Reduce the heat as needed if the steaks are browning too quickly.) Transfer them as they finish to the towel-lined rack. Repeat with the second batch, adding oil and adjusting heat as needed. Once the steaks are finished cooking, carefully discard the towels. Spread out the kohlrabi on the wire rack, set the rack inside a sheet pan, and transfer to the oven to keep warm.

7 Make the Orange Beurre Blanc. Combine the shallot, wine, and vinegar in a small saucepan and bring to a boil over medium heat. Immediately reduce the heat to medium low and simmer until there's roughly 1 to 2 teaspoons of liquid left in the pan, 3 to 5 minutes. Whisk in the cream. Quickly grab the butter from the fridge. Whisking vigorously and continuously, add the butter 1 piece at a time until well incorporated and smooth. (Each addition of butter should take 20 to 30 seconds of whisking until it melts into the sauce.) Continue to cook, whisking constantly, until the sauce thickens, another 1 to 2 minutes. Remove the pan from the heat and stir in the orange zest and salt to taste.

8 Serve the steaks immediately on individual plates with a couple of generous spoonfuls of sauce and the steamed rice. Top with fresh herbs if using.

To reheat the steaks, see Tips and Takeaways on page 196.

Cauliflower Steaks
with Pickled Pepper Relish and Arugula Salad

MAKES 6 STEAKS;
SERVES 4 AS A MAIN

PREP TIP: Make the salad dressing and start the pickled pepper relish before you put the steaks into the oven so that everything is ready as soon as the steaks finish cooking.

ALL PLANTS: The goat cheese is optional, as is the honey (feel free to use maple syrup or agave instead).

BUTCHER TIP: I call for two medium to large heads (1½ to 2 pounds each) of cauliflower to ensure a yield of at least three sturdy steaks each. (Cuts along the sides of the crown don't always hold together well.) If you are looking for one or two portions out of this recipe, use just one large 2-pound head of cauliflower. Reserve uncooked extra, "fallen" cauliflower florets for other recipes. See page 200 for how to cut cauliflower steaks.

This is a golden and delicious cauliflower steak that you serve hot, right out of the oven, with an arugula salad piled high on top. It's my fork-and-knife take on a warm cauliflower salad by chef John Little. The combo of cauliflower, pickled pepper, and peppery arugula is simply outstanding.

FOR THE PICKLED PEPPER RELISH

½ medium onion, ⅛-inch diced

1 medium red bell pepper, ⅛-inch diced

1 small yellow or orange bell pepper, ⅛-inch diced

1 jalapeño, seeded, ⅛-inch diced

2 tablespoons apple cider vinegar

1 tablespoon plus 1 teaspoon sugar

½ teaspoon celery seeds (optional)

¼ teaspoon fine sea salt

FOR THE CAULIFLOWER STEAKS

2 medium to large heads of cauliflower (see Butcher Tip)

About 3 tablespoons extra-virgin olive oil

Fine sea salt and freshly ground black pepper

FOR THE SALAD

1 tablespoon white wine vinegar

1 teaspoon freshly grated lemon zest

1 tablespoon freshly squeezed lemon juice

1 tablespoon honey

1 teaspoon Dijon mustard

Fine sea salt and freshly ground black pepper

¼ cup extra-virgin olive oil

2 teaspoons fresh thyme leaves, minced

6 to 7 cups baby arugula or to taste

About ¾ cup freshly crumbled goat cheese (3 ounces), optional

1 Heat the oven to 475°F with one rack on the lowest shelf and another in the top third of the oven.

2 Make the pepper relish. Combine the onion, peppers, apple cider vinegar, sugar, celery seeds, and salt in a small saucepan over medium heat. Bring the mixture to a simmer and cook, stirring occasionally, until the onion and peppers are tender and the pan is dry, about 12 minutes. Remove the pan from the heat to cool briefly or completely.

3 Meanwhile, cut the cauliflower into 1-inch-thick steaks to make at least 3 steaks per head (see Butcher Tip). These cuts may be held together precariously, so use a wide spatula to transfer the steaks off your board and to two sheet pans (to prevent crowding).

(recipe continues)

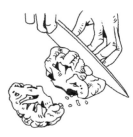

Cut the stalk flush with
the base of the crown.
Make sure not to cut into
any part of the core that
is attached to the florets.
Stand the cauliflower
upright. Cut 1-inch-thick
slices from the crown
down through the core.

4 Brush the steaks evenly on both sides with the oil and season generously with salt and pepper, carefully turning them to ensure the oil gets in between any grooves of the stalk. When the relish is ready or "working," place the steaks in the oven. Roast the steaks, turning them halfway through cooking with a wide metal spatula and rotating the pans between racks, until they are nicely browned on both sides and tender, but not overly soft or falling apart, 17 to 20 minutes.

5 Meanwhile, make the salad dressing. Whisk together the white wine vinegar, lemon zest, lemon juice, honey, Dijon mustard, ¼ teaspoon salt, and ¼ teaspoon pepper in a small bowl. Stream in the oil while mixing constantly and vigorously until the mixture emulsifies. Whisk in the thyme.

6 Place the arugula in a large bowl and add just enough dressing to lightly coat the leaves, tossing to combine. Stir in half the cooled pickled pepper relish. Adjust the dressing, salt, and pepper to taste. Set aside.

7 When the steaks are ready, remove them from the oven and use the wide spatula to transfer them carefully to plates or a serving platter. Top each with a generous portion of salad, some of the remaining relish, and crumbled goat cheese (if using). Serve hot.

To reheat the steaks, see Tips and Takeaways on page 196.

Pan-Fried Celery Root Cutlets
with Lemon-Cashew Aioli

MAKES 8 TO 10 CUTLETS;
SERVES 4 AS A MAIN

Dredge slabs of celery root in flour, egg, and breadcrumbs, then fry them in oil. The result is a crisp-on-the-outside, tender-on-the-inside root steak—a great idea from Joshua McFadden, in his *Six Seasons* cookbook. I think this version calls for for a squeeze of lemon juice, a sprinkle of flaky sea salt, and my Lemon-Cashew Aioli. A couple of spoonfuls of sweet relish will punch the aioli up to tartar sauce status—you can add it or not. (It's so good though, I recommend it!)

(recipe continues)

BUTCHER TIP: See page 197 for how to cut a root into steaks.

HOW TO PEEL CELERY ROOT:

Cut off the top, stem end, just under any leafy stalks (if present). Cut off the gnarly root end. Stand the root upright on its broadest cut surface. Slide your knife down the side of the root, just under the skin. Follow the curve of the root, turning as you go to remove all of the skin. Go back around with your knife or a vegetable peeler to remove any skin burrowed into the flesh.

2 pounds celery root (3 medium), trimmed, peeled, and cut into ½-inch rounds

Extra-virgin olive oil, for coating and pan-frying

Fine sea salt

1 cup all-purpose flour

2 eggs

1 cup panko breadcrumbs

½ teaspoon freshly ground black pepper

Flaky sea salt, such as Maldon

½ cup packed fresh flat-leaf parsley, chopped, for topping (optional)

Lemon wedges

Lemon-Cashew Aioli (recipe follows)

1 Heat the oven to 400°F with a rack in the center position. Place a wire rack topped with a couple of paper towels (or a clean dish towel) near the stovetop.

2 Brush both sides of the celery root cutlets evenly with oil (about 1½ tablespoons in total) and season lightly with fine sea salt. Spread the cutlets out in an even layer on a sheet pan or two. (If using two pans, evenly space the racks in the upper and lower parts of the oven.) Roast the cutlets until just tender, but not overly soft, about 15 minutes. Remove the cutlets from the oven, transfer them to the towel-lined rack, and flip them as necessary to blot some oil; let stand until they are cool enough to handle. Move the oven rack to the lower-middle position and reduce the oven temperature to 200°F.

3 Meanwhile, set up an assembly line to dredge and coat the cutlets: Pour the flour onto a plate. Crack the eggs into a shallow bowl and beat them with a fork. Place the panko in another shallow bowl and combine with the pepper. Place an empty plate at the end of the line.

4 Working one at a time, dip a cutlet into the flour to coat both sides, gently shaking to release excess, then dip into the egg, allowing excess to drip off. Gently drop the cutlet into the breadcrumbs, sprinkling and pressing the breadcrumbs on both sides to evenly adhere. Carefully lift the cutlet and transfer it to the empty plate. Repeat to dredge the remaining cutlets.

5 Replace the towels on the wire rack if needed. Heat a scant ½ cup oil in a medium skillet over medium-high heat until it just begins to shimmer. Add 4 to 5 cutlets or enough to fit comfortably without crowding, and cook until both sides are golden brown, 2 to 3 minutes per side. (Reduce the heat, as needed, if the cutlets are browning too quickly.) Transfer them as they finish to the towel-lined rack and season lightly with flaky sea salt. Add more oil to the skillet if needed and repeat with the second batch. Once the cutlets are finished cooking, carefully peel back and remove the towels and spread out the cutlets on the wire rack. Place the rack inside the previously used sheet pan and transfer to the oven to keep warm until ready to serve.

6 Serve the cutlets hot and crispy with a wedge of lemon and Lemon-Cashew Aioli for topping.

To reheat the steaks, see Tips and Takeaways on page 196.

Lemon-Cashew Aioli

MAKES ABOUT 1 CUP

1 cup raw cashews

¾ cup boiling water

¾ cup water

1½ tablespoons freshly squeezed
   lemon juice

½ teaspoon tamari or soy sauce

¼ teaspoon fine sea salt

1 tablespoon minced shallot

1 small to medium garlic clove,
   finely grated with a Microplane
   or minced

2 tablespoons sweet pickle relish
   (optional)

1 tablespoon finely chopped fresh
   flat-leaf parsley leaves

Place the cashews in a heat-safe bowl or in the base of a high-speed blender
and cover with the boiling water. Let stand for an hour and drain. (You can
let the cashews stand for less time, no problem. The sauce will be less smooth
and creamy, it but will still taste great.) Place the drained cashews back into
the blender with the water, lemon juice, tamari, and salt. Blend until smooth,
scraping down the side as needed and blending again until well incorporated.
Transfer the mixture to a small bowl and stir in the shallot, garlic, relish if you
are adding it, and the parsley. Adjust salt to taste. Cover and refrigerate until
ready to serve, up to 3 days.

The Fritter

The Fritter, a savory must-make vegetable cake, is made of shredded or finely chopped vegetables like carrots, broccoli, cauliflower, sweet potatoes, or zucchini; herbs; a little flour; and a binder like egg. Once pan-fried (or deep-fried) in oil they turn golden and crisp on the outside and tender on the inside. Serve them piping hot with a sauce and a salad. The technique is a gem.

GOOD VEGETABLES FOR FRITTERS: broccoli; carrots; cauliflower; celery root; corn; fava beans; hearty greens, such as collards, kale, mustard greens, and Swiss chard; parsnips; peas; potatoes; romanesco; tomatoes; sweet potatoes; zucchini

TIPS AND TAKEAWAYS

- Grate vegetables against the large holes of a box grater; shred them in a food processor with the shredding attachment; or finely chop them in a food processor or with a chef's knife.

- Don't let the batter sit for too long. Set up for frying before you add salt to the batter.

- Don't add flour all at once, just enough to soak up liquid and hold the batter together. Add more as needed for subsequent rounds of frying.

- The oil needs to be hot to properly crisp up the fritter's exterior. Check its readiness by dropping a pinch of batter into the oil. If it sizzles and bubbles, it is ready. If it falls flat, it's not, so wait a little longer or turn up the heat, reducing it later to prevent burning.

- Pay attention to the heat and adjust as needed. If the fritters start browning too fast, turn the heat down. If they aren't crisp enough, turn the heat up.

- Caution: Take special care when you add corn to fritters. The kernels will burst if they get too hot for too long.

- Keep fritters warm between batches: Transfer fritters to towels to absorb excess oil then hold them in a 200°F oven on a wire rack set in a sheet pan.

- Fritters are best served immediately, but you can refrigerate leftovers (completely cooled) in an airtight container for up to 2 days and reheat them with good results. To reheat, heat the oven to 425°F. Place the fritters on a sheet pan and heat until crisp on the outside and sizzling hot through the center, 8 to 10 minutes.

Carrot-Cilantro Fritters
with Tahini-Lime Yogurt Sauce

Simple and simply delicious, these fritters come together with a vegetable drawer mainstay and a cupful of fresh herbs. The Tahini-Lime Yogurt Sauce is made with always-on-hand refrigerated basics and adds another layer of bright, earthy, and tangy flavor. If preferred, a squeeze of lime (or lemon) will do just fine. Plan on two fritters per eater with a salad on the side or serve 3 fritters per person on their own. Thinly sliced avocado and a sprinkle of toasted sesame seeds are always excellent additions.

---

1 pound carrots, peeled and trimmed

½ large red onion, cut in half lengthwise

2 large eggs

½ cup all-purpose flour, plus more as needed

¼ teaspoon fine sea salt

¼ teaspoon freshly ground black pepper

1 tablespoon minced garlic

Heaping ½ cup freshly crumbled feta cheese (2 ounces)

1 cup loosely packed fresh cilantro leaves and thin stems, roughly chopped

⅓ cup plus 2 tablespoons extra-virgin olive oil, plus more as needed

1 lime, cut into wedges, for serving

Tahini-Lime Yogurt Sauce (page 207), for serving

---

1 Fit a food processor with a shredding disc. Cut the carrots crosswise to fit the feed tube. Place the carrot pieces horizontally on their sides in the feed tube and press down with the pusher and process. (One pound of carrots should yield about 4 cups.) Cut each onion half lengthwise and shred the quarters in the same fashion. Let the mixture stand briefly.

2 In a large bowl, lightly beat the eggs. Whisk in the flour, salt, and pepper until evenly combined. Stir in the shredded carrots and onion, then gently stir in the garlic, feta, and cilantro until just evenly combined. If the mixture appears watery, add more flour, a tablespoon at a time, until the mixture holds together.

3 Set a couple of paper towels or a clean kitchen towel on a wire cooling rack. Heat the oil in a medium nonstick or cast-iron skillet over medium-high heat. Drop a pinch of batter into the pan to test the oil—it should sizzle when it is ready.

4 Working in batches of four, use a spoon to scoop batter into a ⅓-cup measure, filling it just shy of level, then use the spoon to carefully drop the batter into the oil. Use the back of the spoon to shape and gently press down to slightly flatten

(recipe continues)

the mound of batter so it will cook evenly through the center. Cook the fritters until the underside is golden brown, about 3 minutes, then flip and cook until the other side is browned and crisp, about 3 minutes more, reducing the heat at any time if the fritters are browning too quickly. Transfer the cooked fritters to the prepared rack. Repeat with the remaining batter, adding a touch more flour if the batter has become watery, and reducing the heat as needed to make sure the fritters don't burn.

5 Serve hot with a lime wedge and/or Tahini-Lime Yogurt Sauce.

To store and reheat, see Tips and Takeaways on page 204.

Tahini-Lime Yogurt Sauce

MAKES ABOUT ½ CUP

1 small garlic clove

2 tablespoons freshly squeezed lime juice

¼ cup plain Greek yogurt

3 tablespoons tahini

2 tablespoons water

½ teaspoon fine sea salt

Use a Microplane to finely grate the garlic into a medium bowl. (If needed, use a garlic press.) Add the lime juice, then whisk in the yogurt, tahini, water, and salt until well blended. Refrigerate in an airtight container for up to 4 days.

Zucchini-Corn Fritters
with Ricotta and Simple Tomato-Basil Salad

**MAKES 10 FRITTERS;
SERVES 4 AS A MAIN**

TAKE NOTE: Flatten these fritters with the back of the scooping spoon to make sure there is more surface area to get nice and crispy.

INGREDIENT INFO: The corn kernels in these fritters can pop and burst if they get too hot for too long. Monitor and if you hear or see popping, reduce the heat as needed.

BUTCHER TIP: To shave the kernels off a cob of corn, see page 120.

This is a fritter for summer's bounty. Make sure to use fresh corn and small to medium zucchini (they won't be as watery) and squeeze as much liquid as possible out of the grated zucchini to keep the fritters from getting too soft on the inside. Stir together the batter just before frying and add more flour as the batter sits—just enough to hold it together.

---

1 pound zucchini

2 large eggs

2 cups raw sweet corn kernels (from 2 large ears; see Butcher Tip)

1 teaspoon ground cumin

¼ teaspoon crushed red pepper flakes

1 garlic clove, finely grated or minced

¼ cup finely chopped sweet onion or shallot

1 tablespoon finely chopped fresh mint (6 to 8 mint leaves)

1 tablespoon roughly chopped fresh basil

½ cup to ¾ cup all-purpose flour

1 teaspoon fine sea salt

Canola or other neutral vegetable oil, for pan-frying

¾ cup whole-milk ricotta cheese

Simple Tomato-Basil Salad (recipe follows), optional

---

1 Heat the oven to 400°F with a rack in the middle position. Shred the zucchini on the large holes of a box grater (yield should be 4½ to 5 cups). Wrap the zucchini in a lightweight kitchen towel. Repeatedly squeeze out water from the zucchini over the sink or a bowl until you cannot release any more liquid.

2 Whisk the eggs in a large bowl and add the zucchini, corn, cumin, red pepper flakes, garlic, onion, mint, and basil. Stir well to incorporate the eggs, then stir in the ½ cup flour and the salt.

3 Place a couple of paper towels or a clean kitchen towel on top of a wire cooling rack. Heat ¼ cup oil in a large skillet over medium-high heat until it begins to shimmer, then reduce the heat to medium.

4 Working in batches of no more than four, use a large spoon to fill a ⅓-cup measure with the batter, then use the spoon to help release the batter directly into the oil. Use the back of the cup measure to flatten the batter in to discs slightly more than ¼ inch. Fry the fritters until they are golden brown and crispy on the edges, 2 to 3 minutes per side. Transfer them to the rack. Repeat with the remaining batter, reducing the heat to low between batches, adding oil as needed, and removing any stray corn kernels from the pan. If the batter becomes runny, add 1 to 2 tablespoons flour and stir to combine.

5 Transfer the fritters to a sheet pan and bake until they are hot, 10 to 12 minutes. Serve immediately, 2 to 3 per eater, topped with a generous dollop of ricotta and a scoop of Simple Tomato-Basil Salad.

To store and reheat, see Tips and Takeaways on page 204.

Simple Tomato-Basil Salad

MAKES ABOUT 4 CUPS

4 cups ½-inch diced summer tomatoes, or a mix of cherry tomatoes, halved or quartered

Balsamic vinegar

Flaky sea salt, such as Maldon

Freshly ground black pepper

2 tablespoons chopped fresh basil leaves

Extra-virgin olive oil

In a medium bowl, gently toss the tomatoes with 2 teaspoons of vinegar, ¼ teaspoon salt, ⅛ teaspoon pepper, and the basil. Add 2 tablespoons olive oil and toss again to evenly combine. Adjust salt and pepper to taste, and add more vinegar and/or olive oil if needed.

Broccoli Fritters

with Lemon Yogurt and Simple Orange-Fennel Salad

MAKES 13 TO 14 FRITTERS;
SERVES 4 AS A MAIN

TAKE NOTE: This batter may seem like it isn't holding together at first. Use your scooping spoon to release any batter sticking to the sides of your portion cup and then, if needed, use it to keep each fritter contained in a mostly round shape. Once the cheese begins to melt they will hold together beautifully.

BUTCHER TIP: See page 167 for how to prep broccoli.

Broccoli is made for fritters. Serve these with the Lemon Yogurt or just top with a sprinkle of flaky sea salt and a squeeze of lemon. To elevate the fritters and make a fuller meal, I pair them with the Simple Orange-Fennel Salad. The brightness of the citrus plus the fresh, raw bite of the fennel balances the richness of the fried and cheesy fritters.

FOR THE LEMON YOGURT

1 cup Greek yogurt

1 teaspoon freshly grated lemon zest

1 tablespoon freshly squeezed lemon juice

Fine sea salt and freshly ground
    black pepper

1 garlic clove

1 tablespoon minced fresh chives or
    other fresh herbs (optional)

FOR THE FRITTERS

2 large eggs

½ cup all-purpose flour

Fine sea salt and freshly ground
    black pepper

⅛ teaspoon cayenne pepper

2 large garlic cloves

1 teaspoon lemon zest

1¼ cups coarsely grated Gruyère cheese
    or aged Cheddar

1¼ pounds bite-size broccoli florets and
    stems (about 8 cups; see Butcher Tip)

Extra-virgin olive oil, for pan-frying

Flaky sea salt, such as Maldon

Simple Orange-Fennel Salad
    (recipe follows)

---

1 Make the yogurt. In a small bowl, whisk together the yogurt, lemon zest, lemon juice, and ¼ teaspoon fine sea salt. Grate the garlic clove with a Microplane directly into the yogurt then whisk it in—reserve the Microplane to use for the garlic in the fritters. Adjust salt and add pepper to taste. Stir in the chives if you are adding them. Cover and refrigerate until ready to serve.

2 Make the fritters. Set a steamer in a medium pot and fill with enough water to just reach the bottom of the steamer. Cover with a tight-fitting lid and bring the water to a boil over medium-high heat.

3 Meanwhile, lightly beat the eggs in a large bowl. Gently whisk in the flour, 1 teaspoon fine sea salt, ¼ teaspoon black pepper, and the cayenne pepper until a loose but thick paste forms. Grate the garlic cloves with the Microplane directly into the batter. With a rubber spatula, stir in the grated garlic, lemon zest, and Gruyère until just combined.

4 Steam the broccoli for 3 to 5 minutes until crisp-tender (not mushy!). Let cool briefly, then transfer to a food processor, in two rounds, and pulse until roughly chopped into more uniformly small bean-size pieces, 3 to 4 one-second pulses. (Alternatively roughly chop it with a chef's knife.) Add the chopped broccoli to the batter in the large bowl and stir and fold well until just evenly combined.

5 Line a plate with paper towels and place it near the stovetop. If you would like to hold the fritters after frying and until serving, preheat an oven to 200°F.

6 Heat a large skillet over medium heat. Add 4 tablespoons olive oil. As soon as the oil begins to shimmer, scoop ¼-cup portions of the batter (with a ¼ cup measure) and carefully release it with a spoon into the oil. (Use the spoon to grab and add any batter sticking to the cup.) Use the back of the spoon to flatten and gently spread each fritter, 2½ to 3 inches in diameter. You should be able to fit 4 to 5 fritters in the skillet.

7 Fry the fritters in batches for 2 to 3 minutes on each side, tilting the pan every so often to evenly distribute the oil, until evenly browned and crisp on the outside and tender and cheesy within. Turn the heat down and transfer the fritters to the paper towels and sprinkle with flaky sea salt. Turn the heat back up to medium and add another 2 tablespoons or more of the oil as needed to coat the bottom of the pan with a thin layer. Repeat with the remaining batter in batches, adjusting the heat and cooking time as needed to prevent burning. To keep the fritters warm and crispy, transfer them to a cooling rack set in a sheet pan and place in the preheated oven until ready to serve. Serve with the Lemon Yogurt or lemon wedges and Simple Orange-Fennel Salad if you wish.

To store and reheat, see Tips and Takeaways on page 204.

Simple Orange-Fennel Salad

SERVES UP TO 4 AS A SIDE

BUTCHER TIPS: See page 40 for how to prep fennel; see page 33 for how to supreme an orange.

2 small to medium fennel bulbs, trimmed, washed well, and quartered

3 to 4 oranges supremed (see Butcher Tip), juices reserved

Fine sea salt and freshly ground black pepper

2 tablespoons extra-virgin olive oil, best quality if possible

Use a mandoline to thinly shave the fennel into ¹⁄₁₆- to ⅛-inch slices. Place the fennel in a medium-size bowl and combine with the supremed oranges and ¼ cup of the reserved orange juice. Season with ¼ teaspoon salt and ¼ teaspoon pepper. Toss gently to combine and let marinate for 5 minutes, tossing occasionally. Drizzle with the olive oil, gently toss to combine, and adjust salt and pepper to taste. Serve immediately for peak crispness, or cover and chill until ready to serve.

The "Meatball"

Lentils, black beans, and chickpeas (or really any legumes) with some grains, herbs, onions, and spices transform into plant-y, protein-rich "meat." It's impressive, you'll see. Meaty, saucy, and just fun to eat, the Meatball delivers on it all.

GOOD SAUCES FOR MEATBALLS:

• Maple-Lime-Chipotle Crema (page 91), Cucumber-Dill Yogurt (page 219), Red Pepper Pesto (page 230), Lemon-Cashew Aioli (page 203), Tahini Sauce (page 217), Simple Tomato Sauce (page 242), spicy tomato sauce (see page 105), Tahini-Lime Yogurt Sauce (page 207), Secret Sauce (page 95)

METHODS FOR MEATBALLS:

• 2 tablespoons of "meat" makes the perfect-size meatball. A measuring spoon or small ice cream scoop will help to evenly portion, but don't worry this doesn't have to be exact.

• Use a light touch—never completely or forcefully squeeze the batter as you form meatballs. Lightly squeeze, press, and shape.

MAKING MEATBALL SHAPES:

A ball: Gently squeeze and press the batter with your fingertips into the palm of your hand as you form it into a roughly 1½-inch ball.

A disc: Gently press and shape the batter into disc-like patties, about ¾ inch thick..

A torpedo: Using your fingers and palm, gently shape the batter into a cylindrical football shape about 1 × 2 inches.

TIPS AND TAKEAWAYS

• All meatballs need sauce, lots of sauce. For just-out-of-the-oven meatballs, it's best to spoon sauce over the top (to keep them from falling apart). Cooled and reheated meatballs can be cooked in sauce.

• Store leftover cooked meatballs in a single layer on a plate or quarter sheet pan and wrap tightly. Refrigerate for 3 to 4 days or freeze for up to 3 months.

• It's easy to reheat cooked meatballs: Place them on a oiled or parchment-lined sheet pan in a 375°F oven for about 10 minutes until hot through the middle and crisp on the outside.

• You can freeze uncooked shaped meatballs and bake them from frozen following recipe instructions exactly, adding a couple more minutes only if needed to heat all the way through. Avoid freezing uncooked meatballs if you want to eventually fry them (like the falafel on page 216). Reheat frozen cooked meatballs in the oven at 375°F for 10 to 15 minutes on each side.

• Extra Credit: Scoop and portion 2 tablespoons of the sweet potato or mushroom-lentil burger "dough" on pages 90 and 93. Shape into round meatballs. Place the meatballs on an oiled sheet pan and bake at 375°F for about 15 minutes on each side. Serve with a sauce and a handful of arugula or chopped spinach instead of a bun.

Spaghetti and Italian-Style Meatballs

MAKES 26 TO 30
MEATBALLS; SERVES
UP TO 6 WITH SPAGHETTI

PREP TIPS:

- **Fresh Mushrooms:** This isn't the time to rinse or dunk mushrooms under water. It's important to avoid adding moisture to the meatballs. Trim any dry ends of the mushrooms. Dampen a tea towel or paper towel and rub off dirt to clean them.

- **Black Beans:** Spread out the rinsed black beans on a sheet pan lined with paper towels or a clean kitchen towel. Place another towel on top to absorb excess water. Let stand to dry.

MAKE AHEAD: Uncooked meatballs freeze well. Freeze them on a sheet pan, spaced apart. Once completely frozen, transfer them to a freezer-safe storage container and store for up to 3 months. You can bake directly from frozen, adding up to a few extra minutes if needed.

These Italian-style meatless meatballs are strongly reminiscent of the real thing. As a vegetable lover, I think they are even better with a base of mushrooms, black beans, bulgur, and ricotta and seasoned with classics—garlic, onion, oregano, fennel seeds, and Parmesan. They are made to serve childhood memories when piled on top of saucy spaghetti and offer equal comfort rolled in a Parmesan–breadcrumb crust and topped with sauce and more Parmesan (see Variation).

FOR THE MEATBALLS

¼ cup #1 fine-grain or #2 medium-grain bulgur wheat

¾ cup water

0.2 ounce dried porcini mushrooms or dried shiitake mushrooms in a pinch

¾ teaspoon fennel seeds

3 small to medium garlic cloves

½ small red onion, cut into 6 chunks

8 ounces cremini or white button mushrooms, cleaned, trimmed, and quartered (see Prep Tips)

1 can (15½ ounces) black beans, drained, well rinsed, and lightly patted dry

⅓ cup Italian-style breadcrumbs

¼ cup whole-milk ricotta cheese

¼ cup finely grated Parmesan cheese

1 large egg, lightly beaten

1 teaspoon dried oregano

¾ teaspoon fine sea salt

¼ teaspoon freshly ground black pepper

Extra-virgin olive oil

FOR SPAGHETTI AND MEATBALLS

Fine sea salt

¾ pound to 1 pound dry spaghetti pasta

3½ to 5 cups Simple Tomato Sauce (page 242) or favorite store-bought sauce

⅔ cup fresh basil leaves, roughly chopped, for serving

Coarsely grated Parmesan cheese, for serving

1 Make the meatballs. Combine the bulgur and water in a small saucepan and bring to a boil over medium-high heat. Reduce the heat to low, cover, and simmer for 10 minutes; remove from the heat. Let stand, covered, for 5 minutes. Fluff with a fork and cool. (If any water remains, cook off until the bulgur is dry and fluffy. Wet bulgur will ruin the texture of the meatballs.)

(recipe continues)

2 In a food processor set with the standard blade attachment, pulse and blend the dried mushrooms until finely ground into a coarse powder. Allow the "dust" to settle before removing the lid. (The porcini or shiitake should yield about 1 tablespoon of coarse powder.) Add the fennel seeds and pulse and blend briefly to coarsely chop them. Add the garlic and blend until completely minced. Add the onion and pulse 6 times, in 1-second intervals, until they are just finely chopped, not completely broken down. Scrape down the sides of the bowl and add the cremini mushrooms. Pulse about 8 times, in 1-second intervals, until they are finely chopped. Transfer the mixture to a large bowl.

3 Place the black beans in the food processor. Briefly pulse 5 times, in ½-second intervals. Scrape down the sides of the bowl and pulse one more time, until coarsely chopped—watch this closely to prevent the mixture from becoming overly pureed and mushy. Transfer the black beans to the large bowl and stir to evenly combine with the mushroom mixture. Add the cooked and cooled bulgur, the breadcrumbs, ricotta, Parmesan, egg, oregano, salt, and pepper and stir well until evenly combined.

4 Shape and cook the meatballs. Heat the oven to 375°F. Evenly oil two sheet pans with 1 tablespoon of oil each. (If your sheet pans are overly worn, you may want to line them with parchment paper and then oil the parchment to prevent sticking.) One at a time, spoon about 2 tablespoons of the mixture into your hands and very gently squeeze and press it into a ball—see page 212. (The mixture should yield 26 to 30 balls, about 1½ inches each.) Transfer the meatballs to the prepared pans, evenly spacing them apart. Bake for about 15 minutes until a crust forms on the underside, then carefully flip them and bake for another 13 to 15 minutes until well browned and a nice crust forms on both sides.

6 Meanwhile, prepare the pasta. Bring a pot of water to a boil and generously salt it until it tastes like the sea. Cook the spaghetti to just under al dente, according to the package instructions. Drain the pasta and return the pot to the stove.

7 Pour 2½ to 3 cups of the tomato sauce into the pot and immediately return the spaghetti to the pot. Toss the spaghetti and sauce until the sauce is just warmed through. Plate the spaghetti, keeping the pot on the stove. Add the remaining sauce to the pot and heat until it begins to simmer. Top the spaghetti with the cooked meatballs, then top with a generous spoonful of sauce. Finish with fresh basil and freshly grated Parmesan cheese. Serve any remaining sauce at the table.

To store and reheat, see Tips and Takeaways on page 212.

VARIATION

To bread the meatballs and serve simply with sauce, combine ½ cup Italian-style breadcrumbs and ¼ cup finely grated Parmesan cheese and gently roll the shaped uncooked meatballs in the mixture. Carefully press to adhere. Bake the meatballs as directed in Step 4. Serve over warmed sauce and spoon some on top. Finish with shaved ricotta salata or Parmesan and torn basil.

Chickpea Falafel
with Tahini Sauce and Simple Tomato-Cucumber Salad

MAKES 27 TO 30 FALAFEL; SERVES 5 TO 6

PREP TIP: Shape the "dough" into disc-like patties to produce a more uniformly crispy result when shallow-frying. If you shape it into balls, plan to move them around in the oil to ensure all sides get crispy.

MAKE AHEAD: You can make the "dough" ahead and store it in the fridge for up to 3 days before frying (or even shape the falafel and store them covered tightly for the same amount of time). Fry the falafel right before serving.

Believe it or not, you can make falafel—a vegetable "meatball"—at home and it's the kind of dish that you can add to your regular line-up. You just need to plan ahead to soak the chickpeas overnight, and you can shape the falafel patties and hold them in the fridge for a couple of days before you cook them. When it's time to prep, your food processor will do most of the work for you. The cooking method that I call for (shallow-frying) is not as fussy as it may seem and the end result is so much better for it—crispy on the outside and soft and delicate on the inside.

2 cups dried chickpeas, rinsed and soaked (see Note on page 217)

5 small to medium garlic cloves, peeled and trimmed

½ large onion, quartered

1 cup fresh cilantro leaves, loosely packed

1 cup fresh flat-leaf parsley leaves

¼ cup fresh mint leaves (optional)

1¼ teaspoons ground cumin

½ teaspoon ground coriander

¼ teaspoon cayenne pepper

2 teaspoons fine sea salt

2 cups canola oil, plus more as needed

Tahini Sauce (recipe follows), for serving

Simple Tomato-Cucumber Salad (recipe follows), for serving

Warm pita, for serving

1 Drain and rinse the chickpeas well. Place the garlic in the bowl of a large food processor and process until it is minced. Add the onion, chickpeas, cilantro, parsley, mint if you are using it, cumin, coriander, cayenne pepper, and salt. Pulse in 4-second intervals to chop and incorporate all the ingredients, scraping down the side of the bowl as needed. Continue pulsing and processing on high, and scraping down the sides as needed, until the mixture is uniformly minced. Stop as soon as the mixture resembles a coarse paste that holds together. You don't want to produce an actual smooth paste. (You can process in two batches if needed then stir together evenly in a large bowl.)

2 Form the falafels. Line a baking sheet with parchment paper and set aside. Scoop a 2-tablespoon portion of the falafel mixture into your hand and gently press and shape it into a roughly ¾-inch-thick disc or 1½-inch ball (see page 212). Place the finished discs or balls on the prepared baking sheet. Repeat with the remaining "dough." (You can refrigerate uncooked falafel tightly covered with plastic wrap for up to 2 days.)

3 When you are ready to cook, heat the oven to 200°F. Set a wire cooling rack in a sheet pan and place the sheet pan in the oven.

4 Pour the oil into a large skillet and heat over high heat until an instant-read thermometer registers 350°F. Working in batches, fry the falafel, turning with a slotted spoon, until golden brown on each side, 2 to 3 minutes per side. You should be able to fit about 10 in the pan at a time. Adjust the heat as you cook and between batches to maintain between 350°F and 375°F and add more oil if needed. Use the slotted spoon to transfer the finished falafel to the rack in the oven.

5 Serve the warm falafel with Tahini Sauce, Simple Tomato-Cucumber Salad, and warm pita.

NOTE: Soak the chickpeas in a large bowl in enough water to cover by 2 to 3 inches, plus 2 tablespoons salt, overnight or up to 24 hours.

To store and reheat, see Tips and Takeaways on page 212.

Tahini Sauce

MAKES ABOUT 1 CUP

⅓ cup plain full-fat or low-fat yogurt (not Greek yogurt)

⅓ cup tahini

3 tablespoons freshly squeezed lemon juice

1 to 2 small garlic cloves, pressed or finely grated with a Microplane

Fine sea salt

3 to 4 tablespoons water

In a small food processor, blend together the yogurt, tahini, lemon juice, garlic, ½ teaspoon salt, and 3 tablespoons of water, scraping down the sides of the bowl and lid as needed until evenly incorporated and creamy. Add up to 1 more tablespoon of water, adding a little at a time, until you reach your desired consistency. Adjust salt to taste. (If you don't have a small food processor, whisk all of the ingredients together in a medium bowl, adjusting water and salt to taste.)

Simple Tomato-Cucumber Salad

SERVES 4 AS A SIDE

TAKE NOTE: Elevate this side salad to a main dish with additions: chopped romaine, chopped avocado, chickpeas, a grain like farro, bulgur, or spelt berries. Add or swap for the parsley, fresh mint, or dill.

2 cups cherry or grape tomatoes, quartered

3 mini cucumbers (such as Persian), quartered lengthwise and sliced into ¼-inch pieces

⅓ cup packed fresh flat-leaf parsley leaves, roughly chopped

2 large scallions, thinly sliced

Freshly squeezed lemon juice or red wine vinegar

2 tablespoons extra-virgin olive oil

Fine sea salt and freshly ground black pepper

In a medium bowl, combine the tomatoes, cucumbers, parsley, scallions, 1 tablespoon plus 2 teaspoons lemon juice, the oil, ½ teaspoon salt, and ¼ teaspoon pepper. Adjust the lemon juice, oil, salt, and pepper to taste.

Kofta-Style Meatballs
with Cucumber-Dill Yogurt

MAKES 24 TO 26
MEATBALLS;
SERVES 4 TO 5

TAKE NOTE:

- The lentil–millet mixture may feel overly wet and porridge-like when it first finishes cooking. That's okay. Spread out the mixture on a sheet pan or in a pie plate to cool, allowing moisture to evaporate.

- The Simple Tomato-Cucumber Salad on page 217 is an excellent, fresh side, too. If you have Chili Oil (page 6) on hand, drizzle a bit over the yogurt—or you could even brush some over the meatballs before serving.

Lentils, pine nuts, and millet—a protein-rich seed operating like a grain—form just the right filling for these deeply spiced, fully vegetable-based meatballs. Enjoy them straight out of the oven with generous spoonfuls of garlicky Cucumber-Dill Yogurt (think tzatziki). The meatballs and yogurt are a plentiful meal on their own, but you can add Crispy Roasted Potatoes (page 272) for a classic pairing.

4½ cups water

1 cup dried red lentils, picked through and rinsed

1 cup millet

Extra-virgin olive oil

1½ teaspoons fine sea salt

1 medium onion, finely chopped

1 teaspoon Aleppo pepper

1 teaspoon ground cumin

½ teaspoon ground allspice

¼ teaspoon ground cinnamon

¼ teaspoon ground sumac (optional)

¼ teaspoon freshly ground black pepper

2 garlic cloves, minced

¼ cup pine nuts

½ cup loosely packed fresh mint leaves, finely chopped

½ cup fresh flat-leaf parsley leaves and thin stems, finely chopped

Chili Oil (page 6), for brushing (optional)

Cucumber-Dill Yogurt (recipe follows), for serving

Crispy Roasted Potatoes (page 272), for serving (optional)

---

1 In a medium-size heavy saucepan or pot, combine the water and the lentils. Stir to break apart the lentils if they are sticking together and bring to a boil over high heat. As soon as the water comes to a boil, skim any foam off the top without taking too much water along with it. Add the millet, 3 tablespoons olive oil, and 1 teaspoon of salt and stir to combine. When the water returns to a boil, reduce the heat to maintain a low and steady simmer and cook, stirring occasionally, until the water has been absorbed and the lentils and millet are tender, 20 to 25 minutes. If there is excess liquid at this point, turn up the heat to medium, stir, and cook for another minute to cook off. Remove the pan from the heat and let cool briefly. The mixture will look like a thick porridge and will dry out a bit as it cools. Scoop out any liquid pooling in places, or stir it in and continue to cook for 2 minutes. If the consistency is extra loose, pour it out in a shallow bowl to cool.

2 Meanwhile, heat 2 tablespoons olive oil in a medium skillet over medium-high heat and add the onion, Aleppo pepper, cumin, allspice, cinnamon, sumac if you are using it, the black pepper, and ¼ teaspoon of salt. Cook, stirring frequently, for 3 to 5 minutes until the onion has softened a bit and the spices are fragrant. Stir in the garlic and pine nuts, reduce the heat to medium, and cook for about another 2 minutes until the garlic is well incorporated and the pine nuts are lightly toasted.

3 In a large bowl, combine the lentil-millet mixture with the onion, mint, parsley, and the remaining ¼ teaspoon of salt.

4 Form the meatballs. Line two sheet pans with parchment. Lightly coat the top with olive oil, about 2 teaspoons each, and place the trays on your work surface. Scoop a 2-tablespoon portion of the lentil mixture into the palm of your hand and gently press and shape it into a roughly 1- × 2-inch torpedo (see page 212). Place the finished meatball on the prepared sheet pan. Repeat with the remaining lentil mixture, spacing the meatballs apart so they are not crowded, no more than 16 per tray. (You can refrigerate the meatballs at this point, tightly covered with plastic wrap, overnight before baking.)

5 When you are ready to cook, heat the oven to 375°F with one rack in the upper third of the oven and one in the lower third.

6 Bake the meatballs for 15 minutes, carefully flip with a firm spatula, and cook on the second side until a crisp crust forms in places, another 10 to 12 minutes.

7 As soon as the meatballs come out of the oven, you can brush them with Chili Oil or olive oil if you would like (this is optional), and immediately serve with the Cucumber-Dill Yogurt (and the roasted potatoes if you wish).

To store and reheat, see Tips and Takeaways on page 212.

Cucumber-Dill Yogurt

MAKES ABOUT 2 CUPS

1 tablespoon freshly squeezed lemon juice, plus more as needed

1 small to medium garlic clove

2 cups full-fat or low-fat plain Greek yogurt

2 small Persian cucumbers, coarsely grated

⅓ cup fresh dill fronds, finely chopped

Fine sea salt and freshly ground black pepper

Best-quality olive oil or Chili Oil (page 6), for drizzling (optional)

Pour the lemon juice into a medium-size bowl and finely grate the garlic with a Microplane into the bowl. Stir to combine and let stand for 3 to 5 minutes. Stir in the yogurt, grated cucumbers, dill, ½ teaspoon salt, and a few twists of pepper. Adjust the salt, pepper, and lemon juice, if needed. Top with a drizzle of olive oil or chili oil as you wish. Chill for at least 30 minutes if possible (this improves the flavor), but don't fret if not.

The Grilled Vegetable Platter

Grilling vegetables concentrates their flavors and adds a smoky, charred aroma that creates complexity in any dish. So when you stack a platter full of them—layering in more flavor and texture, filling in every last gap with crudités, dips and spreads, a favorite cheese, and flatbread or crackers—a very special meal is born.

HOW TO BUILD A PLATTER

- **SELECT YOUR STAR:** Select a vegetable that stands on its own and that everyone at your table will love. Asparagus, avocado, broccoli, broccolini, cauliflower, corn, eggplant, mushrooms, and zucchini are always a hit.

- **ADD SECONDARY VEGETABLES:** Grill or serve raw for balance.

- **ADD OTHER GOODIES:** Offer a smaller quantity of each of the following ingredients in a supporting role.

  - Add dips, spreads, yogurt, or cheeses.

  - Top with olive oil, flaky sea salt, citrus juice and/or zest, wine vinegar, herbs to sprinkle over the top

  - Piles of flatbread (always flatbread), crostini, crackers, breadsticks, or steamed grain to serve on the side

TIPS AND TAKEAWAYS

- Get organized: For outdoor grilling, gather all of your ingredients, tools, supplies, and seasonings and use a sheet pan to transport them outside. (For indoor grilling, place everything beside the stovetop.) Don't forget a grill brush for cleaning the grates, olive oil or vegetable oil for oiling the grates and the veg, salt, a heatproof pastry brush, long-handled tongs, paper towels and/or a kitchen towel, and a clean platter.

- Heat the grill. We will be grilling at medium-high heat 375°F to 450°F.

- Clean the grates well with a long-handled grill brush.

- Soak a couple of paper towels or a kitchen towel in olive oil or vegetable oil. Working quickly, use tongs to grease the grates before applying food.

- If you are still building confidence at the grill, focus on one or two vegetables at a time so that you can pay attention, listen for flare-ups, and flip vegetables as soon as needed. If your grill is large enough, move finished vegetables to the side of the grill with low or no flame to keep them warm. (Turn off one section of a gas grill; for a charcoal grill, pile the coals on one side.)

- Cover the grill while you are cooking and listen for flare-ups.

- If vegetables are charring too quickly, reduce the heat, uncover, and move them away from hot spots to finish cooking.

- Use a grill basket for small veggies like cherry tomatoes, radishes, baby turnips, and snow peas.

NOTE: Not up for grilling? Swap grilled vegetables for roasted vegetables to make a Roasted Vegetable Platter.

Grilled Asparagus and Snap Pea Mezze

with Beet Hummus, Green Goddess Dip, and Burrata

SERVES 2 TO 4

TAKE NOTE:

- Both dips can be made several days ahead of time and held in the fridge until ready to serve. You'll need a food processor to make the hummus. For the green goddess, a high-speed blender is best.

- I prefer to grill outside to avoid a smoky kitchen, but this requires minimal grilling and will work fine with a small grill pan on the stovetop. If you are using a large outdoor grill, you will need a grill basket and note that you can grill more items at once.

SWAP: Instead of the flatbread, slice ciabatta or good-quality sourdough, brush it with olive oil, and grill it for 2 to 3 minutes on each side until toasted. Storebought naan or good crackers are fine swaps, too.

This vibrant and bountiful spring board is all about variety, which means there are multiple (totally worth it) components to make the full grazing experience possible. It is so much fun to eat and share, and you can make the dips ahead to cut down on prep time (see Take Note). Feel free to dial back the offerings, mix and match, adjust, or add based on the time you have.

---

2 discs (8 ounces each) homemade pizza dough (see page 129) or 1 ball (16 ounces) store-bought dough (optional; see Swap)

Beet Hummus (page 224)

Green Goddess Dip (page 224)

8-ounce ball burrata cheese

Extra-virgin olive oil

2 teaspoons chopped fresh tarragon

1 pound asparagus, woody ends snapped off and discarded

Fine sea salt and freshly ground black pepper

8 ounces sugar snap peas, trimmed and strings removed (see page 223)

1 bunch red radishes, halved or quartered

Canola oil, for the grill

8 to 10 rainbow carrots, cut into sticks

1 watermelon radish, thinly sliced

1 Chioggia or candy-stripe beet, thinly sliced (optional)

1 fennel bulb (8 ounces), cut into quarters or strips (optional)

Flaky sea salt, such as Maldon, for finishing

---

1 If you are making the flatbread on the grill, lightly oil a sheet pan with olive oil and divide the pizza dough evenly into four (4-ounce) pieces. Gently shape the dough into ¼-inch-thick rounds and place them on the prepared sheet pan. Set aside.

2 Place the dips in small bowls and set them on a large serving platter or board. Blot the burrata dry and place it on the platter. Leave space on the platter for the vegetables. Combine 2 tablespoons olive oil with the tarragon and set aside.

3 Set up your outdoor grill for direct grilling and heat it to medium-high (375°F to 400°F). Alternatively, heat a grill pan over high heat.

(recipe continues)

**HOW TO STRING
SUGAR SNAP AND
SNOW PEAS:**

Use a paring knife to
trim the stem end of the
pod and pull the string
down toward the other
end along with it. Some
pods may need stringing
on both sides so repeat
on the other side as
necessary. If you cut the
stem carefully, often you
can pull down both sides
at once.

4 Meanwhile, place the asparagus in a large, shallow bowl, drizzle with a scant tablespoon of olive oil, and season with fine sea salt and pepper. Toss until evenly coated. In a separate bowl, combine the sugar snap peas and red radishes, drizzle with a generous teaspoon of olive oil, and season with fine sea salt and pepper. Gather a pair of tongs and a tightly folded paper towel soaked in canola oil. Take them to the grill along with the bowls of prepared vegetables. Take the platter (or use the oiled prep bowls) to hold the vegetables as you finish grilling them.

5 Brush the grates. Working quickly, use the tongs to oil the grates with the oil-soaked paper towel. Place the asparagus on the grill (or grill pan) and cook, undisturbed, until they begin to sweat and brown lightly on one side, about 3 minutes. Use tongs to turn the asparagus and cook until char marks appear and the asparagus is crisp-tender, about another 2 minutes. Transfer the asparagus to the platter.

6 Place the snap peas and radishes in a grill basket and cook until they just begin to soften in places, about 2 minutes, then turn or shake to move them around. Cook until grill marks appear in places and the vegetables are crisp-tender, about another 2 minutes. Transfer the vegetables to the platter.

7 Place the flatbreads on the grill, evenly spaced; close the lid. (If using a grill pan, place the rounds on the pan one at a time.) Grill until the bottoms are golden brown and the tops are bubbling, 2 to 3 minutes, then flip and cook until grill marks appear and the breads are cooked through, another 2 to 3 minutes. Let the flatbreads cool briefly, then cut them into wedges and arrange them on the platter. Add an assortment of carrots, watermelon radish, beet, and fennel to the platter.

8 Sprinkle the burrata with flaky sea salt and drizzle with the tarragon oil. You can serve any remaining oil on the side.

Beet Hummus

MAKES ABOUT 2 CUPS

INGREDIENT INFO: Feel free to use store-bought, precooked beets here. To roast beets, see the Butcher Tip on page 88, or to gently boil the beets, see page 98.

8 ounces cooked beets, stem ends trimmed and quartered (see Ingredient Info)

1 cup canned chickpeas, drained and rinsed

1 small garlic clove, finely grated with a Microplane or minced

3 tablespoons freshly squeezed lemon juice, plus more as needed

2 tablespoons stirred tahini

2 tablespoons extra-virgin olive oil

Fine sea salt

¾ teaspoon ground cumin

Place the beets in a food processor and pulse to finely chop them. Add the chickpeas, garlic, lemon juice, tahini, olive oil, ½ teaspoon salt, and the cumin and blend until smooth. Scrape down the sides of the bowl with a rubber spatula; adjust salt and lemon juice to taste and blend again to combine. The hummus will keep in an airtight container in the refrigerator for up to 5 days.

Green Goddess Dip

MAKES ABOUT 1½ CUPS

1 cup raw cashews

¾ cup boiling water

1 medium avocado, halved and pitted

About ¾ cup water

2 tablespoons freshly squeezed lemon juice, plus more as needed

1 tablespoon red wine vinegar

Fine sea salt

1 medium garlic clove, finely grated with a Microplane or minced

½ cup packed fresh cilantro, finely chopped

½ cup loosely packed fresh flat-leaf parsley, finely chopped

1 tablespoon minced fresh chives

2 teaspoons finely chopped fresh tarragon

1 Place the cashews in a heat-safe bowl and cover with the boiling water. Let stand for 1 hour to soften, then drain. (You can let the cashews stand for less time, no problem. The sauce will be less smooth and creamy, but it will still taste great.)

2 Transfer the cashews to a high-speed blender and add the avocado, ½ cup plus 2 tablespoons of water, the lemon juice, vinegar, ½ teaspoon salt, garlic, cilantro, parsley, chives, and tarragon. Blend until creamy and smooth, scraping down the side and blending again until well incorporated. Thin with more water as needed (thicker is best for dipping). Adjust salt and lemon juice to taste. Cover and refrigerate until ready to serve, 2 to 3 days.

Grilled Summer Bounty
with Peaches, Halloumi, and Flatbread

SERVES 2 AS A MAIN.
4 AS AN APPETIZER OR
MAIN WITH SIDES

SWAPS: If you can't procure halloumi, use fresh burrata (not grilled). Blot it dry, pull it apart, and place it on top of and between the grilled produce on the finished platter.

TAKE NOTE: If you don't have homemade pizza dough, you can use store-bought dough or good-quality naan or pita. (Throw the premade breads on the grill, then brush them with olive oil and sprinkle with flaky salt and za'atar to finish.)

This is a simple and super-delicious preparation of quick-grilling summer produce and Cypriot halloumi (a goat's- and sheep's-milk cheese) that counts on super-hot grates, olive oil, and flaky sea salt to do the heavy lifting. If you are working with produce in its prime and have seasoned it properly, this should taste amazing. Adjust salt, pepper, and olive oil to taste and make sure you don't forget the fresh herbs.

The flatbread is made with Classic Pizza Dough (page 129); it's extraordinary here.

---

4 tablespoons olive oil, plus more as needed

1 large cucumber, sliced on a diagonal in ¼-inch-thick planks

8 ounces halloumi cheese, cut crosswise into ¼-inch slices

1 large avocado, halved lengthwise and carefully pitted, skin left intact

2 ripe summer peaches, pitted and cut into ¾-inch wedges

Fine sea salt

½ cup mixed fresh cilantro and parsley

2 heirloom tomatoes or other medium-to-large in-season tomatoes

Best-quality olive oil

Flaky sea salt, such as Maldon

Freshly ground black pepper

2 discs (8 ounces each) Classic Pizza Dough (page 129; see Take Note)

Canola oil, for the grill

½ teaspoon za'atar (optional)

⅓ cup Quick-Pickled Onions (page 100) or red wine vinegar to taste

---

1 Pour 3 tablespoons of oil in a small bowl and set it to the side along with a silicone brush. Prepare a sheet pan to carry your ingredients to the grill. Assemble the cucumber, halloumi, avocado, and peaches on the sheet pan, and brush the cut sides of everything lightly with olive oil, then season with fine sea salt. Finely chop the mixed cilantro and parsley; set aside for finishing. Core and slice the tomatoes and arrange them on a large serving platter, drizzle with about 1 tablespoon of your best olive oil, sprinkle lightly with flaky sea salt and pepper, and set aside.

2 If you are making the grilled flatbread, lightly oil another sheet pan with olive oil or flour a lightweight cutting board. Roll or press each disc of dough into a ¼-inch-thick rectangle or oval and place it on the board or sheet pan.

3 Set up your grill for direct grilling and heat it to medium-high heat (375°F to 400°F). Alternatively, heat a grill pan over high heat.

(recipe continues)

EQUIPMENT TIP: If you are using a grill pan, you don't need to cover it. You will need to grill in batches depending on the size of your pan, and cook each item a bit longer.

ALL PLANTS: Omit the cheese and add extra avocado and hummus or eggplant caponata (see page 115).

4 Meanwhile, gather a pair of tongs, a tightly folded paper towel soaked in canola oil and flaky sea salt. Take them to the grill along with the tray of prepared produce. If you are making the grilled flatbread, take the prepared dough, the remaining olive oil and a silicone brush, and the za'atar spice, if using.

5 Working quickly, use the tongs to oil the grates with the oil-soaked paper towel. Place the cucumber planks and halloumi slices on the grill, across the grates, working in batches if needed. Cook until grill marks appear on one side, 2 to 3 minutes, then flip and cook until grill marks appear on the other side, 2 to 3 minutes more. (If using a gas or charcoal grill, cover it while cooking.) If anything sticks or isn't properly charring during the grilling process, give it another minute and then turn. Listen for flare-ups and move items or pull them from the grill as needed. Once cooked, transfer the cucumbers and halloumi back to the sheet pan or to a part of the grill without fire to keep warm.

6 Next, place the avocado and peaches cut sides down on the grill. Cook until grill marks appear, about 2 minutes, then rotate and continue cooking until both fruits have hashmarks and are sweating, about 2 minutes more. (Again, cover if using a gas or charcoal grill.) Transfer all items to the tray, peel the skin from the avocado and cut the halves in thick slices. Sprinkle everything lightly and evenly with flaky sea salt.

7 Grill the flatbread. Place the shaped dough oiled side down on the grill. Cover and grill until golden, puffed up, and bubbling in places, 2 to 3 minutes. Brush the top with oil and sprinkle with about ¼ teaspoon flaky sea salt, flip, and cook until golden and crispy around the edges and soft in the center, and good grill marks appear in places, about another 2 minutes. Remove the flatbread, brush the other side generously with oil, and sprinkle with another ¼ teaspoon or more of flaky sea salt and the za'atar.

8 Assemble the platter. Scatter the grilled items over the tomatoes on the platter. Sprinkle lightly with flaky salt, pepper, and za'atar, and drizzle with about 1 tablespoon of your best olive oil. Add pinches of pickled onions in places, or slowly and evenly drizzle the vegetables with the red wine vinegar, adjusting to taste. Top with the reserved chopped herbs and serve with the warm flatbread, torn or cut into pieces.

Grilled Broccolini, Potato Wedges, and Hakurei Turnips
with Red Pepper Pesto

SERVES UP TO 4 AS A MAIN

SWAPS:

- Use broccoli or romanesco in place of the broccolini.

- Feel free to use a different sauce instead of the pesto—there are many to explore (see A Guide to Sauces, Dips, and Spreads on page 317).

At the farmers market in the fall, there is a moment when broccolini, Hakurei turnips, and a fresh new crop of potatoes seem to arrive at the same time. It's a good thing, because the broccolini (more mild and less bitter than broccoli) with long tender stalks and loose, wispy florets (perfect for soaking up oil and delivering crispy grilled bits), the sweet baby turnips, and earthy, creamy potatoes play so well together.

FOR THE VEGETABLES

Fine sea salt

1¼ to 1½ pounds broccolini, ends trimmed, thick stalks halved or quartered lengthwise to make equal in size

1½ pounds medium-size red, russet, or Yukon gold potatoes, halved lengthwise and cut into ½-inch wedges

4½ tablespoons olive oil

Crushed red pepper flakes

Grated zest and freshly squeezed juice of 1 lemon

1 bunch Hakurei turnips, scrubbed and cut into 1- to 1½-inch wedges

Freshly ground black pepper

½ teaspoon paprika

¼ teaspoon garlic powder

Canola oil, for the grill

3 small watermelon radishes, thinly sliced into rounds or half-moons, or 1 bunch petite radishes, whole or halved

1 bunch baby rainbow carrots, left whole or halved lengthwise

Red Pepper Pesto (page 230), for serving

FOR SERVING (OPTIONAL)

Sliced pear or apple, grapes, or figs

Toasted nuts

Good-quality cheese, for slicing or dipping

Good-quality crackers or grilled flatbread (see page 221) or store-bought flatbread (warmed on the grill)

EQUIPMENT TIP: You can cook the broccolini and turnips on a grill pan (open the windows) and roast the potatoes in a 425°F oven on a parchment-lined sheet pan. Roast until golden on one side, about 20 minutes, then turn the potatoes and roast until golden brown, tender through the middle and, crisp on the edges, another 10 to 15 minutes. Adjust salt to taste.

1 Bring a pot of water to a boil and salt it generously until it tastes like the sea. Boil the broccolini for 1 minute to begin to tenderize the stalks. Lift with a spider or tongs to a colander to drain. Rinse with cold water briefly to preserve its color and drain. Add the potatoes to the pot and boil until tender, 8 to 10 minutes; drain.

2 Meanwhile, pat the broccolini mostly dry and place it in a large bowl. Add 1½ tablespoons of olive oil, a light sprinkling of salt, a couple of pinches of red pepper flakes, the lemon zest, and 1 tablespoon of lemon juice and toss to evenly coat the stalks and florets. Transfer the broccolini to one side of a sheet pan. Place the turnips in the bowl and toss with 1 tablespoon of olive oil, season lightly with salt and pepper, and transfer to the other side of the sheet pan. Wipe the bowl clean.

3 Place the potatoes in the reserved large bowl and add the remaining 2 tablespoons of oil, ½ teaspoon salt, the paprika, and the garlic powder. Toss to coat.

4 Heat an outdoor grill to medium-high heat. Brush the grates clean. Gather a pair of tongs and a tightly folded paper towel soaked in canola oil. Take them to the grill along with the sheet pan and bowl with prepared vegetables.

5 Working quickly, use the tongs to oil the grates with the oil-soaked towel. Place the potatoes across the grill grates, and cook, covered, until lightly browning and grill marks begin to appear, 5 to 7 minutes. Flip the potatoes and cook, covered, until they are tender, browning, and lightly charred in places, another 5 to 6 minutes. If you have room on the grill, continue; or hold off and cook in batches. Place the broccolini directly on the grill, across the grates. Close the grill and cook, flipping halfway through, until the stalks are tender, 6 to 8 minutes. Place the turnips in a grill basket and cook, covered, stirring them once, until crisp-tender and golden brown in places, 4 to 5 minutes. Transfer the vegetables as they finish to the sheet pan or to a cool part of the grill to keep warm. If anything sticks or isn't charring, give it another minute and then turn.

6 Arrange the grilled vegetables on a large serving platter with the raw radishes and carrots and a bowl of the Red Pepper Pesto. Add any optional accompaniments, sprinkle the potatoes with salt if needed, and serve.

Red Pepper Pesto

TAKE NOTE: You can char the peppers on the grill, then let them steam to loosen their skins for peeling while you grill the other vegetables. (Have everything else for the pesto ready so you can quickly blend and serve when the broccolini and potatoes are off the grill.) Broil the peppers if you want to make the dip ahead.

ALL PLANTS: Hold the feta and adjust salt and olive oil to taste.

2 large red bell peppers

½ cup toasted pistachios

4 ounces feta cheese (optional)

½ teaspoon Aleppo pepper flakes, plus more as needed

1 tablespoon freshly squeezed lemon juice, plus more as needed

Fine sea salt

3 tablespoons extra-virgin olive oil

1 To grill the peppers on an outdoor grill, set up your grill for direct grilling and heat it to medium-high heat (375°F to 400°F). Roast the peppers, covered, over medium-high heat, turning, until just tender and evenly charred all over, 10 to 12 minutes. To broil the peppers, adjust an oven rack 6 inches from the broiler element and heat the broiler. Line a sheet pan with foil. Place the whole red peppers on the sheet pan and broil, turning halfway through with tongs, until the peppers are soft all over and charred and blistering in places, 10 to 15 minutes.

2 As soon as the peppers finish cooking, transfer them to a large bowl. Cover and seal the bowl with a pot lid to briefly steam the peppers. Let cool to the touch.

3 Meanwhile, place the toasted pistachios in the bowl of a food processor. Pulse until they are very finely chopped (don't overprocess them into a paste).

4 When the peppers are cool enough to handle, place them in a sieve set over a bowl and peel them with your fingers. Transfer the peeled peppers as you work to the food processor, then add the strained pepper juices (discard the solids in the sieve). Add the feta (if using) breaking it apart in large pieces as you place it in the processor. Add the Aleppo pepper, lemon juice, and ¼ teaspoon salt and process until mostly blended. Scape down the sides of the bowl. With the processor running, stream in the oil. Continue to blend until the pesto is well blended but retains some texture. Adjust the Aleppo pepper, lemon juice, and salt to taste. The pesto will keep, refrigerated in an airtight container, for up to 4 days.

The Sheet Pan Meal

The beauty of a sheet pan meal is that you can prep as you go. Place your sheet pans next to your cutting board and pile on each ingredient as you gather, chop, and measure. Know that some ingredients may require more time to cook than others so pay attention to placement and choreography. There will be a rhythm to follow as you place and pull sheet pans in and out of the oven. Get into the groove so that you can optimize the efficiency of this technique and get a beautiful meal to the table with no fuss.

TIPS AND TAKEAWAYS

- A sheet pan–made meal can be so much more than a tray of roasted vegetables. Take the time to consider a mix of compatible vegetables, then toss in fresh or dried herbs and spices. Add something crunchy with nuts or seeds. Maybe dried fruit or a drizzle of maple syrup? Consider olives or capers for a touch of brine. Choose the right acid like wine vinegar, wine, or citrus juice. Bring it all together with olive oil, coconut milk, or, perhaps, a good cheese. A nice balance of textures and flavors, as always, is the goal.

- Adjust your prep-ahead thinking. Here, you prep as you go.

- All of these recipes require two sheet pans.

- Pay special attention to which ingredients go where and to cook times. Often one sheet pan will go into the oven after the first. When you are riffing on your own, keep in mind that vegetables need more or less time depending on their density and water content. Dense, firm, and starchy vegetables including potatoes, winter squashes, and roots require the most time. Firm but pliable vegetables like broccoli, broccolini, broccoli rabe, Brussels sprouts, cauliflower, and romanesco fall in the middle. Naturally crisp-tender and soft vegetables including asparagus, bok choy, cabbage, eggplant, fennel, green beans, hearty greens, mushrooms, peppers, tomatoes, and zucchini need the least amount of time. The size of the cut matters, too. Larger cuts need more time.

Sheet Pan Cauliflower Marbella
with Polenta

SERVES 3 TO 4 AS A MAIN

TAKE NOTE: If you are feeding four hungry adults for dinner, stir in 1 cup cooked cannellini beans when you add the pine nuts.

BUTCHER TIP: See page 123 for how to cut cauliflower florets.

INGREDIENT INFO: If you would like to crisp the polenta slightly, use a spatula to turn over each round after 10 minutes in the oven. Broil it for 3 to 4 minutes until a light crust forms.

This sheet pan dinner is a modern take on The Silver Palate's famous "Marbella" braise. Cauliflower and onion are layered with chile, olives, currants, capers, and oregano, then tossed with olive oil and sherry vinegar, sprinkled with brown sugar, and bathed in some white wine. The finished cauliflower, roasted and caramelized, is sweet, sour, and a little briny with just a hint of heat. It is a prize destined to be scooped over sheet pan–roasted polenta (or, really, any favorite grain).

FOR THE CAULIFLOWER

2 pounds cauliflower and/or romanesco

1 medium yellow onion

1 serrano chile or jalapeño (optional)

3 large garlic cloves

½ cup pitted green olives, rinsed and drained

Heaping ⅓ cup dried currants

2 tablespoons drained capers

1 tablespoon dried oregano

1 teaspoon fine sea salt

¼ teaspoon freshly ground black pepper

2 bay leaves

¼ cup plus 1 tablespoon extra-virgin olive oil

1 tablespoon sherry vinegar

2 tablespoons brown sugar

½ cup dry white wine

Scant ¼ cup pine nuts

FOR THE POLENTA

1 tube (about 18 ounces) polenta, cut into ½-inch rounds

1½ tablespoons extra-virgin olive oil

Fine sea salt

Manchego, Pecorino, or Parmesan cheese (optional)

1 Position one oven rack in the top position and one in the middle. Heat the oven to 450°F.

2 Make the cauliflower (and/or romanesco). Place one sheet pan near your cutting board. (Transfer vegetables to it as you work.) Quarter the cauliflower lengthwise, from crown to stem end, then remove the core at an angle. Break apart the florets with your hands or a knife, then cut any large florets into 1¾-inch pieces. Chop the upper part of the core into bite-size pieces; discard the end if dry. Peel and thinly slice the onion and scatter over the cauliflower. If using the serrano, stem and seed it, removing the white membranes, and mince it. Add it to the pan, distributing it evenly. Thinly slice the garlic, as thin as you can, and sprinkle it evenly over the pan.

(recipe continues)

3 Halve the olives and scatter them and the currants, capers, oregano, salt, pepper, and bay leaves over the vegetables in the pan. Drizzle the ¼ cup of oil over the top, then the sherry vinegar, and use your hands to toss and evenly coat everything in oil. Spread out all of the ingredients, lifting the onion and currants to the top as much as possible in places (but don't fuss). Sprinkle the brown sugar evenly over the top of the ingredients, then pour the white wine all around, directing the wine mostly in between the cauliflower pieces. Place the sheet pan on the middle rack and cook until the cauliflower is starting to turn golden in places, about 20 minutes.

4 Meanwhile, get the polenta ready to go into the oven: Brush both sides of the rounds with the oil and sprinkle lightly with salt. Spread out the rounds in a single layer on another sheet pan.

5 Remove the cauliflower from the oven and scatter the pine nuts over the top. Carefully give everything a flip and a stir, then spread out in the pan. Return the pan to the middle rack and place the polenta on the top rack. Roast for another 10 to 15 minutes until the cauliflower is nicely browning and tender and the polenta is sizzling. If you would like, grate Manchego over the hot polenta.

6 To serve, top the polenta with the cauliflower mixture, making sure to evenly scoop and distribute all of the smaller ingredients and bits in the pan.

Reheat leftovers on a sheet pan at 425°F for about 10 minutes until warmed through and the cauliflower is crisp in places.

Sheet Pan Potatoes and Green Beans
with Walnuts, Olives, and Feta

SERVES 4 AS A MAIN

This outstanding sheet pan meal is perfectly balanced with nutty, salty, creamy, and bright citrus accents. The whole dish comes together, quite literally, when you toss the potatoes and beans with walnuts, roasted olives, lemon zest, and fresh feta. Chives are the finishing touch.

---

2 pounds Yukon or other gold potatoes, washed, scrubbed if needed, and cut into ¾- to 1-inch pieces

4 tablespoons extra-virgin olive oil

Fine sea salt

1 to 1¼ pounds green beans or haricot verts

Heaping ½ cup pitted green olives, rinsed, drained, and cut in half

½ teaspoon sugar

Freshly ground black pepper

Heaping 1 cup walnuts

6-ounce block feta cheese, cut into ½-inch cubes

2 tablespoons minced fresh chives

1 teaspoon packed lemon zest

Lemon wedges, for serving (optional)

---

1 Position one rack on the lowest shelf in the oven and another in the top third. Heat the oven to 450°F.

2 Toss the potatoes with 3 tablespoons of olive oil and ½ teaspoon salt on a sheet pan and evenly spread them out. Roast the potatoes on the bottom rack for 20 minutes, until they are mostly tender and beginning to brown.

3 Meanwhile, wash and trim the green beans. On another sheet pan, toss the green beans and olives with the remaining 1 tablespoon of oil, ¼ teaspoon salt, the sugar, and ½ teaspoon pepper until evenly coated. Spread them out in an even layer; some overlapping is fine. Cover and seal the pan with a piece of foil (or another inverted sheet pan). Set it aside.

4 After the potatoes have roasted for 20 minutes, move them to the top rack and place the sheet pan with the beans on the bottom rack. Continue to roast the potatoes and beans for another 10 minutes, then pull the green beans from the oven and carefully uncover them, avoiding the release of steam. Carefully shake the pan to turn the beans; they should be browning in places. Return the pan, uncovered, to the bottom rack. Remove the potatoes from the oven and turn them with a metal spatula, forcefully scraping under the potatoes if needed. Sprinkle the walnuts over the potatoes. Return the pan to the top rack.

(recipe continues)

5 Continue to cook for another 5 to 8 minutes until the beans are tender and browned in places, the walnuts are toasted, and the potatoes are tender, golden brown, and crisp.

6 Immediately transfer all of the oven-roasted ingredients to a serving bowl to toss them together. Stir in the feta. Toss with 1 tablespoon of chives and the lemon zest. Adjust salt and pepper to taste. Sprinkle the remaining 1 tablespoon of chives on top. Serve hot or at room temperature with lemon wedges if you wish.

Reheat leftovers on a sheet pan at 425°F for about 10 minutes until warmed through and the potatoes are crisp in places.

Smoky Sheet Pan Coconut Greens and Sweet Potatoes

SERVES 4 AS A MAIN

INGREDIENT INFO: The quality and thickness of canned coconut milk varies by brand. If you are using extra-thick and creamy coconut milk, 1 cup should be enough. If you are using a more watery coconut milk, or if you simply prefer a saucier end result, add another ½ cup well-stirred coconut milk with the chickpeas.

SWAP: Use collard greens or Swiss chard in place of kale.

Complex, rich, smoky flavor makes this dish taste like it was on the stove for hours. But actually, the prep is a breeze and it cooks almost completely hands-free in the oven for 30 minutes. (Perfect for a weeknight.) It's also extremely dense in nutrients—super-powered food—that will make you feel nourished, balanced, and energized.

3 medium sweet potatoes (about 2 pounds), peeled and ¾-inch diced

2 tablespoons extra-virgin olive oil

1 teaspoon fine sea salt, plus more as needed

1 bunch curly kale, stemmed and roughly chopped and slightly damp from rinsing

1 red onion, halved and thinly sliced

3 garlic cloves, thinly sliced

½ teaspoon ground cumin

½ teaspoon smoked sweet paprika

Freshly ground black pepper

1 cup stirred canned coconut milk, plus more as needed

2 teaspoons apple cider vinegar

1 can (15½ ounces) chickpeas, rinsed and drained

Cooked white quinoa (or other favorite grain), for serving

Lemon yogurt (see page 210), for serving (optional, but recommended)

1 Position the oven racks in the upper and lower thirds of the oven. Heat the oven to 425°F. Combine the sweet potatoes with the olive oil and ½ teaspoon of salt on one sheet pan, tossing with your hands until well coated and evenly combined. Spread the sweet potatoes out in as much of an even layer as possible—potatoes will overlap in places, that's fine.

2 On another sheet pan, combine the kale, onion, garlic, the remaining ½ teaspoon of salt, the cumin, paprika, and a few twists of pepper. Drizzle with about ½ cup of coconut milk and the vinegar and use two serving spoons to toss to coat. Spread out the mixture into an even layer on the pan and drizzle the remaining ½ cup of coconut milk over the top. Cover the sheet pan with foil.

3 Place the pan with the sweet potatoes on the lower rack and the pan with the kale on the upper rack. Roast for 20 minutes, then carefully and just briefly transfer the pan with the kale to the stovetop or to a wire rack, and close the door to the oven. Carefully remove the foil from the tray as steam is released. Add the chickpeas to the kale and stir to combine, then evenly spread out the mixture. Return the kale, uncovered, to the upper shelf. Turn the sweet potatoes and spread them out again. Continue to roast the sweet potatoes and the kale-chickpea mixture for another 10 minutes until the sweet potatoes are tender and the greens and onion are soft and stewed in the coconut milk. Stir the greens well and adjust salt and pepper to taste.

4 To plate this dish, spoon quinoa or other grain in the bottom of a shallow bowl. Layer the greens and sweet potatoes over or spoon them side by side. Top with a dollop of lemon yogurt or other yogurt if you wish.

To reheat leftovers, spread out and separate the sweet potatoes and greens mixture on a parchment-lined sheet pan and heat at 400°F for about 10 minutes until warmed through and the sweet potatoes are crisp in places. (If you made a saucier version or if you have a lot of leftovers, use two sheet pans.)

LAYERED CASSEROLES. SAVORY PIES.

The Lasagna

There's a peace of mind that comes with having a lasagna in the oven. Maybe it is a blissful knowing that everyone at the table is going to love it or perhaps it's a sense of relief, for the cook, that comes with simply pulling it out of the oven with no additional fuss. (Likely, there will be leftovers, too, the real prize.)

TIPS AND TAKEAWAYS

- You need a deep lasagna pan, or a 9 × 13-inch glass or ceramic baking dish or metal baking pan for making lasagna.

- As the name suggests, no-boil lasagna noodles don't require cookng, which saves you a step in the lasagna-making process. Don't worry about them fitting the bottom of your pan exactly; there will be some small gaps around the edges. If the gaps are wide, feel free to add another noodle or two (up to 6 per layer), overlapping with noodles as necessary to fill in. (Note: Extra noodles may require an extra box.) No-boil noodles, especially the ones on the top layer, require plenty of sauce to properly cook through and avoid drying out and becoming crisp in places. Make sure to add sauce anywhere that is without.

- Standard lasagna noodles deliver a bouncy, thick, just-right texture. Use a large pot to give them plenty of room to boil. When you have the time, I encourage you to use them. I always prefer them with the Mixed Mushroom and Kale Lasagna.

- Lasagna needs sauce, lots of good sauce. (It bears repeating: When it comes to no-boil noodles especially, don't skimp. They won't cook sufficiently without it.)

- Use any of the vegetable sauces on pages 188–193 to make a lasagna.

- Add extra vegetables between the layers; make sure to cut them into small bite-size pieces that will meld into the layers. Before adding them to the lasagna, sauté or roast them until crisp-tender and long enough to cook off excess liquid.

- You can also make a lasagna the day before serving it. (Its flavors will improve overnight.) Leave plenty of time to reheat it as a whole: cold lasagna can take a while. To reheat a whole lasagna, cover it with foil and bake at 350°F until hot through the center and gently bubbling around the edges, 30 to 40 minutes. Reheat individual pieces, covered with foil, in a 375°F oven until hot through the center, about 20 minutes. To microwave, zap individual pieces with a damp paper towel over the top to prevent it from drying out, 2 to 3 minutes until hot. Alternatively, you can assemble a lasagna the day before serving it and bake it the next day, according to the cooking instructions, just ahead of serving.

- Leftover lasagna will keep, covered in the refrigerator, for up to 4 days. You can also freeze leftover lasagna and thaw it overnight in the fridge; follow the reheating instructions above when you are ready to cook it. To cook a fully frozen lasagna, bake at 375°F, covered with foil, until hot through the center, 1 hour 5 minutes to 1 hour 15 minutes.

- Make a salad dressed with a good balsamic vinaigrette to serve with lasagna. Try red cabbage; a mix of arugula, radicchio, and endive; or mixed greens and chickpeas.

Classic Lasagna
with Spinach-Ricotta Filling and Simple Tomato Sauce

SERVES UP TO 8 AS A MAIN

SWAP: Try chopped kale in place of baby spinach; a mix of kale and spinach is lovely, too.

SHORTCUT: Break off a 1½ ounce chunk of Parmesan cheese and process it in the food processor (so you don't have to do it by hand) before you blend the spinach-ricotta filling. Then use half in the filling and the other half on top. Note: This will produce a smaller volume than the recipe calls for, but that's fine, just divide it evenly.

For me, the ultimate tomato-sauce lasagna is this crowd pleaser with layers of whipped ricotta, spinach, and basil and a classic, simple tomato sauce. The delicious sauce is a quick one, but feel free to use a store-bought sauce that you truly love. Whatever sauce you decide to use, don't skimp on it.

FOR THE FILLING

2 tablespoons unsalted butter

1 tablespoon extra-virgin olive oil

2 large garlic cloves, smashed, peeled, and trimmed

8 ounces baby spinach or chopped spinach leaves

½ teaspoon fine sea salt

1 container (15 ounces) ricotta cheese

1 egg

½ cup finely grated Parmesan cheese

½ cup packed fresh basil

¼ teaspoon freshly ground black pepper

FOR THE LASAGNA

5 to 6 cups Simple Tomato Sauce (recipe follows) or store-bought sauce

16 no-boil lasagna noodles (or boiled noodles)

4 cups low-moisture shredded mozzarella cheese (or 16 ounces fresh mozzarella, torn into small pieces)

½ cup finely grated Parmesan cheese

1 Make the spinach-ricotta filling. Melt the butter with the oil in a large skillet over medium heat. Add the garlic and cook, stirring frequently and tilting the pan to submerge the garlic in the oil, allowing it to simmer until fragrant and slightly translucent (don't let it burn), about 2 minutes. Add the spinach, in batches if needed, and cook, stirring occasionally, until it is wilted and tender, about 2 minutes. Season with the salt and remove it from the heat.

2 Transfer the spinach (leaving any liquid in the pan behind) and garlic to a food processor and blend until finely chopped. Add the ricotta, egg, Parmesan, basil, and pepper and blend on high until fully combined.

3 Heat the oven to 375°F with a rack in the center.

4 Assemble the lasagna. Spread ¾ to 1 cup of sauce over the bottom of a lasagna pan or 9 × 13-inch baking dish. Place 4 noodles on top, covering the sauce and overlapping each of the noodles slightly. Spoon about 9 heaping tablespoons of the ricotta mixture over the noodles, then use an offset spatula or the back of a spoon to spread the mixture evenly over the noodles and out to the sides of the baking dish. Scatter 1 cup of the mozzarella evenly over the top. Next, spoon

(recipe continues)

TAKE NOTE: Serve with a side salad of greens and chickpeas dressed with balsamic vinegar and olive oil or Kale–Radicchio Caesar with Crispy Chickpea "Croutons" (page 29).

EQUIPMENT TIP: To avoid the food processor in step 3, mince the garlic ahead of cooking it, let the cooked spinach and garlic cool briefly, chop the basil, add them to the remaining filling ingredients, and stir together in a medium bowl.

MAKES ABOUT 6 TO 7 CUPS

1 to 1¼ cups of sauce in different spots on the top of the lasagna and then use the spatula or spoon to evenly distribute the sauce. (You will only need about 1 cup of sauce or even a little less to cover if it is on the looser side.)

5 Repeat step 4 two more times, starting with 4 more noodles, then ricotta, then mozzarella, then sauce. Finally, top with 4 more noodles. Evenly spread out enough of the remaining sauce to evenly and generously cover the entire top, then layer with the final cup of mozzarella and the Parmesan.

6 Cover the lasagna with aluminum foil and bake for 15 minutes. Remove the foil and bake until the edges are bubbling and the cheese is melted and golden brown, 25 to 30 minutes longer. Let rest at room temperature for about 10 minutes before cutting into pieces and serving.

To store and reheat lasagna, see Tips and Takeaways on page 240.

Simple Tomato Sauce

3 tablespoons extra-virgin olive oil

4 garlic cloves, thinly sliced

1 small yellow onion, finely diced

2 cans (28 ounces each) whole peeled tomatoes and their juice

Fine sea salt and freshly ground black pepper, plus more as needed

1 teaspoon sugar

1½ teaspoons dried oregano (or Italian seasoning or dried basil)

1 tablespoon unsalted butter (or 1 additional tablespoon best-quality olive oil)

A handful of fresh basil leaves, chopped (optional)

1 Heat the oil and garlic in a large, deep sauté pan or large saucepan over medium heat. When it begins to simmer, cook for about 90 seconds, stirring frequently until the garlic is fragrant and just turning translucent in places, without browning. Add the onion and continue to cook, stirring occasionally, until the onion begins to soften, about 2 minutes. Add the tomatoes and juice. Fill the cans with a splash of water (about 1 tablespoon), swirl to release remaining tomato juice from the sides of the can, and add the water and juice to the pan. Use a potato masher to gently and carefully crush the tomatoes, breaking them apart into smaller pieces. Stir in 1 teaspoon salt, ¼ teaspoon pepper, the sugar, and oregano.

2 Bring the sauce to a simmer, reduce the heat to medium-low, and cook, partially covered, stirring occasionally, until the tomatoes have melted and the sauce has thickened, 20 to 25 minutes. Stir in the butter until it melts (or stir in 1 tablespoon of your best olive oil). Crush the tomatoes further if you'd like or for a smoother sauce, puree it in a blender or food processor. Adjust salt and pepper to taste. Stir in the basil to finish the sauce (if using).

Butternut Squash and Swiss Chard Lasagna

SERVES UP TO 8 AS A MAIN

MAKE AHEAD: Make all of the components up to 3 days ahead and assemble the lasagna the day before or the day you want to bake it. Alternatively, bake the lasagna up to one day in advance.

TAKE NOTE:

• The butternut squash will have a sharp vinegar-forward flavor when just prepared. Once layered and baked into the lasagna, it will relax and add welcome acidity to the lasagna.

• Serve the lasagna with a simple salad of arugula and chickpeas, shredded red cabbage, or a tricolore arugula, radicchio, and endive mix—all options dressed with balsamic vinegar and olive oil sweetened with honey or maple syrup.

BUTCHER TIP: See page 164 for how to cut Swiss chard.

This savory and sweet lasagna is as decadent, delicious, and autumnal as it sounds. It's an elegant make-ahead dish for a fall dinner party or any holiday meal. Feel free to add more Swiss chard to the sautéed filling for "greener" layers and add a bulb of fennel, thinly sliced, to elevate further with added sweetness and subtle anise flavor. The fenugreek is optional, but it's the secret ingredient that adds complexity and balances the sweetness of the squash with just a touch of bitterness.

FOR THE BUTTERNUT SQUASH FILLING

1 large (3½- to 4-pound) butternut squash

1 tablespoon extra-virgin olive oil

½ teaspoon ground fenugreek (optional, but recommended)

Scant ¼ teaspoon ground nutmeg

¾ teaspoon fine sea salt

2½ teaspoons unfiltered apple cider vinegar

1 tablespoon pure maple syrup

FOR THE CHARD FILLING

2 tablespoons extra-virgin olive oil

1 large yellow onion, thinly sliced

1 small to medium fennel bulb, thinly sliced (optional)

2 bunches (1 to 1¼ pounds) Swiss chard, stems cut into ¼-inch dice, leaves cut into ¼-inch ribbons (see Butcher Tip)

3 large garlic cloves, thinly sliced

½ teaspoon fine sea salt

¼ teaspoon freshly ground black pepper, plus more as needed

FOR THE CREAM SAUCE

1 container (15 ounces) low-fat cottage cheese

1½ cups shaken heavy cream

1½ cups finely grated Parmesan cheese

2 teaspoons finely chopped fresh rosemary leaves

½ teaspoon fine sea salt

¼ teaspoon freshly ground black pepper

A small pinch of ground nutmeg

FOR THE LASAGNA

16 no-boil lasagna noodles (or boiled noodles)

Heaping 2½ cups coarsely shredded Italian fontina cheese (6½ ounces)

Heaping ¼ cup finely grated Parmesan cheese

Freshly ground black pepper

---

1 Make the butternut squash filling. Heat the oven to 400°F with a rack in the middle position and line a sheet pan with parchment paper. Trim the ends of the butternut squash. Cut the squash in half crosswise through the middle to separate the bulbous bottom of the squash from the slender and solid neck. Next, cut the bulbous bottom in half lengthwise. Stand the neck of the squash upright on its widest cut surface and cut it in half lengthwise. Brush the squash lightly with the oil and roast for 50 to 60 minutes until the squash flesh is completely tender. Once cool enough to handle, scoop out the seeds and discard them. Now, use a spoon to separate the flesh from the skin. Place 3½ to 3¾ cups of the flesh in a food processor. Add the fenugreek (if using), nutmeg, salt, vinegar, and maple syrup and blend on high until completely smooth. Set aside.

2 Make the chard filling. Heat the oil in a large skillet over medium heat. Add the onion, fennel (if using), and chard stems and cook, stirring occasionally, until the onion is beginning to turn translucent and soften, 4 to 6 minutes. Add the garlic, ¼ teaspoon of salt, and the pepper and cook, stirring occasionally, until the onion is lightly browning in places, about 3 minutes. Add the chard leaves, cooking down a little at a time to fit the skillet, along with the remaining ¼ teaspoon of salt and a few twists of pepper. Once all of the chard is in the pan, cook, stirring frequently, until wilted and all of the liquid has evaporated, about 4 minutes. Set aside.

3 Make the cream sauce. In a medium bowl, whisk together the cottage cheese, cream, Parmesan, rosemary, salt, pepper, and nutmeg.

4 Make the lasagna. Heat the oven to 375°F with a rack in the middle position. In the bottom of a lasagna pan or 9 × 13-inch baking dish, evenly spread out ¾ cup of the cream sauce with an offset spatula or the back of a spoon. Spread out 4 lasagna noodles on top, covering the sauce and overlapping each of the noodles slightly. Spoon about 9 heaping tablespoons of the squash puree over the noodles, then spread the mixture evenly over the noodles and out to the sides of the baking dish. Sprinkle a heaping 1 cup of the chard mixture evenly over the top, followed by ½ cup of fontina. Spoon ¾ cup of the cream sauce over the top, making sure to pull in bits that have settled at the bottom of the bowl, and spread it out to evenly distribute it.

5 Repeat the layering process 2 more times. Place the remaining 4 noodles on top, then evenly spread out the remaining squash puree (using a spatula to collect the last of the puree from the sides of the blender or storage container), then white sauce over the top. Spread out the sauce—evenly covering the noodles and gently mixing the sauces together. Top evenly with the remaining fontina and the Parmesan, and give it a few twists of pepper. Lightly oil a piece of foil to cover the baking dish and place the oiled side down to seal it. (This will help prevent it from sticking.) Bake for 15 minutes. Remove the foil and bake for 25 to 30 minutes longer until the edges are bubbling and the cheese is melted and browning in places. Let rest at room temperature for 15 minutes or so before cutting and serving.

To store and reheat lasagna, see Tips and Takeaways on page 240.

Mixed Mushroom and Kale Lasagna

This is a wintery, white lasagna chock-full of umami from the mushrooms and Asiago cheese, with a hint of green from the kale and rosemary. A true mix of mushrooms is the key to achieving texture and complex flavor. Maitake, shiitake, cremini, and trumpet are my go-to woodsy crew.

INGREDIENT INFO:

- Use a mix of mushrooms. I like to use 8 ounces cremini or white, 6 ounces maitake, 6 ounces shiitake, and 4 ounces white trumpet. Shiitake stems should be removed completely, but the other ends just need a trim.

- You can use no-boil noodles here, but since this isn't an overly saucy lasagna, I recommend taking the time to boil real-deal lasagna noodles. That will ensure even cooking, tenderness, and added lift.

Fine sea salt

3 tablespoons unsalted butter

2 tablespoons olive oil

1½ pounds mixed mushrooms, cut or torn into bite-size pieces

Freshly ground black pepper

2 large shallots (or ½ medium to large onion), finely chopped (1¼ to 1½ cups)

2 to 3 large garlic cloves, minced

⅓ cup dry white wine

3 small sprigs fresh rosemary, stemmed, leaves minced (about 1 tablespoon)

1 package (16 ounces) lasagna noodles (see Ingredient Info)

1 container (15 ounces) whole-milk ricotta cheese

1 cup shaken heavy cream

1 large egg

4 to 6 curly kale leaves, stemmed, leaves finely chopped (4 cups)

12 ounces Asiago fresco cheese (or fresh mozzarella cheese), shredded

1 cup finely grated Parmesan cheese

---

1 For the lasagna noodles (if you are boiling them), bring a large pot of water to a boil and generously salt the water until it tastes like the sea.

2 For the mushrooms, heat 1 tablespoon of butter with 1 tablespoon of oil in a large cast-iron or stainless-steel skillet over medium-high heat. Add half of the mushrooms, ¼ teaspoon salt, and ⅛ teaspoon pepper. Cook, stirring occasionally, until the mushrooms are tender and browning in places, about 6 minutes. Transfer the mushrooms to a small bowl and return the skillet to the heat. Add another 1 tablespoon of butter and the remaining 1 tablespoon of oil to the pan and stir to encourage the butter to melt quickly. Add the remaining mushrooms, ¼ teaspoon salt, and ⅛ teaspoon pepper and cook, stirring occasionally, as done previously until browning, about 6 minutes. Transfer the second batch of mushrooms to the bowl.

(recipe continues)

3 Reduce the heat to medium-low. Add the remaining 1 tablespoon of butter, then stir in the shallots and garlic. Add the wine and cook, stirring to deglaze the pan, for about 30 seconds. Turn the heat up to medium and continue to cook, stirring frequently, until the shallots are translucent, about 3 minutes, being careful not to let them burn, reducing the heat if needed. Add all of the mushrooms and juices back to the pan and add the rosemary. Cook for another minute or two until the pan is mostly dry. Set aside to cool briefly to use immediately (or to cover and refrigerate for up to 2 days before assembling the lasagna).

4 When ready to make the lasagna, carefully add the noodles to the boiling water, crisscrossing them as you add them to help keep them from sticking together. Cook, stirring occasionally, for about 2 minutes less than indicated in the package instructions to ensure you don't overcook them. Carefully lift the noodles with tongs and transfer them to a colander to drain and cool briefly until you can handle them.

5 Meanwhile, in a medium bowl, stir together the ricotta, cream, egg, ¼ teaspoon salt, and a sprinkling of pepper until evenly combined.

6 Heat the oven to 375°F with a rack in the middle position.

7 To assemble the lasagna, spread about ½ cup or a touch more of the ricotta mixture over the bottom of a 9 × 13-inch baking dish. Place 4 noodles on top, covering the bottom of the pan and overlapping each of the noodles slightly. (Place boiled noodles lengthwise, and place no-boil noodles crosswise in the dish.) Scoop about ½ cup plus 1 tablespoon of the ricotta mixture over the noodles, then use an offset spatula or the back of a spoon to spread the mixture evenly over the noodles. Scatter about 1¼ cups of the mushroom mixture evenly over the top, then follow with enough raw kale, then grated Asiago, to cover (about 1 cup each).

8 Repeat step 7 two more times starting with 4 more noodles, then ricotta, then mushrooms, then kale, then Asiago. Finally, top with the remaining 4 noodles and top with the remaining ricotta mixture, then sprinkle evenly with the Parmesan. Crack some black pepper over the top.

9 Cover the lasagna with aluminum foil and bake for 15 minutes. Remove the foil and bake until the edges are bubbling and the cheese is melted and golden brown, about 25 minutes. Let rest at room temperature for 15 minutes or so before cutting and serving.

To store and reheat lasagna, see Tips and Takeaways on page 240.

The Enchilada

With vegetables packed into both the filling and the sauce, enchiladas are an every-season delight for the vegetable eater. In the spring (and fall), we will cover Swiss chard, mushrooms, and pinto beans in a charred poblano salsa verde. In the summer, we will give zucchini, red bell peppers, and onions a red ancho chile sauce. In the fall and winter, we are dressing up cauliflower and kale enchiladas with pumpkin cream sauce.

HOW TO ASSEMBLE ENCHILADAS

1. Warm the tortillas. Microwave a stack between two plates until just warmed through. (Brush them with oil before warming if you are working with tortillas that stick together.) To warm in an oven, preheat the oven to 400°F. Brush them with oil and place them on an unlined sheet pan, heat until just warm and pliable. In an oven you can also warm a stack wrapped in foil.

2. Set up your workstation as an assembly line from left to right: bowl with filling, stack of warm tortillas, 9 × 13-inch baking dish, sauce, cheese.

3. Cover the bottom of the dish with sauce.

4. Working quickly so the tortillas remain pliable, fill a tortilla (don't overfill it), roll it up, and place it lengthwise and seam side down, in the upper left corner of the dish. Repeat, working left to right, with the remaining tortillas and filling, to make two rows of rolled tortillas—6 in each row.

5. Cover the tortillas generously with sauce and sprinkle with cheese.

TIPS AND TAKEAWAYS

- To prevent soggy filling, cook vegetable fillings until vegetables are tender and the liquid has cooked off.

- Keep a store-bought sauce around for when you don't have the time to make your own.

- Don't overdo the cheese. Keep the focus on the delicious sauce and vegetable filling and finish with a dusting of cheese on top.

- Fresh toppings to finish enchiladas can really take them over the top. Try to serve at least one like cilantro or mint, avocado, pickled onions (see pages 66 and 100), radishes, sour cream, or toasted pepitas (see Prep Tip, page 26).

- Leftovers may be the best part. Refrigerate, tightly covered, for up to 2 days. Try to save some extra sauce to refresh them.

- To microwave small quantities, transfer 3 enchiladas at a time to a large microwave-safe plate. Cover them with a damp paper towel or invert the same size plate over the top to cover. Microwave for about 2 minutes or longer if needed until hot through the center and the cheese is melted.

- To reheat enchiladas in the oven, heat the oven to 400°F. Place them in a baking dish and cover with aluminum foil, tenting it to prevent the cheese from sticking. Bake small portions for about 15 minutes until the cheese is melted and the enchiladas are hot through the center. A full pan of cold enchiladas can take up to 35 minutes to reheat.

Mushroom and Swiss Chard Enchiladas
with Salsa Verde

MAKES 12 ENCHILADAS

SHORTCUTS:
- Use a store-bought sauce (a little less than the sauce we make here, 1½ to 1¾ cups, about 15 ounces).

- Try a prewashed mix of baby Swiss chard, kale, and tatsoi for a punch of super-greens. You'll miss out on some texture from the chard stems, but it's a quick trick when you are short on time.

BUTCHER TIP: The size of chard bunches, and of their leaves and stems, can vary. You may find a bunch with much of its weight attributed to its stems or others to its leaves. You need 1 cup chopped stems and 6 to 7 cups sliced leaves. The cooking time assumes that the chard will be slightly wet from rinsing. If you prep the chard ahead you may need to decrease the cooking time or add a couple of splashes of water to encourage wilting. See page 164 for how to prep Swiss chard.

You will love these enchiladas so much! The portobello and chard filling is earthy and green. It's balanced with a bright, tart, and smoky salsa verde and topped with sour cream and red radishes. Quick-Pickled Onions on page 100 or 15-Minute Pickle-y Onions on page 66 are an excellent topping, too. Try to save some sauce to serve fresh on top; it adds another dimension of flavor to a dish that is already full of it.

FOR THE ENCHILADAS

1 can (15½ ounces) pinto beans, rinsed and drained

2 tablespoons canola oil

1 tablespoon minced garlic

1 medium yellow onion, ⅛-inch sliced

1 bunch (8 to 10 ounces) Swiss chard, stems ⅛-inch diced, leaves thinly sliced (see Butcher Tip)

2 large portobello mushrooms caps, halved and ¼-inch sliced crosswise

2 teaspoons ground cumin

1¼ teaspoons fine sea salt

1 teaspoon apple cider vinegar

¼ teaspoon freshly ground black pepper

Twelve 5- to 6-inch mixed corn-and-wheat tortillas or corn tortillas

2 to 2½ cups Salsa Verde (page 252) or store-bought green enchilada sauce

1 to 2 cups shredded Monterey Jack or Oaxaca cheese, or a Mexican blend

FOR TOPPING (ANY OR ALL)

Sour cream

2 to 3 red radishes, sliced into 1/16-inch coins

Sliced avocado

Toasted pepitas (see Prep Tip, page 26)

Pickled onions (see pages 66 and 100)

1 Heat the oven to 400°F and set a rack in the middle position.

2 In a medium mixing bowl, mash half of the pinto beans with a fork; set aside.

3 Heat the oil and the garlic in a large skillet over medium heat. When the garlic just begins to simmer, cook for about 60 seconds, stirring frequently, until fragrant. Turn the heat up to medium-high, add the onion and the chard stems, and cook, stirring occasionally, for about 5 minutes until they just begin to soften and appear golden on the edges. Add the mushrooms, cumin, and ½ teaspoon of salt and cook, stirring occasionally, for about another 3 minutes until the mushrooms begin to soften. Stir in the chard leaves and ½ teaspoon of salt and cook, stirring occasionally, for about 4 minutes until the chard is wilted and the pan is almost dry. (If the pan becomes dry before the chard wilts, add a couple of tablespoons of water.) Add the vinegar, turn the heat up to high, and cook, stirring, until there is no liquid remaining. Stir in the smashed and whole pinto beans, season with the remaining ¼ teaspoon of salt and the pepper, and cook until just warmed through. Remove the pan from the heat and allow it to cool briefly.

• Use 8 ounces baby
bella mushrooms or any
combination of other
mushrooms in place of
portobello. Spinach or
kale can be subbed for
the Swiss chard, and
black beans for the
pinto beans.

• Use the (red) Ancho Chile
Sauce on page 254
instead of the Salsa
Verde.

4 Place the tortillas on a microwave-safe plate and cover them with a second plate of the same size. Microwave for 60 to 90 seconds until the tortillas are warm and pliable without breaking. Alternatively, brush the tortillas with a thin coating of olive oil. Spread them out on an unlined sheet pan and place in the preheated oven until just warm and pliable.

5 Cover the bottom of a 9 × 13-inch baking dish with about ½ cup of Salsa Verde. Position the dish lengthwise on your work surface. Working quickly while the tortillas are warm and pliable, place a scant ⅓ cup of the filling in the center of each tortilla and roll up the tortilla to keep the filling in place. Place the rolled tortilla, lengthwise and seam side down, in the upper left corner of the dish. Repeat, working left to right, and make two rows of rolled tortillas—6 in each row. Cover the tortillas with the remaining Salsa Verde and sprinkle them evenly with the cheese. Cover with foil and bake for 15 minutes until the cheese is beginning to melt. Uncover and cook for another 10 to 15 minutes until the enchiladas are warmed through and the cheese is completely melted and golden in places. (Continue to bake for another 5 minutes or longer if you prefer the cheese to brown in places.) Let the enchiladas cool for at least 10 minutes to set before serving. Serve with the toppings of your choice.

To store and reheat enchiladas, see Tips and Takeaways on page 249.

Salsa Verde

MAKES ABOUT 2½ CUPS

TAKE NOTE: This sauce comes together quickly and can be made ahead and stored for at least a few days for your convenience. Consider making it again to serve with good-quality tortilla chips (add a splash of apple cider vinegar or lime juice) or spoon it over Pinto Beans and Rice (page 65).

**2 poblano peppers (about 8 ounces),
  halved lengthwise, stemmed, and seeded**

**1 pound fresh tomatillos or 2 cans
  (11 ounces each) tomatillos, drained and
  rinsed**

1 small onion, cut into 8 pieces

2 tablespoons canola oil

1 garlic clove

Fine sea salt

1 to 1½ teaspoons sugar

Place an oven rack 6 inches from the top element and heat the broiler. Line a sheet pan with foil. Directly on the pan, toss the peppers, tomatillos, and onion pieces with the oil until evenly coated. Turn the peppers so that they are skin side up and press down to flatten them. Broil for 7 to 10 minutes, rotating the pan halfway through, or until tender and blackened. Let cool for 10 minutes or until the peppers are cool enough to handle. Peel the charred poblano skins and discard them. (Leave the tomatillo skins on for flavor.) In a food processor, pulse the onion and garlic to chop them, about five 1-second pulses. Scrape down the sides of the bowl. Transfer the peeled peppers and the tomatillos to the processor along with any juices on the sheet pan. Add ½ teaspoon salt and 1 teaspoon of sugar, then pulse until well blended and slightly chunky, about ten 1-second pulses. Scrape down the sides of the bowl and process on high just for a few seconds to smooth it out a bit. If you'd like to loosen the sauce add some drops of water until you reach your desired consistency. Add up to ½ teaspoon more sugar if it's too tart and adjust salt to taste.

Summer Vegetable Enchiladas
with Ancho Chile Sauce

MAKES 12 ENCHILADAS

BUTCHER TIP: Quarter the zucchini lengthwise, then thinly slice crosswise to produce quarter moons.

INGREDIENT INFO:

- Use your favorite corn tortillas. I like La Tortilla Factory white or yellow corn and wheat tortillas that have some flour in them.

- Ancho chile powder is made from dried poblano peppers and offers mild to medium heat. If needed, use chili powder in its place.

You may have avoided making enchiladas at home thinking they were too complicated or ruled them out as fried or too cheesy—never a candidate for a nourishing and delicious family meal. I am here to tell you these red sauce enchiladas packed with summer vegetables will change your mind.

FOR THE ENCHILADAS

4 tablespoons canola oil

1½ cups finely diced onion (½ large onion)

1 large red bell pepper, cored, seeded, and thinly sliced

Fine sea salt

1 medium to large zucchini, cut into ⅛-inch quarter moons (see Butcher Tip)

1½ to 2 cups sweet corn kernels (from 2 large ears or frozen)

3 packed cups baby spinach

1 can (15½ ounces) black beans, drained and rinsed

Ancho Chile Sauce (recipe follows)

Freshly ground black pepper

Twelve 5- to 6-inch mixed corn-and-wheat tortillas

1 to 2 cups shredded Monterey Jack or Oaxaca cheese, or a Mexican blend

FOR TOPPING (ANY OR ALL)

Diced or sliced fresh avocado

Lime wedges

Pickled onions (see pages 66 and 100)

Toasted pepitas (see Prep Tip, page 26)

Sour cream or Greek yogurt

Chopped fresh cilantro leaves

Thinly sliced radishes

1 Heat the oven to 450°F and set a rack in the middle position. Heat 2 tablespoons of oil in a large skillet over medium-high heat. Add the onion, bell pepper, and ½ teaspoon salt and cook, stirring occasionally, for about 5 minutes until the vegetables begin to soften. Stir in the zucchini and another ½ teaspoon salt, and cook, stirring occasionally, for 3 minutes until the zucchini is just tender. Stir in the corn and the spinach, a little at a time, until the corn is incorporated and warmed through and the spinach wilts. Reduce the heat at any time or add 1 tablespoon water if the veggies are browning too quickly. Remove the pan from the heat.

2 In a small mixing bowl, mash half of the black beans with the back of a fork. Stir the mashed and whole beans into the vegetable filling along with ¼ cup of the sauce. Adjust salt and add pepper to taste.

(recipe continues)

3 Stack the tortillas on a microwave-safe plate and cover them with a second plate of the same size. Microwave for 60 to 90 seconds until the tortillas are warm and pliable without breaking. Alternatively, lightly brush the tortillas with olive oil. Spread them out on an unlined sheet pan and place in the preheated oven until just warm and pliable.

4 Cover the bottom of a 9 × 13-inch baking dish with ½ cup of the sauce. Position the dish lengthwise on your work surface. Working quickly while the tortillas are warm and pliable, place ⅓ cup of filling in the center of each tortilla and roll up the tortilla to keep the filling in place. Place the rolled tortilla, lengthwise and seam side down, in the upper left corner of the dish. Repeat, working left to right, and make two rows of rolled tortillas—4 in each row. (If you happen to have any filling remaining you can stuff it in any gaps in the pan or reserve it to enjoy on its own.) Cover the tortillas evenly with the remaining sauce and sprinkle them evenly with the cheese. Cover with aluminum foil and bake for 15 minutes until the cheese is beginning to melt. Uncover and cook for another 10 to 15 minutes until the enchiladas are warmed through and the cheese is completely melted. (Continue to bake for another 5 minutes or longer if you prefer the cheese to brown in places.) Let the enchiladas cool for at least 10 minutes to set before serving. Top with any or all of the suggested toppings or serve them on the side.

To store and reheat enchiladas, see Tips and Takeaways on page 249.

Ancho Chile Sauce

MAKES ABOUT 2 CUPS

1 tablespoon canola oil

½ large onion, very finely diced

6 large garlic cloves, minced

2 tablespoons ancho chile powder
  (or chili powder)

2 teaspoons sugar

2 teaspoons ground cumin

1 teaspoon Mexican or Italian oregano
  (optional)

½ teaspoon ground coriander

Fine sea salt

¼ teaspoon freshly ground black pepper

2 cans (8 ounces each) tomato sauce

½ cup water

1 tablespoon pure maple syrup

Heat the oil in a medium saucepan over medium heat. Add the onion and cook, stirring occasionally, for about 5 minutes, until translucent and tender. Add the garlic, ancho chile powder, sugar, cumin, oregano if you are using it, coriander, ½ teaspoon salt, and the pepper and cook, stirring frequently, 60 to 90 seconds until evenly incorporated and fragrant. Stir in the tomato sauce and water and bring to a simmer. Reduce the heat to maintain a simmer and cook, partially covered, for about 7 minutes until the sauce thickens. Stir in the maple syrup and adjust salt to taste. Once cooled, the sauce will keep in the refrigerator in an airtight container for up to 3 days.

Cauliflower Enchiladas
with Pumpkin-Chipotle Cream Sauce

MAKES 13 ENCHILADAS

INGREDIENT INFO: Adjust the heat by using fewer chipotle peppers without their seeds or more with a few seeds depending on their size. To remove the seeds, halve the chipotle peppers lengthwise and use a paring knife to scrape out the seeds. (Then wash your hands.)

SWAPS:
- Feel free to use 2 cups of pureed roasted pie pumpkin or butternut squash in place of the canned pumpkin.
- Use baby spinach or chopped mature spinach in place of the kale.

BUTCHER TIP: See page 123 for how to prep cauliflower.

Pumpkin is a prime candidate for cool-weather enchiladas. Canned pumpkin puree saves time and gives this sauce a consistent, creamy texture. The filling—onion, cauliflower, and curly kale braised with spices and orange zest and juice—is equally straightforward to make. Just before serving, dry-toast the pumpkin seeds (pepitas), then top the enchiladas and enjoy!

FOR THE SAUCE

2 large garlic cloves

1 small onion, quartered

2 to 3 chipotle peppers in adobo

1 can (15 ounces) pumpkin puree

1 cup shaken heavy cream

½ cup water

1 tablespoon freshly squeezed lime juice

1 tablespoon pure maple syrup

1 teaspoon fine sea salt

½ teaspoon ground cumin

FOR THE FILLING

2 tablespoons olive oil

1 medium onion, halved and thinly sliced

Fine sea salt

2 large cloves garlic, minced

1 large head cauliflower, cut into ¾-inch florets

1 teaspoon ground cumin

Heaping 1 teaspoon dried oregano

1 teaspoon ancho chile powder or chili powder

1 teaspoon finely grated orange zest plus 3 tablespoons orange juice

1 bunch curly kale, stemmed and chopped

1 can (15½ ounces) black beans or pinto beans, rinsed and drained (optional)

Freshly ground black pepper

Twelve 5- to 6-inch mixed corn-and-wheat tortillas

1½ cups grated Cheddar, jack, or Cotija cheese (about 3 ounces)

FOR TOPPING (ANY OR ALL)

Heaping 1 tablespoon toasted pepitas (see Prep Tip, page 26)

Thinly sliced radishes

Chopped fresh cilantro

Quick-Pickled Onion (page 100)

1 Make the pumpkin-chipotle sauce. In a food processor or blender, process the garlic until finely chopped. Add the onion and chipotle peppers and pulse until coarsely chopped, about 5 times. Scrape down the sides of the bowl. Add the pumpkin puree, ¾ cup of cream, and the water, lime juice, maple syrup, salt, and cumin. Blend on high until completely smooth. Scrape down the sides of the bowl, add the remaining ¼ cup of cream, and blend until incorporated.

(recipe continues)

2 Make the filling. Heat the oil in a large, deep sauté pan or Dutch oven over medium heat, add the onion and ½ teaspoon salt, and cook, stirring occasionally, for 5 minutes until the onion begins to soften and appear golden in places. Stir in the garlic, cauliflower, ½ teaspoon salt, the cumin, oregano, and chili powder and cook, stirring occasionally, for about 3 minutes until the cauliflower just begins to soften.

3 Stir in the orange zest and juice, then add the kale, a bit at a time if needed to fit the pan. Turn up the heat to medium-high and cook for another 3 to 4 minutes until the liquid in the pan has cooked off and the cauliflower is tender, but not soft, and the kale is tender. If you are adding beans, move the cauliflower mixture to the sides of the pan and add half of the beans to the center of the pan. Use a potato masher or fork to mash the beans. Add the remaining beans and stir to incorporate the smashed and whole beans into the mixture. Season with more salt and add pepper to taste. Remove from the heat and stir in ½ cup of the pumpkin sauce, then let the mixture cool until cool enough to handle.

4 Assemble and bake the enchiladas. Heat the oven to 450°F and set a rack in the middle position. Place the tortillas on a microwave-safe plate and cover them with a second plate of the same size. Microwave for 60 to 90 seconds until the tortillas are warm and pliable without breaking. Alternatively, brush the tortillas with a thin coating of olive oil. Spread them out on an unlined sheet pan and place in the preheated oven until just warm and pliable.

5 Cover the bottom of a 9 × 13-inch baking dish with ¾ to 1 cup of the sauce. Position the dish lengthwise on your work surface. Working quickly while the tortillas are warm, place a heaping ⅓ cup of the filling in the center of each tortilla and roll up the tortilla to keep the filling in place. Place the rolled tortilla, lengthwise and seam side down, in the upper left corner of the dish. Repeat, working left to right, and make two rows of rolled tortillas pressing them together as needed to fit 6 in each row. Tuck one more tortilla crosswise along the bottom. Cover the tortillas with the remaining pumpkin sauce and sprinkle them evenly with cheese.

6 Cover with foil and bake for 15 minutes until the cheese is beginning to melt. Uncover and cook for another 10 to 15 minutes until the enchiladas are warmed through and the cheese is completely melted and golden in places. Let the enchiladas cool for at least 10 minutes to set before serving. Top with the just-toasted pepitas, and radishes, cilantro, and/or pickled onions if you wish.

To store and reheat enchiladas, see Tips and Takeaways on page 249.

The Free-Form Savory Tart

Whether you call it a free-form tart, a galette (as they do in France), or a crostata (an Italian version), when you combine a flaky crust with vegetables, you get a world of delicious possibilities. I am offering you two crust options to use with a bunch of seasonal variations: a sweet wheat-and-butter crust (see page 261) and an olive oil crust (see page 264). You may also try making individual mini tarts, dividing the dough into about 4 servings. Serve your savory pastries with a simple green salad, a grain salad, or a soup to round out the meal.

GOOD VEG FOR SPRING: asparagus, leeks, Swiss chard, onions, mushrooms, potatoes

GOOD VEG FOR SUMMER: tomatoes, eggplant, peppers, zucchini

GOOD VEG FOR FALL/WINTER: beets, broccoli rabe, celery root, kale, mushrooms, rutabaga, spinach, sweet potatoes, Swiss chard, turnips, winter squash

---

TIPS AND TAKEAWAYS

- A food processor is the key to bringing the dough together quickly, but for an extra-flaky crust you can also make it by hand. When short on time, use store-bought puff pastry (thawed following package instructions).

- For a more tender crust, stop mixing the dough when it just comes together and give it a rest before you roll it out.

- Make the dough ahead. Flatten it into a disc, wrap it tightly, and place it in an airtight container. Refrigerate for a couple of days or freeze it for up to 6 months. Thaw frozen dough in the refrigerator overnight. Bring the dough to room temperature and roll out when just pliable.

- Remove moisture from vegetables to prevent a soggy crust. Salt tomatoes and let them drain (see page 262). Sauté or grill watery vegetables, such as zucchini, mushrooms, and greens, to cook off excess liquid and concentrate flavors. To further protect the crust, layer the vegetable filling over dough lined with breadcrumbs, cheese, thinly sliced potatoes, or a bean puree. If your tarts are still getting soggy, try brushing the interior bottom of the crust with egg white, before filling it, to seal it.

- Tuck sautéed greens into the pie or stir them together with ricotta and egg to make a filling of its own.

- These pies are rustic. Roll out the dough into a circular shape; no precise measuring here. To pleat the dough, lift one edge and fold it over the filling, then lift and fold another section over the first, continuing around the tart and pleating every couple of inches.

- If the dough feels too soft or difficult to work after you roll it out, stop and let it chill in the fridge to firm up before you move on to filling and pleating the galette.

- These tarts can be made up to one day in advance. Reheat leftovers in a 375°F oven until warm through the middle, 10 to 12 minutes, or longer depending on the portion size. A toaster oven works well to reheat individual slices. (Slices are also excellent at room temperature.)

Potato and Creamed Leek Galette

SERVES 4 TO 6 AS A MAIN

SWAPS:

- Rosemary can substitute for the thyme; or replace the thyme with additional minced chives: Use 1 tablespoon for the filling and ½ tablespoon to garnish the top after it comes out of the oven.

- Consider adding asparagus in place of the potatoes when the season is right.

MAKE AHEAD: Prepare the leek filling, let cool, cover, and refrigerate for up to 3 days before assembly. Make the dough ahead. Wrap it in plastic and refrigerate one day before assembly or freeze for longer storage. Bake the galette in advance and it reheats beautifully.

BUTCHER TIP: See page 269 for how to thinly slice potatoes with a mandoline vegetable slicer.

I first developed a version of this rustic pie for a magazine, where it was featured as a main dish for the Thanksgiving table. The combination of the potatoes and creamed leeks is such a special treat. With additions of lemon and chives, it feels right to serve it at springtime celebrations, too. Take note, you can make this pie with the olive oil crust on page 264, but the whole wheat flour in this crust is a nice touch to offset the galette's wonderful richness.

Sweet Wheat-and-Butter Galette Dough (recipe follows)

2 tablespoons unsalted butter, plus more as needed

2 large leeks, white and light green parts only, halved lengthwise, thinly sliced, and well rinsed (about 6 cups)

1 teaspoon fine sea salt

Freshly ground black pepper

½ cup shaken heavy cream

1 pound Yukon gold potatoes, peeled and ⅛-inch sliced

2 tablespoons extra-virgin olive oil

1½ teaspoons finely chopped fresh thyme leaves

1 teaspoon finely grated lemon zest

1 large egg

1 teaspoon water

Flour, for rolling out the dough

½ cup whole-milk ricotta cheese

Flaky sea salt, such as Maldon

3 ounces aged provolone cheese, coarsely grated (or 1½ ounces Parmesan cheese, finely grated on a Microplane)

½ tablespoon freshly minced chives (optional)

---

1 Let the dough rest at room temperature (or bring it to room temperature if chilled) while you prepare the filling.

2 Melt the butter in a large skillet over medium heat. Add the leeks, ½ teaspoon of the salt, and ¼ teaspoon pepper and cook, stirring occasionally, until the leeks are tender, adding more butter if the pan becomes too dry, about 8 minutes. Reduce the heat to low, add the cream, and cook, stirring frequently, until thickened, 1 to 3 minutes. Set the leeks aside to cool.

3 In a large bowl, toss the potatoes with the oil, the remaining ½ teaspoon of salt, 1 teaspoon of thyme, and ½ teaspoon of lemon zest. In a small bowl, lightly beat the egg with the water to make an egg wash; set aside.

4 Make the galette. Heat the oven to 400°F with a rack in the middle position. Lightly flour the dough, a rolling pin, and a piece of parchment paper cut to fit a sheet pan. Roll the dough from the center outward on the parchment to form a 14-inch-diameter circle. (Don't fret about making a perfect circle, but try to maintain even thickness.) Transfer the parchment and dough to the sheet pan (the dough will hang over the edges at this point).

5 Leaving a 2-inch border, evenly spread the leek mixture in the center. Stir the potatoes, then lift them from the bowl with a slotted spoon, leaving behind any liquid, and distribute them evenly over the leek mixture, fanning and overlapping the slices. Tuck any irregularly shaped potato slices under or between more even rounds, making sure to maintain the 2-inch border. Dollop the ricotta over the potatoes and sprinkle with ½ teaspoon flaky sea salt and the remaining ½ teaspoon of lemon zest. Top the filling with the provolone (or Parmesan), the remaining ½ teaspoon of thyme, and a grind of fresh pepper.

6 Fold the edge of the dough up and over the filling, pleating as you go. If the dough sticks to the parchment, refrigerate for 5 to 10 minutes, then continue folding. Brush the folded edges with the egg wash, and sprinkle with ½ teaspoon flaky sea salt.

7 Bake the galette, rotating the sheet pan halfway through until the crust is golden brown, the cheese is golden in places, and the potatoes are tender, 45 to 50 minutes. If the crust is browning too quickly, before the filling sets, shield the crust with foil, tenting a few small pieces to cover the edges, and continue baking until the potatoes are tender. Transfer to a cooling rack and let cool for at least 10 minutes. The longer you let it cool, the more it will hold together for serving. If you are using them, sprinkle with the chives. Serve warm or at room temperature.

The galette will keep placed flat on a plate or sheet pan (avoid stacking pieces) and refrigerated for up to 3 days. To reheat it, see Tips and Takeaways on page 258.

Sweet Wheat-and-Butter Galette Dough

MAKES A 14-INCH-ROUND OF ROLLED-OUT DOUGH

1¼ cups all-purpose flour

½ cup plus 2 tablespoons whole wheat flour

2 teaspoons sugar

¾ teaspoon fine sea salt

10 tablespoons (1¼ sticks) cold unsalted butter, cut into small pieces

1 teaspoon apple cider vinegar

6 to 7 tablespoons ice water

Pulse the flours, sugar, and salt in a food processor. Add the butter, breaking the pieces apart and scattering them over the flour. Pulse until the mixture looks like coarse meal, 10 to 12 times. Add the vinegar, then, while pulsing, one at a time, add 6 tablespoons of water until the dough just begins to come together, about 15 times. Add up to another tablespoon of water if needed. Turn the dough out onto a board. Fold the dough on top of itself a few times and shape it into a disc. Wrap it in plastic. If you are making the galette right away, let the dough rest at room temperature for 15 to 30 minutes while you make the filling. Otherwise, store it in the refrigerator for up to a day in advance of assembling the galette. Bring it to room temperature before rolling it out.

Summer Tomato Crostata
with Olive Oil–Parmesan Crust

SERVES 4 TO 6 AS A MAIN

ABOUT THE YIELD:
To serve 6, pair the crostata with a simple side salad, one of the kale salads on pages 26 to 29, or Marinated "Agrodolce" Sweet Peppers and Cannellini Bean Salad (page 41).

A crostata is an always-perfect way to showcase and enjoy luscious in-season tomatoes. Use several varieties and colors to really make it pop. Try rounds of eggplant or zucchini, or winter squash in the fall. Change up the herbs and the grated cheese additions. This belongs in your repertoire.

Olive Oil–Parmesan Crostata Dough (page 264)

2 pounds slicer or heirloom tomatoes

1 teaspoon fine sea salt

1 cup ricotta cheese

½ cup finely grated Parmesan cheese

Heaping ½ cup shredded mozzarella cheese

⅓ cup chopped fresh basil leaves (10 to 12 large leaves)

2 tablespoons extra-virgin olive oil

1 medium garlic clove, minced

1 large egg

1 teaspoon water

Flour, for rolling the dough

Flaky sea salt, such as Maldon, for finishing

---

1 Let the dough rest at room temperature (or bring it to room temperature if chilled) while you prepare the filling.

2 Core the tomatoes and slice them into ¼-inch-thick rounds. Spread them out on a kitchen towel or paper towels. Sprinkle the tomatoes with ¾ teaspoon of salt and let stand to drain, 15 to 30 minutes. Gently place a towel over the tops and blot to dry them.

3 Meanwhile, stir together the ricotta, Parmesan, mozzarella, about half of the basil, and the remaining ¼ teaspoon of salt in a small bowl. In a separate small bowl, combine the oil and garlic. In a third small bowl, lightly beat the egg with the water to make an egg wash. Set all aside.

4 Make the crostata. Heat the oven to 375°F with a rack in the middle position. On a piece of parchment paper, flatten the crostata dough and roll it from the center outward with a lightly floured rolling pin. Turn the dough and the parchment as you go to create a circular shape about 14 inches in diameter. (Even thickness is more important than a perfect circle.) Transfer the parchment and the dough to a sheet pan.

(recipe continues)

5 Evenly spread the cheese mixture over the dough, leaving a border of about 1½ inches. Starting from the outside and working in, fan the tomatoes in concentric circles to cover the cheese mixture. Brush the tomatoes with the oil–garlic mixture. Gently fold the dough border up and over the filling, pleating it as you go. Brush the dough lightly with the egg wash.

6 Bake for 50 to 55 minutes on the center rack until the crust is golden brown and the tomatoes are just wilted. (Move the crostata to the top rack of the oven for the last 10 minutes of cooking if the crust is still very light and needs color.)

7 Cool on a wire rack until close to room temperature, at least 15 minutes. (The tart will set and its flavors will develop as it cools.) Top with the remaining basil and a sprinkle of flaky sea salt, then cut and serve.

The crostata will keep, placed flat on a plate or sheet pan (avoid stacking pieces) and refrigerated, for up to 3 days. To reheat it, see Tips and Takeaways on page 258.

Olive Oil–Parmesan Crostata Dough

MAKES A 14- TO 15-INCH
ROUND OF ROLLED-OUT
DOUGH

ALL PLANTS: Omit the
Parmesan and add
another pinch of salt.

2 cups all-purpose flour

½ teaspoon fine sea salt

½ cup freshly grated Parmesan cheese
  (see All Plants)

½ cup extra-virgin olive oil

About ¾ cup ice water

1 In a food processor or large bowl, briefly pulse or stir together the flour, salt, and Parmesan until just incorporated. Add the oil and pulse or stir to combine. While the processor is running, or while stirring, pour in ½ cup of ice water (no ice) and process until the dough just begins to hold together and to form a ball. If needed, add up to 2 tablespoons more water, 1 tablespoon at a time, while pulsing, until it comes together. The dough should be wet and smooth, but should not stick to your fingers.

2 Flatten the ball of dough just slightly to form a disc and wrap in plastic wrap. If you are making the crostata right away, let it rest at room temperature for 15 to 30 minutes while you make the filling. Otherwise, store it in the refrigerator for up to a day or freeze it for up to 3 months then defrost it in the refrigerator. Bring it to room temperature before rolling it out.

Caramelized Onion and Apple Crostata
with Gorgonzola

TAKE NOTE: This crostata is best cut and served when it is almost completely cooled, but if you can't wait, allow it to stand for at least 15 minutes.

SWAP: Replace the Gorgonzola with ½ cup grated Parmesan and a heaping 1 cup shredded Gruyère.

This crostata is made for fall and winter days, delivering on everything warm, cozy, and delicious. The blue cheese melts into the ricotta and plays a subtle but vital role in balancing the sweetness of the onions and apple and adds a bit of tang. Serve a slice with a tangle of arugula dressed simply with balsamic vinegar or lemon and olive oil.

Olive Oil–Parmesan Crostata Dough (page 264)

¼ cup extra-virgin olive oil

3 large onions, halved and thinly sliced

1¾ teaspoons fine sea salt

1 large Honeycrisp, Fuji, or EverCrisp apple, unpeeled, cored, and ⅛-inch sliced

4 teaspoons finely chopped fresh rosemary leaves

2 tablespoons balsamic vinegar

1 tablespoon pure maple syrup

⅛ teaspoon freshly ground black pepper

1 cup ricotta cheese

½ cup freshly crumbled Gorgonzola cheese (about 2 ounces)

1 large egg

1 teaspoon water

Flour, for rolling out the dough

Flaky sea salt, such as Maldon, for finishing

1 Let the dough rest at room temperature (or bring it to room temperature if chilled) while you prepare the filling. Heat the oven to 375°F with a rack in the middle position.

2 Heat the oil in a large, deep sauté pan or Dutch oven over medium-high heat. Add the onions, stir, and evenly sprinkle 1½ teaspoons of salt over the onions. Cook, stirring occasionally, until the onions are translucent and beginning to soften, about 7 minutes. Stir in the apple and 3 teaspoons of rosemary and cook, stirring frequently, until the onions are completely tender and golden and the apples are just tender, about 5 minutes. (Reduce the heat and add a tablespoon of water if the onions brown too quickly at any point.) Add the balsamic vinegar, maple syrup, and pepper to the pan and stir constantly until incorporated and all liquid is absorbed, about 3 minutes.

(recipe continues)

3 In a small bowl, stir together the ricotta, Gorgonzola, the remaining 1 teaspoon of rosemary, and the remaining ¼ teaspoon of salt. In a separate small bowl, lightly beat the egg with the water to make an egg wash. Set all aside.

4 On a piece of parchment paper, flatten the crostata dough and roll it from the center outward with a lightly floured rolling pin. Turn the dough and the parchment as you go to create a circular shape about 14 inches in diameter and a little less than ¼ inch thick. (Don't bother trying to make a perfect circle but do try to even out the thickness of the dough.) Transfer the parchment and the dough to a sheet pan. The dough can hang over the edges for now.

5 Evenly spread the cheese mixture over the dough, leaving a border of about 1½ inches. Spread out the onion-apple mixture evenly on top, covering the cheese completely. Gently fold the dough border up and over the filling, pleating it as you go. Brush the dough lightly with the egg wash.

6 Bake for 45 to 50 minutes on the center rack until the crust is golden brown. (Move the crostata to the top rack of the oven for the last 10 minutes of cooking if the crust is still very light and needs color.)

7 Cool on a wire rack for at least 15 minutes before cutting and serving. Top with a sprinkle of flaky sea salt. Serve warm or, ideally, close to room temperature.

The crostata will keep placed flat on a plate or sheet pan (avoid stacking pieces) and refrigerated for up to 3 days. To reheat it, see Tips and Takeaways on page 258.

The Frittata

Think of the Frittata as a crustless, no-fuss quiche—essentially whipped eggs and tons of vegetables baked in a skillet. It's a trusty must-know dish (that's easy to get the hang of) and can be made with nearly any vegetable. The ones I share with you will anchor any brunch and are always welcome at dinner with roasted potatoes and a simple salad. Keep a frittata in mind, too, as you score something beautiful at the farmers market, pull veggies from your garden, or find bits and pieces of produce hanging around your kitchen that you aren't quite sure what to do with. An improvised frittata is always a safe bet.

GOOD VEGETABLES TO FILL A FRITTATA:
artichokes, arugula, asparagus, broccoli, broccoli rabe, butternut squash, cauliflower, corn, eggplant, fennel, garlic, garlic scapes, hearty greens (such as collard greens, kale, mustard greens, and Swiss chard), herbs, leeks, onions, mushrooms, nettles, peas, peppers, potatoes, ramps, scallions, spaghetti squash, spinach, sweet potatoes, tomatoes, zucchini

GOOD METHODS FOR FRITTATA FILLINGS:
Sautéing is the most straightforward cooking method for frittata filling, but you can also roast vegetables like broccoli, cauliflower, eggplant, winter squashes, potatoes, sweet potatoes, and tomatoes. Don't overcook firm and dense vegetables, as they will continue to cook when they are baked into the frittata. They should be al dente before going in. Add herbs, scallions, and ramps raw or cook them briefly with other vegetables. You can add small quantities of raw spinach and/or tomatoes to a frittata, too. Raw microgreens can give a nutrient boost and a pop of fresh flavor. Use them as a garnish for the top when serving.

TIPS AND TAKEAWAYS

- Use a well-seasoned cast-iron skillet or an oven-safe nonstick skillet to prevent sticking.

- Be careful of the hot handle when it comes out of the oven. Place an oven mitt over the handle as a reminder.

- Before adding vegetables to a frittata, cook and season them to remove moisture and concentrate their flavor.

- Season the whisked eggs with salt and pepper before adding them to the pan. A layer of salt on top is not enough.

- Take care to not overbake the frittata. Take it out of the oven as soon as the center sets and is slightly firm to the touch.

- Don't cut into a frittata too soon. The longer it cools, the easier it is to pull from the pan.

- Frittata can be served hot or at room temperature. To serve hot, let it rest for 10 to 15 minutes before cutting. Run a rubber spatula around the edges (and underneath if sticking) and slide it onto a platter for serving or serve it directly out of the pan.

- Serve frittata with arugula or baby greens dressed in a simple, bright vinaigrette like House Lemon Vinaigrette (page 21) or a simple vinaigrette with shallots (see page 17) and/or Crispy Roasted Potatoes (page 272).

Potato and Spring Pea Frittata

TAKE NOTE: Have a jar of your favorite chili crisp nearby; a spoonful drizzled over the top is always welcome.

INGREDIENT INFO: Don't skip the fresh peas. You can buy them already shelled to save time.

HOW TO SLICE POTATOES WITH A MANDOLINE:

1. Peel the potatoes. Leave smaller potatoes whole; halve larger potatoes lengthwise.

2. Adjust the slicer to cut ⅛-inch slices. Wearing a cut-resistant glove, carefully press each potato (or short end of each half) against the blade. Using even pressure, glide back and forth to make thin slices. Don't glide too quickly, but do build some momentum in order to easily push the potato through. Stop when you get close to the blade.

Spanish tortilla, an adored open-faced omelet packed with potatoes simmered in olive oil, inspired this frittata. It's heavy on the potatoes and light on the egg. It's a hit at a special-occasion brunch sliced and served with a colorful salad. Cut into small squares, it can anchor a happy hour grazing board. It's also a wonderful dinner, perhaps with sautéed asparagus on the side. You can serve this frittata warm, room temp, or even cold, so feel free to make it a day ahead.

½ cup extra-virgin olive oil

3 garlic cloves, smashed

1½ pounds Yukon gold potatoes (or red potatoes), peeled and ⅛-inch sliced

1 cup fresh shelled peas (1 pound in the pod)

1½ teaspoons fine sea salt

½ teaspoon freshly ground black pepper

8 large eggs

¼ cup shaken heavy cream

1½ teaspoons lemon zest

1 tablespoon plus 1 teaspoon minced fresh chives for topping

1 tablespoon chopped fresh dill

3 ounces goat cheese

Flaky sea salt, such as Maldon, for finishing (optional)

1 Heat the oven to 375°F with a rack in the middle position. Heat the oil and garlic in a large skillet over medium heat. When the garlic just begins to simmer in the oil, cook, stirring frequently, for about 90 seconds until golden and fragrant. Add the potatoes, making sure to separate them as you stir them as they have a tendency to stick together. Cook the potatoes, stirring occasionally, until they are tender and lightly browning in places, 8 to 10 minutes. (Reduce the heat if the potatoes brown too quickly or begin to burn on the edges before cooking through.) Remove large pieces of the smashed garlic with a slotted spoon and stir in the peas. Evenly season the potatoes and peas with 1 teaspoon of salt and ¼ teaspoon of pepper and cook, stirring occasionally, for 1 minute until the peas are warmed through. Transfer the potato-pea mixture with a slotted spoon to a colander set over a large liquid measure or bowl to further drain the oil. Reserve 2 tablespoons of the oil for this recipe.

2 In a large bowl, whisk together the eggs, cream, 1 teaspoon of lemon zest, the 1 tablespoon of chives, the dill, the remaining ½ teaspoon of salt, and the remaining ¼ teaspoon of pepper. Stir in the potatoes and peas until evenly combined.

(recipe continues)

3 Heat the reserved oil in a medium cast-iron skillet or oven-safe nonstick skillet over medium-low heat. Brush the oil evenly over the bottom and lower sides of the skillet, being careful not to allow the hot oil to spill over the sides. Pour the filling carefully into the skillet and use tongs to evenly spread out the potatoes if needed. Cook for 5 to 6 minutes, allowing the egg to set along the outer edges of the pan. Crumble the goat cheese over the top, evenly dispersing it. Sprinkle the remaining ½ teaspoon of lemon zest over the goat cheese crumbles. Transfer the dish to the oven and bake for 15 to 18 minutes until the center is just set. Remove the skillet from the oven, being mindful of the hot handle. Allow the frittata to cool for at least 5 minutes. Run a rubber spatula around the sides to loosen it from the sides of the pan. (If you do not want to cut the frittata in the pan, run the spatula under as well to lift it gently and transfer it to a cutting board.)

4 Sprinkle the frittata lightly with the remaining minced chives and with flaky sea salt if you wish. Cut in wedges to serve as an entrée or small square shapes for an appetizer.

Zucchini-Basil Frittata
with Caramelized Red Onion and Ricotta

MAKES A 10-INCH FRITTATA;
SERVES 4 TO 6 AS A MAIN

This summer frittata, packed with basil, garlic, and zucchini and topped with ricotta, is based on the one my grandmother and her mother so lovingly used to make. It hits the spot in the summer months at breakfast, lunch, or dinner.

¼ cup extra-virgin olive oil

1½ tablespoons minced garlic

1 medium red onion, thinly sliced

1¼ teaspoons fine sea salt

1 pound (2 small to medium) zucchini, ½-inch diced

Freshly ground black pepper

¾ cup loosely packed fresh basil leaves, chopped

12 large eggs

⅓ cup shaken heavy cream

Heaping ½ cup whole-milk ricotta cheese

Heaping ⅓ cup finely grated Parmesan cheese, for topping

1 Heat the oven to 350°F with a rack in the middle position.

2 In a medium cast-iron skillet or oven-safe nonstick skillet, heat the oil and garlic over medium heat until it begins to simmer, then cook, stirring, for about 30 seconds until fragrant. Add the onion and ½ teaspoon of salt and sauté for 4 to 5 minutes until the onion is translucent and turning golden in places. Reduce the heat as needed, being careful not to burn the garlic and onion. Add the zucchini,

¼ teaspoon of salt, and ⅛ teaspoon pepper and cook, stirring occasionally, for about 3 minutes until the zucchini is just about tender. Turn up the heat to medium-high if you are using a nonstick skillet, or keep it at medium heat if using a cast-iron skillet. Stir in half of the basil and cook, stirring often, for about 2 minutes more until the zucchini is just tender and browning. Remove the pan from the heat to cool briefly.

3 Meanwhile, in a large bowl, whisk together the eggs, cream, all but about 1 tablespoon of the remaining basil, the remaining ½ teaspoon of salt, and ¼ teaspoon pepper. Return the pan to medium-low heat. Spread out the zucchini mixture and pour the egg mixture evenly over the top. Rearrange the zucchini and onion to evenly distribute them as needed. Cook for about 5 minutes until the eggs set along the edges, spoon the ricotta over the top in places, sprinkle with the Parmesan, and place the pan in the oven. Bake for 18 to 20 minutes until set in the middle and puffed up and browning in places. Carefully remove the pan from the oven and transfer it to a cooling rack to cool for at least 15 minutes.

4 To serve, run a rubber spatula or offset spatula along the edges to help release it from the sides and bottom of the pan. Cut and serve in wedges, topped with the remaining fresh basil and freshly cracked pepper.

Simple Broccoli-Cheddar Frittata
with Crispy Roasted Potatoes

MAKES A 10- OR 12-INCH FRITTATA: SERVES 4 TO 8 AS A MAIN

Broccoli and Cheddar just go together. There are no fancy bells and whistles here—just a classic match that makes for a no-fuss, everyday frittata that comes together in no time. To feed a crowd at a brunch or lunch event, where a frittata is always welcome, see Variation on page 272. I think you'll find you'll use both recipes all the time.

10 large eggs

⅓ cup shaken heavy cream

½ teaspoon baking powder

1¼ teaspoons fine sea salt

¼ teaspoon freshly ground black pepper

2 pinches of cayenne pepper (optional)

½ cup finely grated Parmesan cheese (about ½ ounce)

About 1 cup coarsely grated aged white Cheddar cheese (2 ounces)

2 tablespoons extra-virgin olive oil

2 teaspoons minced garlic

3 cups ½-inch (bite-size) broccoli florets

2 tablespoons water

Crispy Roasted Potatoes (recipe follows)

(recipe continues)

To make a
12-inch frittata that serves
8 to 12, use 16 eggs, ½ cup
cream, 1 teaspoon baking
powder, 1 teaspoon salt
(with the eggs), increase
the Cheddar to 3 ounces
(1½ cups), and increase the
olive oil to 3 tablespoons,
garlic to 1 tablespoon, and
broccoli to 4 cups. Leave all
other ingredients the same.
Sauté the broccoli for 7 to
8 minutes total and add an
extra tablespoon of water
if needed. Cook it on the
stovetop until set around
the edges, 3 minutes,
and then in the oven until
cooked through the middle,
about 25 minutes.

1 Heat the oven to 350°F with a rack in the middle position. In a large bowl, whisk together the eggs, cream, baking powder, ¾ teaspoon of salt, the black pepper, and the cayenne pepper if using. Stir in half of the Parmesan and half of the Cheddar. Set aside.

2 In a medium cast-iron skillet or oven-safe nonstick skillet, heat the oil and garlic over medium heat. When the oil begins to simmer, cook for about 30 seconds until fragrant. Add the broccoli and the remaining ½ teaspoon of salt and cook, stirring occasionally, for about 3 minutes until just tender. Add the water to prevent burning and encourage steaming, and cook, stirring occasionally, for about 3 minutes more until the broccoli is tender and browning in places and no liquid remains. Give the egg mixture a stir and then add it into the skillet. Reduce the heat to medium-low and gently stir to evenly distribute the broccoli and eggs. Cook for about 2 minutes until the egg begins to set around the edges. Evenly distribute the remaining cheeses over the top. Bake until the frittata puffs up, the edges are set, and the middle is just slightly firm, 15 to 18 minutes.

3 Serve hot or cooled to room temperature, cut into wedges, with the potatoes on the side.

Crispy Roasted Potatoes

SERVES 4 TO 6 AS A SIDE

Fine sea salt

2 pounds Yukon gold potatoes or
   red potatoes, unpeeled and scrubbed,
   ¾-inch to 1-inch diced

3 tablespoons plus 2 teaspoons extra-
   virgin olive oil

Freshly ground black pepper (optional)

1 Bring a large pot of water to a boil and salt it generously until it tastes like the sea. Add the potatoes and when the water has returned to a boil, boil the potatoes for 7 to 8 minutes until they are just tender. Drain the potatoes in a colander and shake the colander up and down to rough up the edges of the potatoes. Let the potatoes stand for a few minutes to dry out. Toss the potatoes with the 3 tablespoons of oil, gradually adding the oil and tossing, to ensure even distribution. Season with ½ to ¾ teaspoon salt. (This will depend on the saltiness of the cooking water.)

2 Heat the oven to 425°F with a rack in the top position.

3 Generously and evenly oil a sheet pan and spread out the par-cooked potatoes in a single layer, leaving some room between them. (If you have used more than 2 pounds, use two sheet pans; do not overcrowd the pan.) Roast for 15 minutes, then flip the potatoes and shake the pan to spread them out. Roast for another 10 minutes then flip the potatoes and shake again. Cook for another 3 to 5 minutes until golden and crispy. Add more salt if needed, and shower the potatoes with pepper (if using), and serve immediately.

The Strata

A savory (sometimes sweet) bread and egg casserole that you can assemble ahead, the Strata is born to brunch. We are making a classic with sourdough bread, asparagus, and spring alliums. There's an untraditional one with tortillas, charred poblanos, and tomatoes, and a breakfast or dinner strata with bacon-like shiitake mushrooms and collard greens. Here's the basic formula so you can freestyle as you wish:

Vegetables + Good-Quality (Dried-Out) Bread or Tortillas + Custard (eggs and milk or cream)

GOOD VEGETABLES FOR STRATAS: artichokes, asparagus, broccoli, Brussels sprouts, cauliflower, celery, fennel, garlic, hearty greens (collards, mustard greens, kale, Swiss chard), leeks, mushrooms, onions, peppers, ramps, spinach, tomatoes, winter squash

---

TIPS AND TAKEAWAYS

- Use good-quality bread or tortillas.

- Try different types of bread like sourdough, multigrain, ciabatta, and brioche. Leave the crust on. It's important to dry out the bread. (Soft, fresh bread makes a soggy strata.) Leave it out uncovered (a turned-off oven is a good spot for it) or toast it at 325°F. Cut bread in ½-inch-thick slices or 1-inch cubes. Anytime you have leftover good bread, think "strata."

- Sauté vegetable add-ins to concentrate flavor and remove excess moisture.

- Strata is a perfect make-ahead brunch dish. Assemble, cover, and store in the fridge for up to 12 hours. Its texture improves with extra time, so soak it overnight.

- If you didn't plan ahead, you can still make strata with good results. Use cans of beans to weigh down the strata and speed up soaking, ideally 40 to 60 minutes. You can get away with 20 minutes if needed.

- Double the recipe, no problem. Size-up the baking dish to a 9 × 13-inch and increase the cooking time by about 10 minutes or until the center is cooked through.

- Stratas are best the day they are made, especially when making for a special occasion, but you can still enjoy leftovers for up to 2 days. Place in a baking dish, cover with foil, and bake for 15 to 25 minutes, depending on the quantity.

Asparagus and Spring Allium Strata

SERVES 4 TO 8

INGREDIENT INFO:

- Spring onions are fresh onions with greens still attached. You may find them in a range of sizes from what appear to be extra-large, bulbous scallions to large tangerine-size bulbs. Shallots are a good substitute.

- Young garlic is pulled from the ground before it has a chance to mature into individual, more pungent cloves. You will find individual heads of young garlic with its stalk and greens attached. Its mild, green flavor is perfect in this strata, but you can use a couple of cloves of standard (mature and cured) garlic if needed.

ABOUT THE YIELD:

- If serving as part of a brunch spread, this can serve up to 8. With a simple salad on the side, it will serve 4 to 6.

- You can easily double this recipe. Use a 9 x 13-inch pan and cook for another 10 minutes or so.

When asparagus, scallions, spring onions, and green, young garlic appear at the farmers market at the same time, you will know to make this strata. The combination of young alliums brings fresh onion and garlic flavors to a dish that tastes like spring. This strata shines at a brunch, but it is savory and very filling, great for dinner, too. Serve it with a light salad for sure.

---

6 to 7 slices white French bread (or sourdough bread)

3 tablespoons unsalted butter

½ cup chopped green garlic (2 to 3 small heads, trimmed and finely chopped) or 1 large garlic clove, minced

1 cup sliced spring onions (2 to 3 small bulbs) or shallots

½ cup chopped scallions

1 pound asparagus, woody ends snapped off, cut into ¼-inch coins or ½-inch pieces

1 teaspoon fine sea salt

¼ teaspoon freshly ground black pepper

¼ cup dry white wine

1 tablespoon chopped fresh tarragon

6 large eggs

2 cups half-and-half

4 ounces fontina cheese, coarsely grated

---

1 Heat the oven to 350°F with a rack in the middle position. Place the bread slices in a single layer on a sheet pan. If needed, tear a slice or two in half to fit the pan. Toast the bread for 10 to 12 minutes until it is dried out and mostly crisp. Pull the pan from the oven and let the bread continue to dry out as it cools.

2 In a large skillet, melt 2 tablespoons of butter over medium heat. Add the garlic, spring onions, and scallions. Cook, stirring frequently, for about 1 minute until well incorporated and fragrant. Stir in the asparagus, ½ teaspoon of salt, and ⅛ teaspoon of pepper. Cook, stirring occasionally, for 3 minutes until the asparagus is crisp-tender. Add the wine, turn up the heat to medium-high, and cook, stirring, for about 2 minutes until the wine cooks off and the pan is dry. Stir in the tarragon. Remove the pan from the heat; let stand.

3 Whisk together the eggs, half-and-half, the remaining ½ teaspoon of salt, and the remaining ⅛ teaspoon of pepper. Butter the bottom and sides of an 8 × 8-inch baking dish with the remaining 1 tablespoon of butter. Place 3½ to 4 pieces of bread on the bottom of the dish, overlapping slightly in places if needed or breaking apart the bread to fit in one layer to cover completely.

(recipe continues)

SWAP: Replace the fontina cheese with 4 ounces of Gruyere or sharp white Cheddar, about 2 loosely packed cups.

Scatter half of the asparagus mixture over the top (about 1 cup). Follow with about half of the cheese. Repeat with the remaining bread, then asparagus mixture then the remaining cheese. Evenly pour the egg mixture over the top and in between gaps. Cover tightly with plastic wrap and gently push down on the top to help encourage the bread to soak up the custard. If you would like to bake as soon as possible, let the strata stand for 20 to 40 minutes with four full cans of food (or something else) to weigh it down and encourage soaking. Alternatively, refrigerate the strata overnight.

4 To bake the strata, heat the oven to 325°F with a rack in the middle position. Uncover the strata. (If the strata was refrigerated, let it stand at room temperature for 15 to 20 minutes.) Bake for 45 to 55 minutes until puffed up, cooked through the middle, and golden brown in places. Transfer the strata to a cooling rack and let stand for at least 5 minutes before cutting into pieces to serve.

Tortilla Strata
with Charred Poblano and Tomatoes

SERVES 4 TO 6

Torn tortillas work like bread in this strata, forming soft, corn-filled layers. Briefly broiled poblano pepper and tomatoes plus onion make a sweet and slightly smoky sauce to spread in between. It's incredible on its own and it's even better with diced avocado and a sprinkle of cilantro or a spoonful of fresh pico de gallo on top.

1 pound tomatoes, cored and cut into 1-inch pieces

1 large poblano pepper, cut in half lengthwise, stemmed, and seeded

3 tablespoons unsalted butter

1 medium onion, ¼-inch diced

1 teaspoon fine sea salt

½ teaspoon dried oregano

1 teaspoon sugar

½ teaspoon apple cider vinegar

5 large eggs

1¼ cups half-and-half

¼ teaspoon freshly ground black pepper

Six 6-inch corn tortillas

About 2 loosely packed cups grated sharp white Cheddar cheese (4 ounces)

1 avocado, pitted and diced (optional)

Pico de gallo or a handful of fresh cilantro, chopped (optional)

1 Adjust an oven rack to the top position, about 6 inches from the broiler element. Preheat the broiler and line a sheet pan with foil. Place the tomatoes on one side of the sheet pan and place the poblano halves skin side up on the other side of the pan. Broil for 5 minutes, rotate the pan, and broil for about another 1 minute or so until the skins of the poblano are mostly charred and the tomatoes have blackened a bit in places. Remove the sheet pan from the oven and let the tomatoes stand. Transfer the poblano halves to a bowl and cover the bowl completely with a pot top or a plate to trap steam in the bowl. Turn the oven off. When the poblano halves are cool enough to handle, peel and discard the skins. Finely dice the flesh.

2 Melt 2 tablespoons of butter in a large nonstick skillet over medium heat. Add the onion and ¼ teaspoon of salt. Cook, stirring occasionally, until softened and translucent, 4 to 5 minutes. Stir in the tomatoes, chopped poblano, ¼ teaspoon salt, and the oregano. Cook, stirring occasionally, for 5 to 6 minutes until the mixture thickens and any liquid released in the pan has cooked off. (The pan should be mostly dry and the mixture should appear to be a chunky sauce.) Sprinkle the sugar over, add the vinegar, and simmer for another 1 minute to incorporate. Remove the pan from the heat; let stand.

3 Whisk together the eggs, half-and-half, the remaining ½ teaspoon of salt, and the pepper. Butter the bottom and sides of an 8 × 8-inch baking dish with the remaining 1 tablespoon of butter. Tear the tortillas into 2-inch pieces and toss them, directly in the baking dish, with two thirds of the cheese followed by the tomato mixture until evenly combined. Evenly spread out the mixture in the dish and evenly pour over the custard. Top with the remaining cheese. Cover with plastic wrap. Let the strata stand for at least 40 to 60 minutes or refrigerate it overnight. (If the strata was refrigerated, let it stand at room temperature for 15 to 20 minutes before baking.)

4 Heat the oven to 350°F with a rack in the middle position. Bake for 45 to 55 minutes until cooked through the center, golden brown all over, and bubbling around the edges. Transfer the strata to a cooling rack and let stand for at least 5 minutes before cutting in to serve. Serve with avocado and pico de gallo or freshly chopped cilantro for topping if you wish.

Mushroom-Collard Strata
with Gruyère and Thyme

BUTCHER TIP: See page 164 for how to prep Swiss chard. Apply the same technique for prepping collard greens, however discard collard stems.

With braised collard greens and meaty mushrooms (browned to taste like bacon), this is the ultimate Sunday brunch strata. Remember this one, too, as a good breakfast-for-dinner option.

6 to 7 slices crusty multigrain or sourdough bread

5 tablespoons unsalted butter

6 ounces shiitake mushrooms, stemmed, caps thinly sliced

Fine sea salt

½ cup finely diced shallot

1 large garlic clove

¼ cup dry white wine

1 bunch collard greens (10 to 12 ounces), stemmed, leaves thinly sliced

Freshly ground black pepper

⅓ cup water

2 packed teaspoons fresh thyme, roughly chopped

7 large eggs

2 cups half-and-half

About 2 cups shredded Gruyère cheese (4 ounces)

1 Heat the oven to 350°F with a rack in the middle position. Place the bread slices in a single layer on a sheet pan. If needed, tear a slice or two in half to fit the pan. Toast the bread for 10 minutes, flip it, and toast for another 5 minutes until it is dried out and mostly crisp. Pull the pan from the oven and let the bread continue to dry out as it cools.

2 In a large, deep sauté pan, melt 2 tablespoons of butter over medium heat. Add the mushrooms with a pinch of salt, and turn the heat up to medium-high. Cook, stirring frequently, for 3 to 5 minutes until the mushrooms have released their liquid and are tender and browning in places. The pan should be dry. Turn the heat off and transfer the mushrooms to a small bowl; let stand.

3 In the now empty sauté pan, melt 1 tablespoon of butter over medium heat. Add the shallot and cook, stirring frequently, for 1½ to 2 minutes until it begins to turn translucent and soften. Add the garlic and cook, stirring, for 30 to 60 seconds until fragrant. Add the wine and cook, stirring almost constantly and scraping any browned bits from the bottom of the pan, for about 1 minute to reduce it.

4 Add the collard greens, a little at a time if needed to fit the pan, then cook for about 1 minute until well incorporated and the collards are just starting to wilt. Season with ¼ teaspoon salt and ¼ teaspoon pepper, and stir in the water. Cover and reduce the heat to medium-low until the collards are tender, 5 minutes. Uncover and stir in 1 tablespoon of butter, the thyme, and the reserved mushrooms. Turn up the heat to medium-high. Cook, stirring frequently, until well incorporated and any remaining excess liquid has cooked off, 1 to 2 minutes. Remove from the heat immediately.

5 Whisk together the eggs, half-and-half, ¾ teaspoon salt, and ⅛ teaspoon pepper. Butter the bottom and sides of an 8 × 8-inch baking dish with the remaining 1 tablespoon of butter. Place 3½ to 4 pieces of bread on the bottom of the dish, overlapping slightly in places if needed or breaking apart the bread to fit in a single layer to cover completely. Scatter half of the collard mixture over the top (about ½ cup). Follow with half of the Gruyère. Repeat with enough of the remaining bread to cover, then collard mixture then the remaining Gruyère. Evenly pour the egg mixture over the top and in between gaps. Cover with plastic wrap and gently push down on the top to help encourage the bread to soak up custard. If you would like to bake as soon as possible, let the strata stand for 40 to 60 minutes with four full cans of food (or something else) to weigh it down and encourage soaking. Alternatively, refrigerate the strata overnight. (Its texture will improve.)

6 To bake the strata, heat the oven to 325°F with the rack still in the middle position. Uncover the strata. (If refrigerated, let it stand at room temperature for 15 to 20 minutes.) Bake for 45 to 55 minutes until puffed up, cooked through the middle, and golden brown in places. Transfer the strata to a cooling rack and let stand for at least 5 minutes before cutting in to serve.

The Classic Dinner Pie

Shepherd's pie, pot pie, and Wellington are getting a vegetable-centric makeover. These are fill-you-up, warm and cozy comfort foods at their best and each one comes to party. For an October dinner with friends, a meal on New Year's Day, even a spring renewal celebration, you can find a pie here that will be perfect there. We will take care to build the base with tons of vegetables, then top or wrap them with flaky puff pastry or a rich and creamy mash of roots. You and your guests will be rewarded and impressed.

FROZEN PUFF PASTRY TIPS

- Plan ahead to make sure that your pastry is thawed and cold when it is time to work.

- For ease of use and best results, defrost puff pastry slowly and evenly in the refrigerator. (It will thaw unevenly on your counter and run the chance of getting too warm.) In a pinch, put it on your counter and monitor it closely. Then work quickly once it is ready to go.

- Handle it gently. To prevent sticking, make sure to dust your cutting board or work surface with flour (and rolling pin, too, if you need to roll it out).

- Use egg wash or dabs of water to help seal or press the pastry together when a recipe calls for it.

- You can decorate the top of the puff pastry as you like. Try a crosshatch pattern by scoring the dough—applying very little pressure and making sure not to cut all the way through the second layer of dough. Create vents cutting all the way through both layers. Use extra dough and small cutters to make shapes that you can place on top.

TIPS AND TAKEAWAYS

- Reserve the Classic Dinner Pie for the spring, fall, and winter when there is a coolness in the air and the moment calls for something substantial and special to serve. (This isn't light summer fare.)

- Hearty root vegetables, potatoes, winter squash, and legumes, a balance of starch and protein, are a natural fit to make a strong, substantial base.

- Classic French puff pastry—used in the Beet Wellington (page 281) and the Celery Root and Apple Pot Pie (page 287)—is made with butter. If you are looking to make a fully plant-based dinner pie, take care to buy an oil-based dough.

- Make 1 day ahead and reheat to serve or bake the base or filling up to 2 days ahead, then assemble and freshly bake to serve.

- There is a depth and richness to these dishes that calls for a crisp salad or something green on the side.

- These classic pies have a ceremonious feel, so make and bring them to the table on a special occasion.

Beet Wellington
with Horseradish Cream

SERVES 6 TO 8 AS A MAIN

ABOUT THE YIELD: With a side like buttered peas, roasted Brussels sprouts, Crispy Roasted Potatoes (page 272), or a salad, you will get up to 8 servings.

PLAN AHEAD: Make sure to thaw the puff pastry for two to three hours in the refrigerator before making this dish.

INGREDIENT INFO:

- You may find an 18-ounce package of puff pastry with two 9-ounce, 9½-inch by 9½-inch sheets of dough. If so, lightly flour a rolling pin and gently roll out each sheet into a roughly 12-inch by 9-inch rectangle. Cut each sheet in half lengthwise then trim an inch or so crosswise to produce four 6-inch-wide by 8-inch-wide pieces of dough. Proceed with step 8 dividing the ingredients evenly between the 4 sheets of dough to make 4 individual pastries.

- If you are having trouble with the pastry sticking together, you can use some of the egg wash to help seal it.

This dish is special—*really special*—and incredibly delicious. It's rosemary-roasted beets, sweet caramelized onions, and sautéed shiitake mushrooms and thyme wrapped up in puff pastry crust. It is meant for a holiday meal, for a get-together with family or friends, or to share with a loved one on a Saturday night at a table set for conversation. I suggest making the beets, onions, and mushrooms a day ahead and then assembling and baking the Wellington just before you are ready to serve it. The horseradish cream can be made up to 3 days in advance.

FOR THE BEETS

2 pounds beet roots, trimmed, peeled and ½-inch diced

2 tablespoons extra-virgin olive oil

1 tablespoon chopped fresh rosemary (2 small sprigs)

½ teaspoon fine sea salt

FOR THE ONIONS AND MUSHROOMS

2 tablespoons extra-virgin olive oil

2 medium onions, thinly sliced

1 teaspoon plus ¼ teaspoon fine sea salt

1 tablespoon pure maple syrup

1 tablespoon balsamic vinegar

¼ teaspoon freshly ground black pepper

2 tablespoons unsalted butter

¾ pound shiitake mushrooms, stemmed, caps thinly sliced

2 sprigs fresh thyme

¼ cup dry white wine

1 teaspoon lemon zest

All-purpose flour, for dusting

1 package (14 to 16 ounces) puff pastry, thawed according to package instructions (see Plan Ahead)

¾ cup toasted walnuts, very finely chopped

1 egg, beaten with 1 teaspoon water

Horseradish Cream (page 284)

---

1 Make the beets. Heat the oven to 400°F with a rack in the middle position. Line a sheet pan with parchment paper. Toss the beets directly on the pan with the oil, rosemary, and salt. Spread out the beets and roast for 20 minutes, stir and flip the beets, and spread them out again. Continue to roast for another 15 to 20 minutes until tender. (Extra-large beets may take longer.)

2 Make the onions and mushrooms. In a large skillet, heat the oil over medium heat. Add the onions and the 1 teaspoon of salt and cook, stirring occasionally, until they begin to soften and lightly brown, about 10 minutes. Stir in the maple syrup, vinegar, and pepper and continue to cook, stirring frequently, for about another 5 minutes until the onions become soft and a deep golden brown. Transfer the onions to a bowl and return the skillet to medium heat. Heat the butter in the pan until almost completely melted. Stir in the mushrooms and the

(recipe continues)

remaining ¼ teaspoon of salt and cook, stirring frequently, until the mushrooms release liquid and it mostly cooks off, 3 to 4 minutes. Stir in the thyme, wine, and lemon zest and continue to cook, stirring, for another 2 to 3 minutes until the mushrooms are golden and tender and the pan is dry. Reduce the heat at any time if browned bits on the pan begin to burn. Transfer the mushrooms to a small bowl. (At this point you can let everything cool and store in separate airtight containers until you are ready to assemble the pastry.)

3 Assemble and bake the pastry. Line a sheet pan with parchment paper and set it nearby. Lightly dust a large cutting board and rolling pin with flour. Unfold the thawed (but still cold and firm) pastry dough. Cut it in half lengthwise to yield two roughly 5- by 14- to 15-inch rectangles. Gently roll out the 5-inch sides crosswise to 6 inches.

4 Evenly divide the mushrooms between the two rectangles and spread them out in the center, leaving a ¾- to ½-inch border all the way around. On top, divide and spread out the caramelized onions, loosely separating them as you place them. Again, leave an untouched border. Sprinkle the toasted walnuts over the onions. Now, carefully divide and spread out the beets on top.

5 Starting toward the ends, gently lift the two long sides, stretching the dough just slightly and carefully to encourage meeting in the middle. When the two sides touch, gather and pinch them together, tucking the seam under itself to seal if you can. Gather, fold, and pinch the ends together, too. Work gently and with a soft touch to prevent holes from forming. Once the pastry is sealed, lightly brush the seam with egg wash. Carefully work your hands under one pastry at a time to transfer it to the lined sheet tray (freeze or refrigerate the filled pastry briefly to firm it up if soft before flipping). Flip it over so that the seam side is down. Repeat, transferring the remaining pastry, making sure to space it evenly apart from the other one. Brush the tops and sides with the egg wash.

1. Gently lift the sides, stretching the dough slightly to encourage meeting in the middle. Gather and pinch the dough together.

2. Lightly brush the seams with egg wash before carefully flipping the pastry over for baking. Brush the tops and sides, too.

(recipe continues)

6 Bake for 30 to 35 minutes until the pastry puffs up and the crust is golden brown all over.

7 Let the Wellington rest for at least 5 minutes before cutting it on a diagonal into 3-inch (or larger) pieces.

To reheat, place a full log or two on a parchment-lined sheet pan, cover with foil, and bake at 375°F for about 10 minutes (less for smaller pieces). Uncover and bake for another 5 minutes until hot through the center and the crust is golden and crispy.

Horseradish Cream

MAKES ABOUT 1 CUP

SWAP: Substitute 2 tablespoons of prepared horseradish plus more to taste in place of the fresh.

1 cup full-fat sour cream

¼ cup finely grated, peeled fresh horseradish (loosely packed), plus more to taste

1 tablespoon freshly squeezed lemon juice, plus more as needed

½ teaspoon fine sea salt

1 tablespoon finely chopped fresh chives (optional)

2 to 3 tablespoons shaken heavy cream (optional)

Stir together the sour cream, ¼ cup horseradish, the lemon juice, salt, and chives, if using, in a medium bowl. Taste and adjust for horseradish (add up to 2 more tablespoons) and lemon juice as needed. If you prefer a thinner sauce, stir in some of the heavy cream. The sauce will keep in an airtight container in the refrigerator for several days. Stir well before serving.

Lentil and Mushroom Shepherd's Pie

SERVES 6 TO 8 AS A MAIN

INGREDIENT INFO: If you add rutabaga or celery root to the topping, try to keep the potato as the main player. You'll need about 2 large potatoes (1½ pounds) and a medium rutabaga or celery root (about 1 pound).

ALL PLANTS: For the mash, use olive oil in place of the butter and some of the cooking water or almond milk in place of the milk. Salt to taste.

TAKE NOTE: For an extra-special touch, bake the pies in individual pie plates, large ramekins, or latte bowls. For the ease of it (and to maximize servings), use a 9 x 13-inch or 8 x 11½-inch baking dish, or a 10-inch broiler-safe skillet.

With hearty root veggies, mushrooms, and lentils as the filling, this shepherd's pie not only lives up to its reputation, but it has an elegance that a meal served out of a casserole dish doesn't always carry. Serve the pie with a pile of dressed greens.

FOR THE MASH

2½ pounds russet potatoes or a mix of russet potatoes and rutabaga or celery root (see Ingredient Info), peeled and 1-inch diced

Fine sea salt

4 tablespoons (½ stick) unsalted butter

½ cup milk

Freshly ground black pepper

FOR THE FILLING

2 tablespoons extra-virgin olive oil, plus more as needed

1 large onion, ¼-inch diced

16 ounces white button mushrooms or a mix of favorite mushrooms, trimmed and chopped or sliced

Fine sea salt

4 large garlic cloves, minced or pressed

2 tablespoons tomato paste

2 tablespoons all-purpose flour

¼ cup white wine

4 cups (1 quart) low-sodium vegetable stock

1 cup green lentils, sorted and rinsed

2 cups ¼-inch diced carrots (3 to 4 carrots)

1 bay leaf

3 to 4 fresh sprigs thyme

1 teaspoon sugar

1 tablespoon tamari or soy sauce

Freshly ground black pepper

¾ cup frozen peas

1 tablespoon aged balsamic vinegar

2 tablespoons minced fresh chives (optional)

---

1 Make the mash. Place the potatoes in a large pot and fill it with enough water to cover them. Add 1 scant tablespoon of salt to the water and bring it to a boil. Reduce the heat to maintain a steady simmer and cook until completely tender—10 to 12 minutes if you are cooking potatoes only or about 15 minutes if you are boiling a combination of potatoes and root veggies. Drain the potatoes (or combination) and return them to the pot. Mash them with a potato masher until mostly smooth. Stir in the butter, allowing it to melt, then stir in the milk, ½ teaspoon salt, and ¼ teaspoon pepper (adjusting both to taste). Set aside.

(recipe continues)

2 Make the filling. Heat the oil over medium-high heat in a Dutch oven or large sauté pan (with top) and add the onion, mushrooms, and ½ teaspoon salt. Cook, stirring occasionally, until the onion is translucent, the mushrooms are tender, and any liquid that has formed in the pan has cooked off, 5 to 7 minutes. Stir in the garlic, tomato paste, and flour. Continue to cook, stirring almost constantly, for about 2 minutes until the mixture is lightly browning. Add the wine and cook, for about 1 minute until it cooks off, gently scraping any browned bits off the bottom of the pan.

3 Add the stock, lentils, carrots, bay leaf, thyme sprigs, sugar, tamari, and ¼ teaspoon pepper. Cover and cook over medium heat, stirring occasionally, for 20 to 25 minutes until the lentils and carrots are tender and the mixture thickens. Uncover the pan, stir in the peas and vinegar, and cook for another 2 to 3 minutes, stirring occasionally, until the peas have warmed through. Adjust salt and pepper to taste. Remove the thyme sprigs and bay leaf.

4 Spread the hot lentil-vegetable mixture out in a 2-quart casserole dish or a 9 x 13-inch baking dish. Top with big spoonfuls of the mashed potatoes, then use the back of the spoon to spread them out evenly to cover the filling. Run a fork gently along the top of the potatoes to create ridges. Place an oven rack 6 inches from the broiler element and broil for about 5 minutes until the potato ridges are evenly and lightly browning, rotating the pan if needed to ensure even browning.

5 Top the pie with chives if you are using them, then scoop out hearty portions to serve.

To reheat, zap portions in the microwave for 90 seconds to 3 minutes (or more) depending on the quantity until evenly warmed through. Alternatively, cover and bake at 375°F, 8 to 10 minutes for a small portion, 15 to 20 minutes for a larger portion, until hot all the way through.

Celery Root and Apple Pot Pie

PLAN AHEAD: Make sure to thaw the puff pastry for two to three hours in the refrigerator before making this dish. The filling can be made up to 2 days in advance. When you are ready to make the pie, spread out the filling in the skillet, top with puff pastry, and bake as directed.

INGREDIENT INFO:

• You can use whole milk or almond milk in the sauce. Almond milk will need to simmer longer than dairy milk in step 4.

• If you would like, add some "green" like peas or spinach to the pie when it's time to add the apple.

• For the pastry, use oil- or butter-based pastry, whichever you prefer.

My celery root pot pie in *The Vegetable Butcher* is one of my favorite classic dinner pie recipes for the winter months. I wanted to reinvent it here with some shortcuts (packaged puff pastry and a single skillet) and the option to make a creamy, all-plants base. The result is magnificently rich, earthy, and sweet.

---

6 tablespoons extra-virgin olive oil (or butter or a combination)

1 medium yellow onion, ¼-inch diced

2 large celery ribs, ¼-inch diced

4 garlic cloves, minced

2 medium celery root (1½ to 2 pounds), peeled and ½-inch diced

2 to 3 small to medium parsnips and/or carrots, ½ inch-diced

1 medium sweet potato, ½-inch diced

1¼ teaspoons fine sea salt

¼ teaspoon freshly ground black pepper

2 cups low-sodium vegetable stock

1 bay leaf

1 large apple, peeled, cored, and ½-inch diced

½ cup frozen peas (optional)

3 tablespoons white miso

¼ cup plus 2 tablespoons all-purpose flour, plus more for dusting

2 cups milk (see Ingredient Info)

4 to 6 sprigs fresh thyme

2 generous pinches of ground nutmeg

1 teaspoon apple cider vinegar

All-purpose flour

1 sheet (8 to 10 ounces) puff pastry, thawed according to package instructions

---

1 Heat 3 tablespoons of oil in a large oven-safe skillet or Dutch oven over medium heat. Add the onion and celery and cook, stirring occasionally, until they start to soften and the onion becomes translucent, about 5 minutes. Stir in the garlic and cook for 1 minute more.

2 Add the celery root, parsnips and/or carrots, sweet potato, 1 teaspoon of salt, and the pepper. Cook, stirring occasionally, for 2 minutes. Add 1 cup of the vegetable stock and the bay leaf, cover, and reduce the heat to medium-low. Cook, uncovering to stir occasionally, until the vegetables are crisp-tender, 10 minutes.

3 Uncover the pot, stir in the apple and peas if you are adding them, and turn up the heat to medium-high. Cook, uncovered, until almost all of the liquid has evaporated, 1 to 3 more minutes. Remove from the heat, discard the bay leaf, and let stand.

(recipe continues)

BUTCHER TIP: Celery root has a gnarly-looking exterior and root, which you'll need to cut off and discard. (Some grocery stores cut off the root before displaying them.) See page 202 for how to peel a celery root.

EQUIPMENT TIP: This recipe is designed to make and bake in a large oven-safe skillet. If you increase the vegetables, you may want to make them in a Dutch oven and then transfer the filling to your baking dish of choice. If you are serving fewer portions and expect that you'll have leftovers, consider a 9 x 13-inch baking dish; it will fit and store leftovers in the fridge more easily. You can always serve the pies individually; you'll need six 5- to 6-inch oven-safe bowls and you'll cut the pastry dough accordingly.

4 In a 2- to 4-cup liquid measure (or medium bowl), whisk the miso into the remaining 1 cup of vegetable stock until it mostly dissolves; place it near the stove. Heat the remaining 3 tablespoons of oil in a medium saucepan over medium heat. Slowly add ¼ cup of flour, whisking to break apart any lumps until a paste forms. Add the remaining 2 tablespoons of flour and continue whisking until well incorporated, about 1 minute. The mixture may become dry and crumbly; make sure it does not brown or burn, reducing the heat if needed. Whisk in the stock–miso mixture a little at a time, whisking constantly until mostly smooth between additions. Gradually whisk in the milk until no lumps remain. Add the thyme, nutmeg, and the remaining ¼ teaspoon of salt. Bring to a steady simmer over medium heat and simmer for 6 to 10 minutes, whisking frequently, until the sauce thickens slightly. Remove the pan from the heat and whisk in the vinegar. Discard the thyme stems.

5 Pour about ½ cup of the sauce into the vegetables and stir to evenly combine. Evenly spread the vegetables out in the skillet and pour the remaining sauce evenly over the top. If you have used a Dutch oven, transfer the mixture to your selected baking dish (see Equipment Tip).

6 When you are ready to bake the pie, heat the oven to 425°F with a rack in the middle position. Line a sheet pan with foil.

7 Lightly flour a cutting board or work surface and a rolling pin. Carefully unfold the thawed pastry dough and transfer it to the board. Roll out the dough to a roughly 12- to 13-inch circle. Transfer it to evenly cover the top of the skillet. Some overhang is fine or you may need to gently stretch the dough in places to cover the skillet. Where there is excess, fold the edges of the dough under and press it together just below the rim of the skillet. Use a fork to crimp the edges and push the dough against the rim of the skillet to seal it. Cut 4 evenly spaced slits in the dough, near the center of the pie, to allow steam to release. Use a sharp knife to score evenly spaced stripes into the top of the dough without cutting through. Place the skillet on the sheet pan, transfer to the oven, and bake until the filling is simmering and the crust is golden brown and cooked through the middle, about 30 minutes.

8 Let the pie stand to cool slightly, 10 to 15 minutes, before serving.

To reheat, bake covered with foil at 400°F for 10 minutes; remove the foil. Continue to bake until warmed through the center and the crust is flaky, 5 to 10 minutes more depending on the amount of leftovers.

SWEETS.

Crumble-Topped Banana Coffee Cake

MAKES A 9-INCH SQUARE OR OR TWO 6-INCH CAKES

SERVING SIZE: To make two 6-inch cakes (they make excellent gifts), divide the batter and crumble between metal or paper baking pans. Reduce the baking time by 5 to 8 minutes.

Don't let the simple title fool you. Yes, this is a coming together of banana bread and coffee cake. But you will have to imagine, and trust me, it is so, so much more. The cake base gives life to spotty bananas (even frozen ones), but it is fluffy, not dense, and never gummy. The sweet and nutty topping is a treat. It is impossible to resist especially if you form it into massive crumbles, which I recommend.

Canola oil, for the pan

FOR THE CRUMBLE TOPPING

1¼ cups all-purpose flour

⅔ cup granulated sugar

¼ teaspoon fine sea salt

¾ teaspoon ground cinnamon

½ cup toasted walnuts or pecans, very finely chopped

½ cup solid unrefined virgin coconut oil

½ teaspoon pure vanilla extract

¼ teaspoon almond extract

FOR THE CAKE

2 cups all-purpose flour

½ cup whole wheat flour

⅔ cup granulated sugar

½ teaspoon fine sea salt

1 tablespoon baking powder

½ teaspoon baking soda

1¼ cups almond milk

2 tablespoons ground flaxseed

3 overripe bananas, peeled

¼ cup canola oil

1 tablespoon freshly squeezed lemon juice

1 teaspoon pure vanilla extract

1 Heat the oven to 350°F with a rack in the middle position. Cut two pieces of parchment paper to line a 9-inch square baking pan so that all four sides are covered with a 1- to 2- inch overhang around the edges. Lightly oil the bottom and sides of the pan, line it with one piece of the parchment, and smooth to eliminate any bubbles. Lightly oil the just-placed parchment with more oil and crisscross the other piece of parchment on top to line the other sides; smooth the bottom to eliminate bubbles. (Alternatively, use a couple of drops of oil to grease a 9-inch round springform pan on the bottom and all sides.)

2 Make the crumble topping. Whisk together the flour, sugar, salt, cinnamon, and walnuts in a medium bowl. Melt the coconut oil in a 1-cup liquid measure in the microwave or in a small saucepan over low heat, then whisk in the vanilla extract and the almond extract. Pour the coconut oil into the flour mixture and use a rubber spatula to stir and mix until evenly combined, the oil has completely moistened the dry ingredients, and clumps start to form. Set aside.

(recipe continues)

3 Make the cake. Whisk together the all-purpose flour, wheat flour, sugar, salt, baking powder, and baking soda in a medium bowl until the mixture is evenly combined. In a 2-cup liquid measure, whisk the almond milk and flaxseed, let stand for at least 5 minutes, then whisk again.

4 Mash the bananas with a potato masher or the back of a fork in a large bowl. Measure and keep 1 to 1¼ cups in the bowl. (Save any leftover for another use.) Whisk in the canola oil, almond milk–flax mixture, lemon juice, and vanilla. Vigorously whisk until mostly smooth and evenly combined. Then, add the dry flour mixture to the bowl and stir and fold until just combined, scraping down the sides of the bowl as needed. Transfer the batter to the prepared pan and let it rest for 10 minutes. (If you have used a springform pan, place it on a baking sheet.) Sprinkle the crumble topping evenly over the top, forming large clumps in places, and bake until golden brown along the edges and cooked through the center, about 55 minutes.

5 Transfer to a wire cooling rack and let it cool for 30 minutes. Remove the cake from the pan and let it cool completely on the wire rack. Tightly wrapped, this cake's texture and flavor will improve overnight. It will last for up to 3 days.

Buttermilk Cornbread
with Honey Butter

MAKES A 9- OR 10-INCH ROUND BREAD OR 20 MUFFINS

EQUIPMENT TIP: You can use a 10-inch cast-iron skillet, a 9-inch cake pan, or one to two standard 12-cup muffin tins. (If you use two muffin tins, space them apart in the upper and lower thirds of the oven, and rotate them after about 10 minutes.).

This easy cornbread has punched-up sweet corn flavor with two full cups of corn pureed into the batter. It's seriously yummy with a smear of honey butter.

8 tablespoons (1 stick) unsalted butter, plus softened butter for the pan

1 cup yellow stone-ground cornmeal or polenta (also packaged as corn grits)

1 cup all-purpose flour

¼ cup granulated sugar

2 teaspoons baking powder

½ teaspoon fine sea salt

½ teaspoon baking soda

2 cups defrosted frozen corn or freshly shaved kernels from 2 large ears sweet corn (see page 120)

1 cup well-shaken buttermilk

¼ cup pure maple syrup

2 large eggs

Honey Butter (recipe follows), for serving

1 Heat the oven to 400°F with a rack in the middle position. Butter the bottom and sides of a 10-inch cast-iron skillet or 9-inch round cake pan, or line a muffin tin with paper liners and bake in batches (or use two tins, see Equipment Tip).

PREP TIP: **PREP TIP:** To defrost frozen corn, place it in a heat-safe bowl with ⅓ cup water. Zap it in the microwave for 1 minute, stir, then zap it again for 1 minute until it is just defrosted. Stir again and drain well. Alternatively, leave the corn at room temperature or in the fridge until defrosted and drain well.

VARIATION: When blueberries are in season, I recommend gently stirring 1½ cups of the fruit into the finished batter; alternatively, fold one or two minced, seeded jalapeños into the batter just before baking.

2 Gently melt the butter in a bowl in the microwave or in a small saucepan over medium heat. Let cool briefly.

3 In a bowl large enough to accommodate the dry and wet ingredients, whisk together the cornmeal, flour, sugar, baking powder, salt, and baking soda.

4 Pulse the corn kernels in the bowl of a food processor 8 to 10 times, 1-second pulses each, until they are coarsely pureed. Scrape down the sides of the bowl with a rubber spatula. Add the buttermilk, butter, and maple syrup and process briefly until all of the ingredients are just evenly blended. Scrape down the sides of the bowl again and add the eggs. Blend again until just evenly combined.

5 Pour the wet ingredients into the bowl with the dry ingredients and stir until just combined. Scrape the mixture into the prepared pan with a rubber spatula. If you are using a muffin tin, use a ¼-cup measure to portion out the batter.

6 Bake until the edges and top of the cornbread are lightly browning in places, the center is cooked through, and a cake tester poked into the center comes out clean: 15 to 18 minutes for a standard muffin tin, 25 to 27 minutes for a 10-inch cast-iron skillet, and 30 to 33 minutes for a 9-inch cake pan.

7 Transfer to a wire cooling rack to cool for 10 to 15 minutes. The bread's texture and flavor will improve when tightly wrapped and stored overnight at room temperature (refrigerate it after 1 day).

Honey Butter

MAKES ABOUT ¾ CUP

8 tablespoons (1 stick) unsalted butter, at room temperature

¼ cup raw honey

Stir together the butter and honey in a small bowl or food processor until it is evenly combined. Transfer it to a ramekin and smooth out the top before serving.

Zucchini and Dried Cherry Scones

MAKES 8 SCONES

PREP TIPS:

- Cut dough freezes well for up to 3 months. Freeze the cut dough on a small lined baking sheet, then transfer to a freezer-safe, airtight container for long-term storage.

- When ready to bake, transfer to a prepared baking sheet, brush with cream, and sprinkle with sparkling sugar according to the instructions. Bake at 400°F for 16 to 19 minutes.

BUTCHER TIP: Trim the zucchini, then grate it on the large holes of a box grater.

TAKE NOTE: These scones are best enjoyed immediately, but you can keep leftovers for up to one day. Wrap them well and reheat leftover scones in an oven or toaster oven at 375°F to revive some of their original texture. Warm through until browned and crisp in places, 5 to 7 minutes. You can also freeze fully baked scones for up to 3 months. Reheat at 400°F until warm through the middle and browned and crisp in places, about 12 minutes. Let cool for 2 minutes.

This extraordinary recipe came from my restaurant team many years ago, thanks to chefs Sophie and Amber, who tinkered until they got it just right. The zucchini is a brilliant addition that not only adds flavor but also keeps the scones moist—preventing the dreaded dry scone. The cherries and orange zest add bright, tart flavor that balances this scone's sweetness.

¾ cup tart dried cherries

1 tablespoon plus ¼ cup granulated sugar

⅓ cup shaken heavy cream, plus 3 tablespoons for topping

1 large egg

1 teaspoon pure vanilla extract

2½ cups (11.3 ounces) all-purpose flour, plus more for dusting

1 teaspoon fine sea salt

1 tablespoon baking powder

8 tablespoons (1 stick) unsalted butter, cubed into about 32 pieces

1 packed cup (3 ounces) coarsely grated zucchini (see Butcher Tip)

1 packed teaspoon finely grated orange zest

1 tablespoon plus 2 teaspoons white sparkling sugar

---

1 Heat the oven to 400°F with a rack in the middle position. Line a sheet pan with parchment paper or a silicone baking mat.

2 Toss the cherries and the 1 tablespoon of granulated sugar in a small bowl until evenly coated. Transfer the mixture to a cutting board and finely chop the cherries. In a separate small bowl or 2-cup liquid measure, whisk together the cream, egg, and vanilla; let stand.

3 Whisk together the flour, the ¼ cup of granulated sugar, the salt, and the baking powder in a large bowl until evenly combined. Scatter the butter over the top, separating the pieces as you go. Use your hands to toss the butter into the flour while gently pressing and rolling the butter through your fingertips to flatten the butter in places and break it down into small pieces. (Some larger pieces may remain, that's fine.)

4 Scatter the zucchini and orange zest over the top and gently toss to break up any clumps of zucchini and zest until evenly combined. Sprinkle the cherries over the top and gently toss again. Pour about half the egg-cream mixture evenly over the top and use a large spoon to toss and fold the liquid into the flour. Scrape down the sides of the bowl, then drizzle the remaining liquid over the top and toss and fold (don't stir or press the dough) until evenly combined. The dough will appear very shaggy and dry to start.

(recipe continues)

5 Directly in the bowl, use your hands to gather and work the dough into one mass, gently pressing dry bits and flour into the dough, and gently folding it a few times until it comes together. Alternatively, if more comfortable, carefully turn the shaggy dough onto a flat work surface and use your hands (plus a bench scraper if you have one) to gather and form the dough in the same way. Gently flatten and shape the dough into a rough circle. Lightly flour a rolling pin, and roll out the dough to about an 8- to 8½-inch round, roughly ¾ inch to 1 inch thick. Use a bench scraper or sharp knife to cut out 8 wedges and transfer them to the prepared baking sheet, spacing them evenly. Alternatively, use a 2½-inch round or square cutter to cut the dough. Gather scraps into a mound and repeat the process of rolling the dough and cutting scones.

6 Brush the tops of the scones with cream and sprinkle evenly with sparkling sugar, a generous ½ teaspoon of sugar per scone. Bake for 15 to 17 minutes until golden around the edges. Transfer to a cooling rack and let the scones cool for at least 5 minutes or completely before serving.

Spiced Pumpkin Waffles
with Orange Zest and Pecans

MAKES 4 TO 6 WAFFLES; SERVES 4 AS A MAIN

SWAP: Try sweet potato puree in place of the pumpkin. Peel and ¾-inch dice 1 pound of sweet potatoes and boil until tender, 10 to 15 minutes. Drain in a colander. Let cool to dry out. Mash with a potato masher or puree in a food processor. Measure ¾ cup and freeze the rest to make another batch of waffles.

When this batter hits the hot iron, *that* autumnal pumpkin spice fragrance hits the air. Once crisp and nicely browned on the outside, with orange zest and pecans hidden on the inside, these waffles turn any fall weekend morning into a seasonal celebration.

¾ cup all-purpose flour

½ cup whole wheat flour

¾ teaspoon fine sea salt

1 teaspoon baking powder

½ teaspoon baking soda

1½ teaspoons ground cinnamon

½ teaspoon ground ginger

¼ teaspoon ground nutmeg

2 pinches of ground cloves

¾ cup canned pumpkin puree (see Swap)

¼ cup packed brown sugar

2 tablespoons unsalted butter, melted, plus softened butter for serving

1 teaspoon pure vanilla extract

1 teaspoon packed grated orange zest, plus more for topping

2 tablespoons freshly squeezed orange juice

2 large eggs

1 cup well-shaken buttermilk (or ¾ cup milk in a pinch, plus up to 2 tablespoons if needed)

½ cup pecans, toasted and finely chopped (optional)

Canola oil for waffle iron (optional)

Pure maple syrup, for serving

(recipe continues)

EQUIPMENT TIP: If you have one, use a classic, thinner-style waffle maker known for making crispier waffles. With a Belgian-style waffle maker, the waffles won't get quite as crispy; use a little less batter and adjust the heat to brown and crisp.

TAKE NOTE: You can store any leftover batter or waffles in an airtight container in the refrigerator for up to 2 days. Reheat waffles in a toaster oven until warmed through and crisp.

1 Heat the oven to 200°F and place a sheet pan on a rack in the middle position.

2 Whisk together the all-purpose flour, whole wheat flour, salt, baking powder, baking soda, cinnamon, ginger, nutmeg, and cloves in a medium bowl.

3 In a separate large bowl, whisk together the pumpkin puree, brown sugar, melted butter, vanilla, orange zest and juice, eggs, and buttermilk. Add the dry ingredients and pecans, if using, to the wet ingredients. With a rubber spatula, stir and fold until just evenly combined. (Don't overmix the batter.)

4 Heat your waffle iron to medium-high. If your iron requires a thin coating of oil, carefully apply it now. Use a measuring cup, portion scoop, or ladle to pour the batter into the center of the iron (making sure not to overfill it) and use the back of your scooping vessel to spread out the batter evenly, stopping short about ¼ inch from the edge. The cooking time and the amount of batter to add will vary depending on your iron; follow the manufacturer's instructions and cook until evenly browned and crisp.

5 Hold the waffles on the sheet pan in the warm oven until ready to serve. Serve with butter and pure maple syrup. Sprinkle more orange zest on top if you wish.

VARIATION

TO MAKE PANCAKES: Add an additional 2 tablespoons buttermilk (or ¼ cup milk) when mixing the batter. Heat a large nonstick skillet over medium heat. Melt butter or brush canola oil over the pan. Working in batches, pour ¼ cupfuls of the batter into the pan. Cook for 2 to 3 minutes until small bubbles appear all over, then gently flip and continue to cook until the pancakes puff up, turn golden brown, and are cooked through the center, adjusting the heat to prevent burning, 1 to 2 minutes on the other side. Makes about 14 pancakes.

Parsnip Morning Glory Muffins

MAKES 22 MUFFINS

PREP TIP: Use the shredding attachment on your food processor to easily and quickly break down the parsnips. Or shred the parsnips on the large holes of a box grater, stopping at the core if it is woody.

SWAP: Use carrots to make a more traditional morning glory muffin or use a little of both parsnips and carrots.

INGREDIENT INFO:
To make your own oat flour, pulse and then blend a heaping ½ cup of old-fashioned oats (2 ounces) in a food processor until it becomes a coarse powder. In a pinch, replace ½ cup of the oat flour with ½ cup all-purpose flour or whole wheat flour.

There's just something about these glorious muffins. They really do start the day off right. (And they make for the best kind of snack, too.) Parsnips are the headliners filling in for the carrots that usually take the leading role in these muffins. You will grate the white, conical roots just like carrots and they'll bring similar texture and moisture, but they'll also assert pleasant licorice-y flavor with a hint of earthiness and fall–winter spice. With apples, cinnamon, coconut, and raisins they offer it all: great taste, a balance of nutrients, and a sense of satisfaction that most sweet breakfast confections don't always provide.

---

10 ounces parsnips, peeled and shredded (2½ to 3 cups)

2 Granny Smith or other tart apples, peeled, cored, and shredded on the large holes of a box grater

2 cups all-purpose flour (9 ounces)

½ cup oat flour (see Ingredient Info)

¼ cup ground flaxseed

1½ teaspoons baking powder

1 teaspoon baking soda

¾ teaspoon fine sea salt

½ teaspoon ground cinnamon

1 can (13½ ounces) coconut milk, well stirred

¼ cup canola oil, plus more for the pan

½ cup granulated sugar

½ cup loosely packed brown sugar

1 teaspoon pure vanilla extract

⅓ cup unsweetened shredded coconut, plus more for topping

½ cup raisins

---

1 Line 2 standard 12-cup muffin tins with paper liners. Heat the oven to 425°F with racks evenly spaced in the upper and lower thirds of the oven.

2 Use your hands or a spoon to evenly mix the parsnips and apples in a medium bowl; set aside.

3 In a separate medium bowl, whisk together the all-purpose flour, oat flour, flaxseed, baking powder, baking soda, salt, and cinnamon until evenly combined.

4 Blend the coconut milk in a large bowl with a handheld electric mixer on low, or whisk by hand until just combined. Add the oil, granulated sugar, brown sugar, and vanilla and continue to blend or whisk until just combined. Increase the speed to high and beat or vigorously whisk by hand for 1 minute, until well combined and smooth. With the mixer running on low or while gently whisking,

(recipe continues)

- If you only have one standard 12-cup muffin pan, you can bake the muffins in two separate batches on the middle rack.

- You can freeze these muffins once cool in an airtight container for up to 6 months. Defrost them in a microwave or in the fridge overnight. Warm or toast as you wish.

add one third of the flour mixture to the wet ingredients, then add half of the parsnip-apple mixture, beating until just combined. Beat in on low or whisk in another third of the flour mixture, then the remaining parsnip-apple until just combined. Scrape down the sides of the bowl as needed and add the remaining flour mixture while beating on low speed or whisking gently. Stop when the final flour addition just disappears. Mix in the coconut and raisins.

5 Scoop the batter into the lined muffin cups with a rounded ¼-cup measure and a spoon to help release it or a ¼-cup portion scoop. Sprinkle each of the tops with a pinch of coconut and bake for 10 minutes. Carefully rotate the pans between shelves. Bake for another 10 to 12 minutes until golden brown and the centers are cooked through; a toothpick or a knife inserted into the middle should come out clean. Transfer the pans to wire racks and let the muffins cool for 5 minutes. Transfer the muffins directly to the racks to cool completely.

Strawberry-Citrus Olive Oil Cake

MAKES A 9-INCH CAKE

SEASONAL SWAPS:

It's just the right special-occasion or tea cake to show off strawberries, but as the season moves on, try 1½ cups blueberries, or 2 cups sliced peaches—or omit the fruit altogether when the season no longer provides it.

This may be my favorite cake. (And I seriously *love* cake.) It wins my affection with a mix of citrus zest, almond extract, vanilla extract, and a whole lot of olive oil. The cake's deep fruity flavors and savory-sweetness matched with bouncy, moist texture and a crisp exterior will have you coming back for more.

3 cups (12 to 14 ounces) strawberries

1¼ cups olive oil, plus more for the pan

¾ cup granulated sugar, plus more for the pan

1¾ cups all-purpose flour (7.8 ounces)

⅓ cup almond flour (1.3 ounces)

¼ cup cornstarch (1 ounce)

2 teaspoons baking powder

Scant ½ teaspoon fine sea salt

½ teaspoon baking soda

2 teaspoons grated orange zest

1 teaspoon grated lemon zest

3 tablespoons freshly squeezed lemon juice (or replace 1 tablespoon with orange juice)

2 tablespoons pure maple syrup

1 tablespoon pure vanilla extract

1 teaspoon almond extract

3 large eggs

1 tablespoon white sparkling sugar, for topping

(recipe continues)

1 Gently wash the strawberries, dunking them in a bowl of cold water, then spread them out on a towel-lined sheet pan to dry thoroughly. Carefully blot to remove excess water and let stand.

2 Cut a round of parchment paper to line the bottom of a 9-inch springform pan. Drizzle the bare bottom of the pan with about 1 tablespoon of oil. Use your fingers to evenly coat the bottom and sides. Line the bottom with the parchment round, then coat with another light drizzle of oil. Sprinkle the bottom of the pan with about 1 tablespoon granulated sugar, shaking to coat, then sprinkle about 1 tablespoon along the sides, turning and shaking the pan to coat the pan evenly. Pour out any excess.

3 Heat the oven to 400°F with a rack in the middle position. Whisk together the all-purpose flour, almond flour, cornstarch, baking powder, salt, and baking soda in a medium bowl; set aside.

4 Combine the orange zest, lemon zest, lemon juice, maple syrup, vanilla extract, and almond extract in a 1-cup liquid measure. Whisk to evenly combine; set aside.

5 In a large mixing bowl with a handheld electric mixer or in the bowl of a stand mixer with the whisk attachment, beat the eggs and the ¾ cup granulated sugar on high speed until the mixture is thick, velvety, and pale in color, about 2 minutes. On high speed, gradually stream in the 1¼ cups olive oil until it is well blended and the mixture appears a bit thicker, 1½ to 2 minutes. Reduce the speed to low and add the vanilla–citrus mixture, blending until just combined. Add the flour mixture in 2 rounds and mix on low speed until just combined. Do not overmix. Let stand briefly.

6 Return to the strawberries and blot them again to dry if needed. Hull the berries. Halve small strawberries and quarter medium strawberries.

7 Return to the batter. Scrape down the sides of the bowl with a spatula and gently fold in a little more than half of the cut strawberries. Pour the batter into the prepared pan. Top evenly with the remaining strawberries and sprinkle with the sparkling sugar.

8 Transfer the pan to the oven. You may want to place the sheet pan on the rack below to catch potential olive oil drips. *Reduce the heat to 350°F.*

9 Bake until the top of the cake is golden brown all over and the center of the cake is cooked through, 54 to 57 minutes. It should be just firm to the touch. If you don't mind puncturing the middle of the cake, a tester or paring knife should come out clean. Transfer the cake to a wire rack.

10 Cool the cake for about 15 minutes in the pan. Carefully slide a knife around the perimeter of the cake to separate it from the pan. Remove the sides of the pan and let the cake cool completely. Wrap leftover cake tightly and refrigerate for up to 4 days. Bring to room temperature before serving.

Blueberry Jam Crostata

MAKES A 10-INCH TART

SWAP: You can use any favorite flavor of store-bought jam.

EQUIPMENT TIPS:

- You can make the dough by hand using a fork or pastry cutter to cut the butter into the flour mixture, then stirring the egg into the mixture and kneading it briefly until the dough holds together.

- You'll need a 10-inch fluted tart pan with removable sides.

- For a quick alternative to the lattice strips, use cookie cutters to make circles, squares, or seasonal/holiday shapes that will adorn the top, gathering and re-rolling dough as needed.

This sweet Italian-style, jam-filled crostata was made famous in my family by my great-grandmother. Its buttery lemon shortbread (press-in) crust calls for a filling of cooked-down, overripe fruit and lattice strips casually placed over the top. My simple and fast blueberry jam filling is perfect (it's thickened with fiber-rich chia seeds, which are undetectable in the finished pie). A scoop of vanilla ice cream is a must when it's time to serve.

---

3 cups all-purpose flour

1½ cups granulated sugar

1 teaspoon baking powder

1 teaspoon fine sea salt

Grated zest from 1 lemon (about 2 teaspoons)

½ pound (2 sticks) cold unsalted butter, cut into 1-inch pieces

2 large eggs

Up to 5 teaspoons water or milk

1¼ cups Blueberry-Lemon Jam (recipe follows) or other favorite jam

1 tablespoon white sparkling sugar (optional)

Vanilla ice cream, for serving (optional)

---

1 Heat the oven to 350°F with a rack in the middle position.

2 Make the crostata dough. Combine the flour, granulated sugar, baking powder, salt, and lemon zest in the bowl of a food processor and pulse until blended. Scatter one fourth of the butter over the flour mixture and pulse to just combine. Add the remaining butter in 3 more rounds, pulsing each addition until just combined and the mixture resembles coarse sand, about twenty 1-second pulses total. (Pea-size lumps of butter are okay.) The bowl will be quite full by the last addition so be careful opening it from here on. Lightly beat one egg in a small bowl and add it through the top feed tube (reserve the bowl). Pulse a few more times until the mixture just begins to stick together in places and is crumbly. It should stick together when pressed with your fingers—add 1 to 4 teaspoons of water (one at a time) if needed.

3 Carefully remove the lid and turn the mixture over a work surface. Gather the dough and all the crumbly bits and press and gently fold the dough together in one mound. Cut off about one quarter of the dough, shape it into a disc, wrap it in plastic, and place it in the fridge.

4 Press the remaining dough into the sides and bottom of a 10-inch fluted tart pan with removable sides. (Place pieces of the dough around the edges of the pan and press it into a mostly even layer, working your way around the pan until the sides are covered. Next, evenly press all of the remaining unchilled dough into the bottom of the pan until it is covered.) Use the clean bottom of a measuring cup to press and

(recipe continues)

flatten the dough evenly. Slide the back of a knife or side of an offset spatula along the sides to level and evenly trim the dough along the top of the sides of the pan. Place the tart pan on a sheet pan and freeze or refrigerate briefly while you prepare the lattice topping.

5 To make lattice strips, roll out the reserved chilled dough on a lightly floured work surface or board, or on a piece of parchment paper, into a rough 11-inch circle. Use a pizza or pastry wheel, ravioli cutter, or knife to cut 6 to 8 strips, roughly 1 inch wide. The dough is quite delicate, but don't worry if it breaks; you can easily press strips back together later. Place on a baking sheet and refrigerate until ready to use.

6 In the reserved small bowl, lightly beat the remaining egg with the remaining teaspoon of water to make an egg wash; set aside.

7 Fill the crust with the blueberry-lemon jam, spreading it out evenly. Carefully and evenly space and place 3 to 4 lattice strips across the top horizontally, then place the other strips vertically on top, using the shortest strips on the sides. (You don't need to weave the strips, just cross them.) You want a fair amount of jam to show through. If the lattice strips or cutouts become too soft, refrigerate or freeze them for 5 to 10 minutes until firm enough to work with. The dough is delicate, but forgiving—if it breaks, gently press it back together. Gently press the edges of the strips into the crust to seal; trim the excess.

8 Brush the strips of dough on top lightly with the egg wash, then sprinkle them with sparkling sugar. Place the crostata on the sheet pan and bake for about 40 minutes until just turning golden in places. Transfer the sheet pan to a cooling rack and let cool until the filling has set, at least 30 minutes. Serve topped with vanilla ice cream, if you like.

Blueberry-Lemon Jam

MAKES 1¼ CUPS

TAKE NOTE: Use fresh or frozen blueberries, or a combination.

4 cups ripe blueberries (about 1 pound), rinsed well and stems removed

1 tablespoon freshly squeezed lemon juice

Fine sea salt

¼ teaspoon pure vanilla extract

2 to 3 tablespoons granulated sugar

1 teaspoon chia seeds

Place the blueberries, lemon juice, a pinch of salt, the vanilla, and 2 tablespoons of sugar in a medium saucepan. Bring to a gentle boil and then reduce the heat to gently simmer the blueberries, 10 to 12 minutes, until the juices have run and thickened slightly. Add up to 1 more tablespoon of sugar to sweeten to taste. (I generally use 2 to 2½ tablespoons.) Stir in the chia seeds and cook for another 1 minute. Remove from the heat to cool and thicken for about 10 minutes, or cool completely.

Fudgy Secret-Ingredient Brownies

MAKES 16 BROWNIES

INGREDIENT INFO: To temper the sweetness, reduce the chocolate chips or some of the sugar.

ALL PLANTS: Replace the eggs with flaxseed "eggs." Combine 2 tablespoons flaxseed meal with 4½ tablespoons water in a small bowl and let stand for 5 minutes. Stir to combine. Bake the brownies for about 50 minutes, testing for doneness as the recipe states.

TAKE NOTE: The brownies will keep, well wrapped in plastic and in an airtight container, in the refrigerator for up to 4 days or in the freezer for up to 3 months. To thaw, leave them out at room temperature or in the refrigerator, or microwave each for 15 to 20 seconds.

These fudgy brownies will satisfy even the most serious of chocolate cravings. I love them so much! The black beans stand in for flour and butter. A splash of coffee amplifies the chocolate. Dark chocolate chips and nuts add texture to balance the fudge-like, dense confection. I swear, they are a miracle in a treat.

---

2 tablespoons canola oil, plus more for the pan

1 can (15½ ounces) black beans, rinsed and drained well and patted dry

½ cup plus 2 tablespoons granulated sugar

½ cup good-quality unsweetened cocoa powder

1 teaspoon baking powder

½ teaspoon fine sea salt

¼ cup pure maple syrup

1 tablespoon cooled coffee or 1 teaspoon fine espresso powder

1 teaspoon pure vanilla extract

2 large eggs

½ cup dark chocolate chips or chopped chocolate, plus a heaping tablespoon for topping

½ cup walnut halves or pecans, toasted

---

1 Heat the oven to 350°F with a rack in the middle position. Cut two pieces of parchment paper to line an 8-inch square baking pan with a 1- to 2-inch overhang around the edges. Lightly oil the bottom and sides of the pan, line it with one piece of the parchment and smooth to eliminate any bubbles. Lightly oil the just-placed parchment with more oil and crisscross the other piece of parchment on top to line the other sides; smooth the bottom to eliminate bubbles. Gently crease the parchment along the bottom edges so it lies flat.

2 Place the beans, sugar, cocoa powder, baking powder, and salt in the bowl of a food processor and pulse 5 times, then process until well combined, the beans are completely pureed, and the paste-like mixture just begins to come together in a ball. Add the maple syrup, the 2 tablespoons of oil, the coffee, vanilla, and eggs. Blend again until just incorporated, scraping down the sides of the bowl as needed with a rubber spatula. The batter will be very thin and glossy. Add the chocolate chips and three quarters of the chopped walnuts. Briefly pulse 3 to 5 times to roughly chop and combine.

3 Pour and scrape the batter into the prepared pan. Evenly sprinkle the top with the remaining chocolate chips then the walnuts, crushing them into slightly smaller pieces with your hand. Bake the brownies on the middle rack for 33 to 35 minutes until they are cooked through the middle—the middle should be firm to the touch and a toothpick should come out clean. (Chocolate from chips is okay, batter is not!) Let cool in the pan on a wire rack.

4 Run a knife around the edge of the pan. Lift the brownies out and cut them into squares with a sharp knife, wiping it between cuts. Serve at room temperature or chilled.

Orange-Pistachio Chocolate Chip Cookies

MAKES 14 TO 16 COOKIES

INGREDIENT INFO: Use light to medium rye flour for subtle, nutty, crowd-pleasing flavor. Dark rye flour offers more robust flavor. Both are excellent.

PREP TIP: For the best texture, I recommend refrigerating these cookies on sheet pans before baking them. If space is an issue, consolidate portioned dough onto one sheet pan and evenly redistribute on two sheet pans before baking.

EQUIPMENT INFO: Use a level #24 or scant #20 portion scoop to portion out the dough.

TAKE NOTE: If you can't chill the dough, bake the cookies for 11 to 12 minutes, checking for doneness at 11 minutes. If you have frozen the portioned dough, let it sit out for 5 minutes, then bake for 14 to 15 minutes.

Orange, pistachios, and rye flour make over the beloved chocolate chip cookie into a dressed-up, sophisticated (fully plant-based) cookie that will stand out against the classic. The rye flour lends nuttiness and tender texture; if you haven't baked it into sweet things before now, get ready to be wowed.

½ cup raw shelled pistachios, lightly toasted and cooled

2 cups stirred, spooned, and leveled rye flour (8 ounces)

1 teaspoon fine sea salt

1 teaspoon baking powder

¾ teaspoon baking soda

½ cup granulated sugar

½ cup lightly packed brown sugar

½ cup canola oil

¼ cup water

1 teaspoon pure vanilla extract

2 teaspoons grated orange zest (from 1 to 2 oranges)

1 tablespoon freshly squeezed orange juice

1¼ cups dark chocolate chips or chunks

---

1 Line two sheet pans with parchment paper or silicone baking mats.

2 Finely chop the toasted and cooled pistachios. Whisk together the rye flour, salt, baking powder, and baking soda in a medium bowl.

3 Combine the granulated and brown sugars in a large bowl. Add the oil, then beat with a handheld mixer starting on low speed and increasing to medium speed to evenly and completely blend the mixture. Add the water, vanilla, orange zest, and orange juice and beat again, starting on low speed and increasing to medium-high speed, until well emulsified, 1½ to 2 minutes.

4 Add the dry ingredients to the wet ingredients and blend with the mixer on low speed until just combined. Use a rubber spatula to scrape down the sides of the bowl and mix in the chocolate chips and pistachios. Scoop 2½ to 3 tablespoonfuls of the dough and drop them evenly between the lined sheet pans. Refrigerate the portioned dough for at least 20 minutes (or up to 24 hours for the best texture and flavor; you can also freeze them—see Take Note).

5 Heat the oven to 350°F with a rack in the middle position. Bake the cookies for about 12 minutes until golden for a soft, chewy cookie. Transfer the sheet pan to a wire cooling rack and let cool. Repeat baking and cooling instructions with the remaining cookies. Store completely cooled cookies in an airtight container and enjoy within 2 days of baking them.

Apple-Almond "Croissant" Galette

This gorgeous, sweet apple galette tastes like an almond croissant stuffed with apples. It is much simpler to make than you may think for such a next-level dessert. Serve it to finish any fall or winter meal and save a slice for breakfast.

FOR THE DOUGH

1¼ cups (about 5.6 ounces) all-purpose flour, plus more for dusting

1 tablespoon granulated sugar

Scant ½ teaspoon fine sea salt

10 tablespoons (1¼ sticks) cold unsalted butter

5½ to 6½ tablespoons water

FOR THE ALMOND PASTE

3 tablespoons unsalted butter, softened

¼ cup granulated sugar

½ cup almond flour or almond meal (about 2 ounces)

1 large egg

1 teaspoon almond extract

1 tablespoon all-purpose flour

FOR THE APPLE FILLING

1¾ to 2 pounds mixed apples, peeled, cored, and sliced in ⅓- to ½-inch wedges (see Ingredient Info)

¼ teaspoon fine sea salt

2½ tablespoons granulated sugar

2½ tablespoons raw honey

Heaping ¼ cup sliced raw almonds

---

1 Make the dough. Whisk the flour, sugar, and salt in a large shallow mixing bowl. Place a piece of plastic wrap near your work space so that you can easily transfer the dough to it once your hands are full of dough.

2 Use a chef's knife to cut the cold butter in thin strips on a sharp diagonal to produce 25 to 30 thin rectangular sheets of butter, ⅛ to 1/16 inch thick. (Lengths will vary, some shorter and some longer than others.) Evenly spread out and dip the butter into the flour, then use your hands to toss and lightly coat the butter with flour. While tossing, use your fingertips to gently crumble the butter into smaller pieces (roughly ½ inch) and evenly incorporate the butter into the flour. (As you break apart the butter you will produce some smaller, pebble-size pieces as well.) The mixture will look very dry and shaggy.

3 Gradually pour 5½ tablespoons of water over the flour-butter mixture while tossing, then gently gather and knead the dough until just incorporated and holding together. (Add another tablespoon of water if needed.) Fold the dough in half 4 or 5 times, then shape it into a ball. The dough should be soft and sticky, but not so much that it completely sticks to your hands. You should also be able to see large pieces of butter in the dough.

(recipe continues)

4 Place the dough on the plastic wrap. Wash your hands, then place another piece of plastic over the top. Use a rolling pin to gently flatten the ball into a disc. Fold over the plastic to wrap the disc and reshape, rounding out the edges if needed. Chill the disc of dough in the refrigerator for 30 minutes or up to overnight.

5 When ready to assemble the galette, let the dough sit out at room temperature until it just becomes pliable. Meanwhile, make the almond paste. Beat the butter and sugar together in a large bowl with a handheld mixer starting on low speed and then increasing to medium speed until well combined and almost fluffy, about 1 minute. Add the almond flour and beat on low speed to combine. Add the egg and almond extract and beat on medium speed to combine. Scrape down the sides of the bowl, add the all-purpose flour, and beat on low to just combine; let stand.

6 Lightly flour a rolling pin and roll out the chilled dough on a piece of parchment paper from the center outward to about 13 inches (a perfect circle is not necessary). If the dough is sticking at any point, sprinkle a couple of pinches of flour over the top. Transfer the parchment and round of dough to a sheet pan. Spread out the almond paste in the center of the round, leaving about a 2-inch border. Chill or freeze the dough on the sheet pan briefly while you prepare the apples and until the dough firms up.

7 Make the filling. Toss the apples with the salt in a clean large bowl. Add the sugar and toss again until evenly coated. Pour the apples evenly over the almond paste (piled slightly higher in the center), containing them within the 2-inch border as much as possible. Carefully and loosely fold the edges of dough up and over the outer apples on the border, folding and gently pressing the dough as you go. Use the parchment (or a bench scraper) to help lift and place the dough if it gets too soft or sticky. This may feel a bit unwieldy, but the end result will not suffer.

8 Heat the oven to 425°F with a rack in the middle position. Place the galette on the sheet pan in the freezer until the dough is firm, 5 to 10 minutes. Then bake it for about 30 minutes until golden brown all over. Drizzle the apples with the honey, top evenly with the almonds, rotate the pan, and bake for another 5 to 10 minutes until the crust is a deeper golden and the almonds are lightly toasted. Cool on a wire rack for 10 minutes, cut into wedges, and serve.

Store leftover galette (completely cooled) on a sheet pan or in pieces on a plate so they lie flat (do not stack) and refrigerate for up to 3 days. Bring the galette to room temperature or reheat it at 400°F until warm and the crust gets crispy in places, 8 to 12 minutes.

CONVERSION TABLES

Approximate Equivalents

1 stick butter = 8 tbs = 4 oz = ½ cup = 115 g

1 cup all-purpose presifted flour = 4.5 oz

1 cup granulated sugar = 7 oz = about 200 g

1 cup (firmly packed) brown sugar = 7½ oz = 215 g

1 cup powdered sugar = 3¾ oz = 115 g

1 cup honey or syrup = 12 oz

1 cup grated cheese = 4 oz

1 cup dried beans = 8 oz

1 large egg = about 2 oz or about 3 tbs

1 egg yolk = about 1 tbs

1 egg white = about 2 tbs

Please note that all conversions are approximate but close enough to be useful when converting from one system to another.

Weight Conversions

US/UK	METRIC	US/UK	METRIC
½ oz	15 g	7 oz	200 g
1 oz	30 g	8 oz	250 g
1½ oz	45 g	9 oz	275 g
2 oz	60 g	10 oz	300 g
2½ oz	75 g	11 oz	325 g
3 oz	90 g	12 oz	350 g
3½ oz	100 g	13 oz	375 g
4 oz	125 g	14 oz	400 g
5 oz	150 g	15 oz	450 g
6 oz	175 g	1 lb	500 g

Liquid Conversions

US	IMPERIAL	METRIC
2 tbs	1 fl oz	30 ml
3 tbs	1½ fl oz	45 ml
¼ cup	2 fl oz	60 ml
⅓ cup	2½ fl oz	75 ml
⅓ cup + 1 tbs	3 fl oz	90 ml
⅓ cup + 2 tbs	3½ fl oz	100 ml
½ cup	4 fl oz	125 ml
⅔ cup	5 fl oz	150 ml
¾ cup	6 fl oz	175 ml
¾ cup + 2 tbs	7 fl oz	200 ml
1 cup	8 fl oz	250 ml
1 cup + 2 tbs	9 fl oz	275 ml
1¼ cups	10 fl oz	300 ml
1⅓ cups	11 fl oz	325 ml
1½ cups	12 fl oz	350 ml
1⅔ cups	13 fl oz	375 ml
1¾ cups	14 fl oz	400 ml
1¾ cups + 2 tbs	15 fl oz	450 ml
2 cups (1 pint)	16 fl oz	500 ml
2½ cups	20 fl oz (1 pint)	600 ml
3¾ cups	1½ pints	900 ml
4 cups	1¾ pints	1 liter

Oven Temperatures

°F	GAS MARK	°C	°F	GAS MARK	°C
250	½	120	400	6	200
275	1	140	425	7	220
300	2	150	450	8	230
325	3	160	475	9	240
350	4	180	500	10	260
375	5	190			

Note: Reduce the temperature by 68°F (20°C) for fan-assisted ovens.

A GUIDE TO SAUCES, DIPS, AND SPREADS

RECIPES BY SEASON

Cooking with the seasons is intrinsic to the recipes in this book and will make everything you cook even more delicious. Keep in mind, this is a general guide based on my own experience with these recipes and the produce available to me. The season's produce may vary where you live. Some vegetables appear locally in multiple seasons and some can feel right in every season (with a little help from our grocery stores).

ENTRÉE-WORTHY SALADS.	Winter	Spring	Summer	Fall
Every Season Green Salad with House Lemon Vinaigrette	✓	✓	✓	✓
Baby Beet and Blueberry Salad with Avocado Basil Vinaigrette	✓	✓	✓	
Delicata Squash and Apple Salad with Arugula and Maple-Balsamic Vinaigrette	✓			✓
Lacinato Kale and Jalapeño Pickled Golden Raisins with Avocado Dressing and Corn Nuts		✓	✓	✓
Kale and Watermelon Panzanella			✓	
Kale-Radicchio Caesar with Crispy Chickpea "Croutons"	✓	✓		✓
Asparagus-Spinach Farro Salad with Almonds and Orange-Sesame Vinaigrette		✓		
Tomato-Green Bean Freekeh Salad with Pistachios and Lemon-Feta Vinaigrette			✓	
Lemony Rainbow Carrot Couscous Salad	✓	✓	✓	✓
Parisian-Style Lentil and Crudités Salad	✓	✓	✓	✓
Tomato-Bean Salad with Shaved Fennel, Spinach, and Tomato Vinaigrette			✓	✓
Marinated "Agrodolce" Sweet Peppers and Cannellini Bean Salad			✓	✓

SOUPS. CHILIES. STEWS.	Winter	Spring	Summer	Fall
Celery Root and Potato-Leek Soup	✓			✓
Charred Zucchini Soup with Sweet Corn and Tomato Crostini			✓	
Classic Butternut Squash Soup with Pepitas and Pomegranate	✓			✓
Spring Vegetable and Orzo Soup with Parmesan-Miso Broth		✓		
Green Summer Vegetable Soup with Basil Pesto			✓	
Winter Minestrone with Kale and Farro	✓	✓		✓
Stewed Lentils and Carrots with Olive Oil and Parmesan	✓	✓	✓	✓
Pinto Beans and Rice with All the Fixings	✓	✓	✓	✓
The Best Cannellini Beans with Orange-Pistachio-Kale Gremolata	✓	✓	✓	✓
Easy White Bean Chili with Tomatoes and Sweet Corn			✓	✓
Ultimate Black Bean Chili	✓	✓	✓	✓
Sweet Potato and Poblano Chili	✓			✓
Spring Artichoke Ragout		✓		✓
Butternut Squash and Kale Coconut-Curry Stew	✓			✓
Root Vegetable Tagine	✓			✓

SANDWICHES. TACOS. PIZZA. QUESADILLAS.	Winter	Spring	Summer	Fall
Classic Beet and Black Bean Burgers	✓	✓	✓	✓
Roasted Sweet Potato-Chickpea Burgers with Maple-Lime-Chipotle Crema	✓			✓
Drive-Through-Style Mushroom-Lentil Cheeseburgers with Secret Sauce	✓	✓	✓	✓
Beet and Avocado Sandwich with Pickled Onions and Chive Goat Cheese	✓	✓	✓	✓
Cucumber and Pesto Sandwich with Arugula and Avocado		✓	✓	
Butternut Squash Steak Sandwich with Kale, Walnuts, and Apple-Onion Jam	✓			✓
Saucy Eggplant and Melted Mozzarella Hero			✓	✓
Butter-Poached Cauliflower Rolls		✓	✓	✓
Broccoli Rabe Grilled Cheese with Olives and Apple	✓			✓
Sweet Peas on Toast with Mint and Quick-Pickled Carrots		✓	✓	
Avocado Toast with Turmeric Nut-Seed Mix	✓	✓	✓	✓
Eggplant Caponata Toast with Arugula and Pickled Raisins			✓	✓
Smoky Beet Tacos with Goat Cheese and Cilantro Salsa	✓	✓	✓	✓
Sweet Corn and Black Bean Tacos with Peach Salsa and Red Cabbage			✓	
Coconut-Cauliflower Tacos with Creamy Apple-Cabbage Slaw	✓	✓	✓	✓
Garlicky Swiss Chard Flatbread with Mozzarella, Olives, and Pine Nuts	✓	✓	✓	✓
Summer Vegetable Grilled Pizza with Burrata			✓	
Pear and Arugula Pizza with Gorgonzola, Honey, and Hazelnuts	✓			✓
Asparagus-Leek Quesadillas with Fresh Strawberry Salsa		✓		
Zucchini and Black Bean Quesadillas with Avocado-Corn Salsa		✓	✓	
Browned-Butter Quesadillas with Butternut Squash and Jammy Onions	✓			✓

GRAIN BOWLS. NOODLE BOWLS.	Winter	Spring	Summer	Fall
Brassicas and Brown Rice Bowls with Peanut Sauce and Crispy Tofu	✓	✓	✓	✓
Asparagus Sushi Rice Bowls with Spicy Tofu "Mayo"		✓		
Tomato-Cucumber Freekeh Bowls with Spiced Chickpeas and Pine Nut-Chili Yogurt			✓	✓
Asparagus and Artichoke Paella (+variations)		✓	✓	✓
Spiced Lentil and Rice Pilaf with Spinach-Currant Salad	✓	✓	✓	✓
Swiss Chard Risotto (+variations)	✓	✓	✓	✓
Once-A-Week Broccoli Stir-Fry	✓	✓	✓	✓
Weeknight Vegetable Stir-Fry Wraps	✓	✓	✓	✓
Fried Rice with Brussels Sprouts and Cashews	✓			✓
Saucy Garlic-Ginger Noodles with All the Green Things		✓	✓	✓
Sesame Peanut Noodles with Crunchy Vegetables and Garlic-Scallion Chili Oil		✓	✓	
Orange-Miso Soba Noodle Bowls with Broccoli and Carrot Ribbons	✓	✓		✓
Cacio e Pepe with Roasted Cauliflower and Spinach	✓	✓		✓
Tomato, Sweet Corn, and Zucchini Pasta with Fresh Basil			✓	
Creamy Eggplant and Tomato Sauce with Rigatoni and Ricotta Salata			✓	✓
Creamy (No Cream) Fennel Alfredo Sauce with Bucatini	✓	✓		✓
Lemon-Beet Sauce with Fusilli with Peas and Poppy Seeds	✓	✓	✓	✓
Broccoli Rabe Pesto with Fettuccine and Chickpeas	✓			✓

STEAKS. FRITTERS. MEATBALLS. GRILLED VEGETABLES.	Winter	Spring	Summer	Fall
Macadamia-Crusted Kohlrabi with Orange Beurre Blanc	✓	✓		✓
Cauliflower Steaks with Pickled Pepper Relish and Arugula Salad			✓	✓
Pan-Fried Celery Root Cutlets with Lemon-Cashew Aioli	✓			✓
Carrot-Cilantro Fritters with Tahini-Lime Yogurt Sauce	✓	✓	✓	✓
Zucchini-Corn Fritters with Ricotta and Simple Tomato-Basil Salad			✓	
Broccoli Fritters with Lemon Yogurt and Simple Orange-Fennel Salad	✓	✓		✓
Spaghetti and Italian-Style Meatballs	✓	✓	✓	✓
Chickpea Falafel with Tahini Sauce and Simple Tomato-Cucumber Salad	✓	✓	✓	✓
Kofta-Style Meatballs with Cucumber-Dill Yogurt	✓	✓	✓	✓
Grilled Asparagus and Snap Pea Mezze with Beet Hummus, Green Goddess Dip, and Burrata		✓		
Grilled Summer Bounty with Peaches, Halloumi, and Flatbread			✓	
Grilled Broccolini, Potato Wedges, and Hakurei Turnips with Red Pepper Pesto				✓
Sheet Pan Cauliflower Marbella with Polenta	✓	✓	✓	✓
Sheet Pan Potatoes and Green Beans with Walnuts, Olives, and Feta			✓	✓
Smoky Sheet Pan Coconut Greens and Sweet Potatoes	✓	✓		✓

LAYERED CASSEROLES. SAVORY PIES.	Winter	Spring	Summer	Fall
Classic Lasagna with Spinach-Ricotta Filling and Simple Tomato Sauce	✓	✓	✓	✓
Mixed Mushroom and Kale Lasagna	✓	✓		✓
Butternut Squash and Swiss Chard Lasagna	✓			✓
Mushroom and Swiss Chard Enchiladas with Ancho Chile Sauce	✓	✓	✓	✓
Summer Vegetable Enchiladas with Ancho Chili Sauce			✓	✓
Cauliflower Enchiladas with Pumpkin-Chipotle Cream Sauce	✓			✓
Potato and Creamed Leeks Galette	✓	✓		✓
Summer Tomato Crostata with Olive Oil-Parmesan Crust			✓	
Caramelized Onion and Apple Crostata with Gorgonzola	✓		✓	
Potato and Spring Pea Frittata		✓	✓	
Zucchini-Basil Frittata with Caramelized Red Onion and Ricotta		✓	✓	
Simple Broccoli-Cheddar Frittata with Crispy Roasted Potatoes	✓	✓	✓	✓
Asparagus and Spring Allium Strata		✓		
Tortilla Strata with Charred Poblano and Tomatoes			✓	✓
Mushroom-Collard Strata with Gruyère and Thyme	✓	✓		✓
Beet Wellington with Horseradish Cream	✓	✓	✓	✓
Lentil and Mushroom Shepherd's Pie	✓	✓		✓
Celery Root and Apple Pot Pie	✓	✓		✓

SWEETS.	Winter	Spring	Summer	Fall
Crumble-Topped Banana Coffee Cake	✓	✓	✓	✓
Buttermilk Cornbread with Honey Butter	✓	✓	✓	✓
Zucchini and Dried Cherry Scones		✓	✓	
Spiced Pumpkin Waffles with Orange Zest and Pecans	✓			✓
Parsnip Morning Glory Muffins	✓			✓
Strawberry-Citrus Olive Oil Cake (+variation)	✓	✓	✓	✓
Blueberry Jam Crostata (+variation)	✓	✓	✓	✓
Fudgy Secret-Ingredient Brownies	✓	✓	✓	✓
Orange-Pistachio Chocolate Chip Cookies	✓	✓	✓	✓
Apple-Almond "Croissant" Galette	✓			✓

INDEX

Note: Page references in *italics* indicate photographs.

C

ACKNOWLEDGMENTS

THANK YOU . . .

KYLIE FOXX MCDONALD (my editor) for your partnership and friendship. I appreciate your willingness to get into the weeds with me and to match my commitment to the details. Thank you for believing in me and trusting my perspective. You are extraordinary, the absolute best, and every page of this book is undoubtedly better because of you.

STACEY GLICK (my agent) for your unwavering commitment to me, to my aspirations, and to this project. I am so grateful for your enthusiasm and your point of view. I still feel pinch-me lucky that I get to partner with you.

ERIN SCOTT (photographer) for generously sharing your brilliant eye and your love of vegetables to capture exactly what I hoped this book could be in pictures. Your energy, talent, and exquisite photographs have given vibrant life to this book. I adore you. **TAMER ABU-DAYYEH** and **BRAD KNILANS** (photo assistants) for bringing your expertise and good energy to the shoots and to the images that appear here.

EMILY CANEER (food stylist) for your creativity and calm confidence that made the food in this book so gorgeous. I am in awe of you and the magic you make (and make look so effortlessly easy). **BECCA MARTIN** (assistant food stylist) for cooking for days on end and being so good at it. Your diligence and focus helped make this food so beautiful.

BECKY TERHUNE (art director) for being the most patient, open, and flexible collaborator. I'm deeply grateful for your tireless work in putting the many parts and pieces of this book together and doing it in such a wonderful way.

To the rest of the genius team at Workman Publishing for supporting me and this book with your talent and vision. I am so fortunate to work with all of you, especially **REBECCA CARLISLE**, **CHLOE PUTON**, **MOIRA KERRIGAN**, and **CINDY LEE**; **BETH LEVY**, **KATE KAROL**, **BARBARA PERAGINE**, and **ANALUCIA ZEPEDA**; and **LIA RONNEN**, **DAVID SCHILLER**, and **CLAIRE MCKEAN**.

SHARON HALKOVICS for jumping fully into this project with me. Your meticulous recipe testing, your organization, and your right-on sense of taste and perspective are in so many recipes. I trust you completely, I love working with you, and can't imagine making a cookbook without you.

ALEX CHRISTIAN for your dedication to Little Eater, for your ongoing recipe testing, and your ability to handle everything with ease. You are one of a kind and I am so proud of everything we accomplished. I am forever grateful for your partnership and friendship which provided vital support and insight throughout the development of this book.

AMBER HERRON, **DIANA WEBSTER**, and **ALL LITTLE EATER TEAM MEMBERS** who inspired me and supported our mission. Your extraordinary hard work helped us turn thousands of people into vegetable eaters and lovers. To my customers and farmers, for all of your vegetable love and support for all those many wonderful years. Your partnership and the eating we all did together are reflected in these pages.

RACHEL BAREHL for generously allowing me to include some of your gorgeous vegetable photos here. For years, you so beautifully captured the rhythm of the seasons for me. I treasure each photograph and the moments in my life they represent—thank you.

BETH for listening, guiding, and supporting me and this project endlessly. You and your real-life experience cooking everyday for your family has influenced so much of this book. Thank you for always, *always* showing up for me. To your vegetable eaters, JORDAN and MY NIECES for tasting and testing, and sharing your excitement for these meals and this project from the beginning to the end. DAD, for cheering me on always. NICK, for being a constant, unyielding force of support that makes everything feel possible. EMILY for your willingness to pitch in always and for putting so many of these recipes to the nightly test. To the many other friends and family members, who brought these recipes into their home kitchens to test and share feedback including DAVE and NANCY YEWELL, VICKI KIRKLAND, and GINA MANION.

To my GRANDMOTHERS and GREAT-GRANDMOTHERS, for inspiring this book with recipes and with their example of cooking every day for the people they loved and of making every meal at the table an occasion to celebrate.

MOM, for the gift of feeding me and nourishing me throughout my life. The love and time you put into every meal for our family is not lost on me—every early morning breakfast, every nutritious lunch, and every balanced dinner pulled together after work—has made its way into this book's framework. I am infinitely grateful to always have you in my corner and to be lifted up by your love and support and by your excitement for this work.

STELLA AND NICO, my sweet, little vegetable eaters, for contributing to this book every morning, day, and night for most of your childhood. I hope these meals always bring you happy, delicious memories.